ABOUT GOVERNMENT INSTITUTES

Government Institutes was founded in 1973 during a time when many of the nation's environmental laws were being enacted, and was one of the first organizations to provide practical environmental information to the business community. That same year, Government Institutes published the **Environmental Law Handbook** by J. Gordon Arbuckle et al., the standard reference in the field and now in its 12th edition. Today Government Institutes conducts more than 150 environmental courses across the country each year. These courses, coupled with the publication of many books covering aspects of both environmental law and science, have earned Government Institutes the reputation as the leader in the environmental information field.

Government Institutes books are widely used throughout industry and government for training as well as guidance by engineers, managers, attorneys, and others who work in the environmental field. In addition to its many highly acclaimed books on federal environmental law, including the standard edition of U.S. environmental statutes, Government Institutes is publishing the first comprehensive series of state environmental law handbooks. When completed, this series will be the most extensive source of information on state environmental laws.

The many conferences sponsored by Government Institutes have ranged from some of the first to explore the relationship and interdependence of energy and the environment to the establishment in 1992 of the Environmental Management Development Institute. Over the years prominent speakers have included leaders in both business and government including Dr. Armand Hammer, J. Peter Grace, President George Bush, as well as senators, congressmen and numerous environmental leaders. Each year Government Institutes conducts the Environmental Management Roundtable. Top environmental managers from business firms such as Anheuser Busch, Hallmark, Texaco, DuPont as well as officials from government agencies, attend this annual forum to discuss major environmental issues.

THE GREENING OF AMERICAN BUSINESS

MAKING BOTTOM-LINE SENSE OF ENVIRONMENTAL RESPONSIBILITY

Editor
Thomas F. P. Sullivan

Ⓖ Government Institutes, Inc.
Rockville, Maryland

Library of Congress Cataloging-in-Publication Data
    The Greening of American business : making
    bottom-line sense of environmental responsi-
    bility / edited by Thomas F.P. Sullivan.
        p.   cm.
    Includes bibliographical references and index.
    ISBN 0-86587-295-3 (alk. paper) : $24.95
        1. United States--Industries--Environmental
    aspects. 2. Business enterprises--United States--
    Environmental aspects. 3. Green movement--United
    States. 4. Environmental policy--United States.
    5. Social responsibility of business--United States.
    I. Sullivan, Thomas F. P.
    HC110.E5G7345 1992
    658.4'08--dc20   92-71551
                                            CIP

Printed on recycled, acid-free paper with soybase ink

ii

72551

General Table of Contents

Table of Contents

v

Preface

Newspapers, television, and radio daily present us with more and more stories about hazardous materials releases and other environmental damages caused by American business.

This continuous flood of environmental horror stories has alarmed people across the country, and they are demanding that businesses be responsible.

As a result, environmentally aware consumers and investors alike are beginning to demand that businesses change their policies and procedures to minimize the adverse effects their companies are having on the environment.

To respond to this new era, seventeen leading business professionals from industry, consulting firms, law firms, and universities share their experience of the impact of the green movement on business to create this practical text on *The Greening of American Business*.

In the chapters that follow, these experts present the most current advice of leaders from the business, legal, and academic communities. Focusing on such diverse topics as labeling and packaging, liability, market opportunities, investing, and insurance coverage for environmental risks, each author shows how industry is responding to the increasing demands that companies engage in environmentally sound business practices.

This book was first conceived of as a guide for corporate managers who must think through the practical challenges of sensible corporate environmental policies. At the same time, we believed it would provide valuable information for future corporate leaders still in business schools.

However, as the book came together, we realized that there is a much wider audience that is concerned with environmental business practices. Since we all have both a moral and a legal obligation to protect the environment, the insights contained in this book should be of interest to virtually everyone concerned with the direction and impact of the environmental movement.

Thomas F. P. Sullivan
Editor

About the Editor

Thomas F. P. Sullivan

Thomas F. P. Sullivan received his B.S. degree in physics and mathematics from St. Louis University, and was awarded a J.D. degree by Catholic University. He has authored or edited over 30 books on environmental and energy law, including the *Environmental Law Handbook*, now in its eleventh edition, the *Environmental Glossary*, and *Environmental Information Sources*. In 1973 he founded Government Institutes, at which he currently serves as president.

About the Authors

Neil A. Belson

Neil A. Belson is an associate with the Washington, D.C. law office of Anderson Kill Olick & Oshinsky. He has worked extensively in all areas of environmental law, and his current practice includes both regulatory counseling and litigation involving questions of federal, state and local environmental law. Mr. Belson is a member of the District of Columbia Bar, the State Bars of Maryland and Colorado, and the Section on Natural Resources, Energy and Environmental Law of the American Bar Association. He received a J.D. from Harvard Law School and an M.S. in agronomy from the University of Maryland.

Roger H. Bezdek

Dr. Bezdek is president of MIS, Inc., a consulting firm in Washington, D.C. He has 22 years experience in consulting and management in various fields, serving in private industry, academia, and the federal government. His consulting background includes market forecasts by product line and industry segment and financial analysis of new environmental and energy technologies. He has been research director in the Energy Research & Development Administration of the Department of Energy, and special advisor on energy and environmental policy in the Office of the Secretary of the Treasury. While with ERDA/DOE, he founded the federal government's program to assess the institutional, economic, and regulatory implications of energy/environmental legislation. Dr. Bezdek received his Ph.D. in Economics from the University of Illinois (Urbana).

Thomas K. Bick

Thomas K. Bick is a partner in the Environmental Practice Group in the District of Columbia office of the law firm of Kilpatrick & Cody. Mr. Bick specializes in environmental and toxic tort litigation. He was formerly with the U.S. Department of Justice, where he served first as trial attorney and later as senior attorney in the department's Environmental Enforcement Section. Prior to serving with the Justice Department, Mr. Bick worked as a litigator and lobbyist in the Toxics Division of the National Wildlife Federation. Before that he was special assistant on environmental matters to the administrator of the National Oceanic and Atmospheric Administration. He graduated from the University of Notre Dame with a BS degree in chemistry and from Antioch School of Law in Washington, D.C.

Grace A. Carter

Grace A. Carter is a partner in the litigation department of the Los Angeles office of Paul, Hastings, Janofsky & Walker. Ms. Carter is a member of the international firm's National Policy Committee and is vice chairperson of the litigation department.

She has practiced extensively in both state and federal courts and has specialized in representing businesses as policyholders in sophisticated insurance coverage litigation. In addition, she has handled a wide variety of general commercial litigation, particularly in the energy field. Ms. Carter received her J.D. from Boalt Hall, University of California at Berkeley.

David R. Chittick

David R. Chittick, as Environment & Safety Engineering vice president, is responsible for environmental, product and occupational safety for AT&T. Currently, he is also a member of the board of directors for AT&T Resource Management. He has held various managerial positions and two vice presidential positions in the company. He was a member of the U.S. mission to the Peoples Republic of China regarding stratospheric ozone depletion, and a member of a U.S. government delegation to the U.S.S.R. and Hungary to exchange technical information regarding CFC solvent replacement. Mr. Chittick is founder and chairman of the board of the Industry Cooperative for Ozone Layer Protection, Inc. (ICOLP). He serves as vice chairman of the Global Environmental Management Initiative and also serves on various EPA advisory committees including the Stratospheric Ozone Protection Council. Mr. Chittick earned a Master of Science degree from the Massachusetts Institute of Technology.

Gabriele G. Crognale, P.E.

Mr. Crognale specializes in RCRA compliance and enforcement issues, and oversees facilities undergoing enforcement-mandated corrective actions, working until recently with the Massachusetts consulting firm of Arthur D. Little. Mr. Crognale has served as a senior compliance officer with the U.S. EPA in Region I where his duties included the preparation of administrative orders, reviewing RCRA Facility Assessment/RCRA Facility Investigation approvals of those orders, and overseeing facilities undergoing corrective action. He is a member of the National Association for Environmental Management and the Air & Waste

Management Association, and is a registered civil engineer in Massachusetts. Mr. Crognale earned a Bachelor of Science degree in civil engineering from the University of Massachusetts and Northeastern University. He currently works with Science Applications International Corporation (SAIC).

Joel Hirschhorn

Joel Hirschhorn is the president of Hirschhorn & Associates, Inc., an environmental consulting firm that provides professional environmental advice and analysis for industry's front-line problem solvers and strategic planners, especially in pollution prevention, waste reduction, and green products. For over a decade, Dr. Hirschhorn was a senior associate at the Office of Technology Assessment. He directed studies on waste reduction, hazardous waste, and Superfund cleanups for Senate and House Committees. Before OTA, he was a full professor of engineering at the University of Wisconsin, Madison, a director of research for a small Ohio manufacturing company, a management consultant, and a researcher at Pratt & Whitney Aircraft. He has published several books, including *Prosperity Without Pollution: The Prevention Strategy for Industry and Consumers.* Dr. Hirschhorn earned his Ph.D. in materials engineering from Rensselaer Polytechnic Institute.

Ciannat M. Howett

Ms. Howett recently graduated from the University of Virginia with a joint law degree and masters in marine affairs. While in law school, she served on the executive board of the Environmental Law Forum. During the summer of 1991, she worked as a summer associate in the Washington, D.C. office of the law firm Kilpatrick & Cody, where she will begin working full time in September 1992 in the firm's Environmental Practice Group.

Sacha Millstone

Ms. Millstone is a vice president at the investment firm of Ferris Baker Watts, Inc. in Washington, D.C., where she is a specialist in socially-responsible investing. Prior to joining the firm, she was associated with Smith Barney, Harris Upham, Inc. and with First American Bank, N.A. Ms. Millstone writes a syndicated column on socially responsible investing for publications nationwide and publishes the *Concerned Investor* newsletter. She holds an MBA in finance from George Washington University.

Stuart A. Nicholson

Stuart Nicholson is associate professor of Environmental Science at New Mexico Highlands University in Las, Vegas, New Mexico. He is involved in teaching and research in several areas, including environmental ethics and policy, especially as they relate to business, environmental law, environmental science, and applied ecology. He has also practiced law with a private firm and worked as a scientist for an environmental firm and state government. Dr. Nicholson has conducted extensive funded environmental research and is currently analyzing and writing on environmental policy and ecological restoration. Dr. Nicholson is a member of the Bar in Minnesota and North Dakota. He has a Ph.D. in botany from the University of Georgia, and a J.D. from the University of North Dakota.

Ronald M. Oster

Ronald M. Oster is a partner in the international firm of Paul, Hastings, Janofsky & Walker, where he also is a member of the firm's Policy Committee and is the chairperson of the Insurance Coverage Group. Mr. Oster has extensive experience representing commercial insureds in complex insurance coverage cases. For the past ten years, he has taught continuing education courses for the California Bar Association on a variety of subjects including Fundamentals of Civil Litigation Before Trial and Recent Developments in Civil Litigation. He has been a lecturer for the American Bar Association National Institute and for the Los Angeles County Bar Association on insurance, bankruptcy and toxic tort issues. He received his law degree from Stanford Law School .

Daniel M. Steinway

Daniel M. Steinway is a partner with the firm of Anderson Kill Olick & Oshinsky in Washington, D.C., and is chairman of its environmental law practice. He is a member of the District of Columbia Bar and the State of Michigan Bar. He also is chairman of the Environmental Law Committee of the Federal Bar Association, vice chairman of the Subcommittee on Alternate Energy Sources of the American Bar Association Section of Natural Resources Law. In the past, Mr. Steinway has served as minority counsel responsible for environmental matters on the Committee on Science and Technology of the U.S. House of Representatives, and as an attorney-advisor with the Office of Enforcement of the U.S. Environmental Protection Agency. He holds a B.S.E. in engineering science from the University of Michigan and a J.D. from George Washington University National Law Center.

Roger Strelow

Roger Strelow is executive vice president of Bechtel Environmental, Inc. He is responsible for BEI's worldwide environmental services business, which includes business development and oversight of projects in the private sector. Besides working in private law for several years in Washington, D.C., Mr. Strelow has served as GE's vice president for corporate environmental programs and as assistant administrator for Air and Waste Management in the EPA. He is on the boards of directors of the Environmental Law Institute and the Climate Institute. Mr. Strelow is a graduate of the Law School of the University of California at Berkeley.

Robert M. Wendling

Robert M. Wendling is a senior economist with 18 years experience in environmental economics, utility planning, regulatory policy, disaggregate regional analysis, alternative energy technologies, macroeconomic and industrial productivity analysis, and computerized data aggregation and mathematical analysis techniques. His consulting background includes economic analysis of environmental legislation, managing utility demonstration projects, capacity planning and forecasting, development of environmental impact statements, and assessing the effects of regulatory policies. He has served as a corporate vice president and in senior positions in the U.S. Department of Commerce and the Department of Energy. Mr. Wendling received an M.A. from George Washington University.

Mark White

Dr. White is an assistant professor with the McIntire School of Commerce at the University of Virginia, where he teaches finance and is developing a new course in Environmental Management. He is also a member of the affiliated faculty of the University of Virginia's Center for Environmental Policy. Dr. White is currently pursuing research on the relationship between environmental and financial performance and is preparing case studies on environmental issues in business. Dr. White holds an MS in ecology from Michigan State University, and MBA and Ph.D. degrees in finance from Michigan State.

Thomas H. Yancey

Thomas H. Yancey is a partner in the Washington, D.C. office of Sidley & Austin where he specializes in tax and corporate matters, including foreign and domestic tax planning and real estate, as well as tax and commercial litigation. He has special expertise in issues involving the income taxation of environmental matters and environmental excise taxes. He is a member of the bars of the District of Columbia and Virginia, and of the Sections of Taxation and Real Property, Probate and Trust Law of the American Bar Association. He also serves as chairman of the General Income Tax Subcommittee of the Environmental Taxes Committee of the ABA Section of Taxation. Mr. Yancey received his J.D. degree from the University of Virginia Law School.

Steven S. Young

Steven S. Young, REM. CEA. is a staff researcher and regular contributor to *Pollution Engineering Magazine.* He is currently assisting in the development of educational programs on environmental accident investigation for the National Registry of Environmental Professionals. He has served as a criminal investigator and administrative assistant for the Illinois, Lake and Cook County Public Defendants' Offices and has provided police- and security-related bibliographic research for the Illinois Academy of Criminology, Northeast Training Council for Police, and the Chicago Crime Commission. He received his undergraduate degree in military and criminal justice history, and has completed graduate and post-graduate work at De Paul and Northwestern Universities.

THE GREENING OF AMERICAN BUSINESS

Chapter 1

Effect of the Green Movement on Business in the 1990s

Sacha Millstone
Ferris Baker Watts

"In the Nineties, environmentalism will be the
cutting edge of social reform and absolutely the
most important issue for business."
Gary Miller, public policy expert at
Washington University, St. Louis, MO.

Worldwide, the momentum of the environmental movement is creating a permanent shift in the way business operates. What began as a grassroots effort identified largely with the liberal agenda is quickly becoming a mainstream issue of concern to consumers, investors, politicians, and businesspeople alike. This evolution results from the growing awareness of elements of both crisis and opportunity inherent in the global environmental situation.

Environmentally-oriented special interest groups have been active for decades, so why has the environmental movement suddenly developed so much momentum? The primary reason may be our growing awareness of global environmental problems, coupled with our increased understanding of global inter-

1

dependence and the fragility of our planet's life sustaining ecosystem. Reports of environmental disasters from every corner of the world have been brought into American households on a regular basis in a way that people experience very personally. Television has shown us the *Valdez* oil spill, complete with oil drenched wildlife and blackened landscapes; and more recently the thick grey air in Kuwait resulting from hundreds of burning oil fires. *People* magazine featured former Olympic champion Olga Korbut and her family's desperate fight against terrifying illnesses five years after the Chernobyl nuclear accident. Scientists' reports of growing holes in the ozone layer and global warming trends have raised fears that our actions as a world community are straining our planet's natural balance.

As these environmental issues are viewed as threatening by more and more people, their growing awareness is translated into public pressure on politicians. While there is some controversy surrounding the extent of the environmental threat, there is widespread public belief that *any* threat should be minimized. Resulting legislation has directly affected businesses in a variety of ways, and created new expenses which businesses have been forced to deal with. Companies have begun to wonder if there isn't a better—more profitable—way.

Business has also been feeling pressure from conscientious consumers and investors who are voting with their dollars. Corporate reaction has been varied, yet it appears that overall, companies who have been slow to comply with environmental regulations or who have demonstrated a lack of concern for the environment have suffered in comparison to companies who have seized the initiative, seen the opportunity, and taken a pro-active environmental stance. Meanwhile, entrepreneurs have sprung up to meet the new demands of the environmental marketplace, seeing opportunities in crisis.

The environmental movement is addressing issues vital to our quality of life on Earth, and thus is no fleeting fad or fancy. Enlightened members of the business community have recognized this truth and are now taking steps which realize many goals of environmentalists, even though in some cases the motivations of the two groups may be very different.

The Growing Influence of Green Organizations

The latest figures show that 14 percent of America's population is actively involved with green organizations. Public opinion is firmly behind the activists.[1] A survey conducted in 1989 reports that 77 percent of Americans said that a company's environmental reputation affected what they buy, 89 percent said they were concerned about the environmental impact of products purchased; and 78 percent said they were willing to pay more for recyclable or biodegradable packaging.[2] With such broad public support, environmental organizations have been effective in lobbying for tough legislation and in using the legal system to ensure legislation is enforced. Green groups have become very sophisticated in fighting for a wide variety of issues. For example, the *Economist* reported that lobbying by the Natural Resources Defense Council "helped bring about a television programme on the alleged carcinogenic properties of Alar, a chemical additive to apples." As a result, in 1989 Uniroyal withdrew Alar from use in foods worldwide.[3]

Because environmental lobbyists have such clout and public trust, some companies are turning to these groups for advice. Some environmentalists are suspicious of cooperative efforts, but as of now, such partnerships seem to have yielded positive results. For example, a long-time activist in California, Cliff Humphrey was hired by the consulting firm of Dames & Moore as director of integrated waste management services. The company wanted the benefit of his years of experience in the field, and his

---

[1] "Seeing the Green Light", *The Economist*, v.317, n.7677, Oct. 20, 1990, p.88.

[2] Iris Rosendahl, "Retailers Joining Fight to Clean Up Environment," *Drug Topics*, v.134, n.6, March 19, 1990, p.63.

[3] "Seeing the Green Light," p.88.

creative solution-oriented thinking. Mr. Humphrey felt the position offered him an opportunity to show other companies how to profit from environmentally responsible actions in a forum in which his advice would be adopted. He still sees himself as an agent of change.

In Midland, Michigan, home of Dow Chemical Company, Mary Sinclair, a prominent environmental activist, accepted a volunteer position on Dow's Midland Citizen Advisory Committee. In the 1960s Ms. Sinclair publicly challenged the company over the issue of a Dow-supported nuclear plant which was built on sinking swamplands, and she has maintained an activist stance ever since. In a recent interview she said that she took on her new role because she was impressed by some recent environmentally oriented Dow initiatives that will address several issues including energy efficiency and waste streams. She believes that Dow has made up its mind to lead the chemical industry in the area of environmental responsibility, and she says, "After a certain period, I'll be able to tell if I'm being manipulated....But I think they have a potential for establishing a pattern for deep industrial change that other companies might follow."[4] After years of agitation and consciousness raising, these activists are now in a position to help make sweeping changes within companies that will achieve many of the objectives they have fought for all along.

Perhaps the most widely publicized example of cooperation between a green organization and a large company is the joint effort between the Environmental Defense Fund (EDF) and McDonald's. The two factions jointly commissioned four scientists to examine ways McDonald's could reduce and recycle waste. The McDonald's Corporation was prohibited from using EDF's name in any marketing campaign, yet EDF was given full access to the corporation and was permitted to publish the findings of

---

[4] Art Kleiner, "The Three Faces of Dow," *Garbage*, July/Aug 1991, pp. 52-58.

the study with an eye toward providing a blueprint for other fast food companies to follow. Indeed, the study produced a set of sound proposals, including phasing out bleached paper; testing reusable cups, coffee filters, and shipping containers; buying recycled materials; and continuing experimentation so McDonald's becomes as creative in reducing and recycling its waste as it is in introducing new foods.

Prior to their link with EDF, there was much controversy over McDonald's approach to the issue of waste. The company's move from polystyrene to paper packaging was one lightning rod. The move was a big blow to the plastics industry because McDonald's used one percent of all polystyrene produced, and because the McDonald's name has high visibility and great public influence. In response, the plastics industry launched a campaign citing a lifecycle analysis study by Franklin Associates, a research organization, which they claimed indicated that cradle-to-grave, paper packaging was less environmentally sound than polystyrene. However, "the pro-plastic counter charges depend on a misinterpretation of the Franklin study," according to *Garbage* magazine. "It never compared the two McDonald's wrappers, but only a choice McDonald's never made—the stiff cardboard box. Franklin themselves said later that the paper wrap was the best of the lot (ecologically speaking)."[5]

The McDonald's/EDF cooperative study broke new ground. It boosted the advocacy power of environmental groups and brought public attention to the practice of lifecycle analysis, giving the practice new legitimacy and increasing the likelihood of its use by more companies as they try to gauge the true environmental impact of their actions and products. The positive results of the project demonstrate that through cooperation among interest groups ecological and economic benefits can be found. For example, by simply reducing the weight of its drinking straws by 20

---

[5] Art Kleiner, "Green Markets: Theatre of the McServed," *Garbage*, Sept/Oct 1991, pp. 52-56.

percent, McDonald's eliminated one million pounds of waste per year, saving both money and landfill space. By inviting assistance from a highly respected environmental organization, McDonald's went from a position of defensiveness vis-à-vis green groups to a position of model citizen—certainly a helpful boost to their public image. Some of the changes McDonald's implements will require one time capital expenditures, yet the company will benefit from reduced expenses on an ongoing basis and thus produce greater profits once the changes are in place. Pollution reduction pays in the long run.

The Effect of Green Legislation on Business

Both environmental lobbyists and public opinion have become major forces in shaping environmental legislation that impacts business. A recent example is the Environmental Defense Fund's work with EPA to draft the Clean Air Act. Such legislation required emissions reporting and criminal penalties for willful environmental pollution, having severe economic consequences for American businesses. The penalties associated with environmental legislation have spurred businesses to rethink their corporate environmental practices, resulting in significant changes in many cases. Some companies are even learning how to profit from environmental legislation.

Superfund, the fund for cleaning up pollution from hazardous waste, has been extremely costly for many companies. The EPA and corporate polluters have already spent $9 billion cleaning up the 1,222 sites on the National Priority List. The EPA estimates completely cleaning up the sites will cost $40 billion more. In the future, 750 more waste sites may be added to Superfund. Most of these sites were polluted before the hazards were understood and before the materials were illegal. Nevertheless, since the cost of cleaning up a typical site is $30 million, companies have surely learned to be more cautious with their waste.

The Justice Department, meanwhile, is becoming more aggressive in pursuing environmental criminals. In fiscal year

1990, the Department returned 134 indictments for environmental violations, 33 percent more than in FY 1989. Of this total, 78 percent of the indictments were against corporations and their top officers. More than half of those convicted were given prison sentences and are serving jail time. Penalty assessments were at record levels. The EPA collected $15 million from Texas Eastern, the largest penalty assessed to one company ever. USX was fined $1.6 million for water pollution violations. Eagle-Picher Industries was fined $1.5 million for Clean Water Act violations, and later declared bankruptcy as a result of penalties assessed in an unrelated asbestos case.

State and local governments, as well as individuals, have also collected large sums from polluting companies. Laidlaw, a waste management company, recently had to close a Cleveland landfill at a cost of $22 million after it was charged with 72 alleged violations. Monsanto was assessed the largest environmental penalty in Massachusetts history for attempting to conceal the discharge of 200,000 gallons of acid-laden waste water—$1.2 million. One individual who lived along a river polluted by Georgia-Pacific was awarded $1 million in damages and subsequently 1800 others joined together to sue the company and International Paper for $2 billion. Some industry observers believe DuPont's decision to abandon chlorofluorocarbons (CFCs) was sparked partly because the company feared future lawsuits from people who contracted skin cancer and blamed it on the damaged ozone layer. Of course, companies want to avoid exposing themselves to settlements so large they can seriously hurt the company's profitability or its very survival. More than ever, it is incumbent upon corporate officers to understand and comply with environmental regulations.

Recognizing the potential degree of environmentally related financial exposure, the SEC has tightened up on disclosure requirements for companies facing potentially large environmental expenditures or liabilities. Companies who fail to comply leave themselves open to shareholder suits. For example, in 1984,

Waste Management shareholders won a suit contending that by keeping its environmental problems from reaching the public, the company artificially inflated the price of its stock.

Even more effective than the threat of large fines has been EPA disclosure requirements whereby companies must report their usage of toxic and hazardous products and their emissions of poisonous chemicals. These emission results are ranked by the EPA and are public information. Some environmental organizations publicize the information in lists such as the National Wildlife Federation's Toxic 500. Companies want to avoid such adverse publicity because it reflects poorly on them in the eyes of their consumers, employees, and investors. This concern has produced instances of radical shifts in corporate behavior, as no company wants to be known as the biggest polluter in its state or industry.

Chemical companies have been especially responsive, because they typically produce 50-70 percent of the hazardous waste incurred in the complete cycle from manufacturing through disposal of final product. In 1987 Monsanto had to report to the EPA that it had released 20 million pounds of toxic emissions into the air. The company's chairman and CEO, Richard Mahoney, was so concerned about the public reaction that he simultaneously announced Monsanto's intention to voluntarily reduce its toxic air pollution to only 10 percent of 1987 levels within four years. Mahoney did not know how the company would achieve this goal when he made the announcement. He said, "The public, which gives us our privilege to operate, has expressed dissatisfaction with the rate of progress on the environment. And even though I think the progress has been quite good...it's critically important to earn the public's approbation for what we're doing."[6] Although Mahoney and environmentalists would disagree on many points, Mahoney's waste reduction

---

[6] Robert McGaugh, "A Matter of Perception," *Financial World*, v.159, n.2, Jan. 23, 1990, p.43.

plan has paid off for the environment and for the company. Emissions are down, although still not to targeted levels, and the company has recognized some savings. In one example, in attempting to reduce the volume of waste leftover from the manufacturer of the herbicide "Roundup," chemists discovered a new formula that is now saving the company $75 million a year in raw materials. Pollution in the manufacture of "Roundup" was cut by 50 percent, and costs were reduced by 22 percent.

DuPont is still the largest producer of toxic chemicals in the U.S., but the chairman and CEO Edgar S. Woolard, Jr. has a goal of reducing emissions 60 percent from the 1987 level by 1993. Thus far, DuPont has spent $1 billion on pollution control equipment, $1 billion to develop substitutes for CFCs, and $500 million to clean up past pollution. Now the company is recycling a billion pounds of its own polymers each year, recycling plastic bottles for use in other products, has the largest waste treatment operation in the country, and has a consulting arm that advises other companies how to clean up for a fee. DuPont has also realized operational savings. For instance, in the production of nylon DuPont produces a chemical byproduct called HMI. The company used to dispose of 3,600 tons of HMI annually. When it began looking for alternatives to solving this problem, DuPont discovered it could use HMI to coat pharmaceuticals. This worked so well that demand for the chemical now exceeds supply, and the company has to make HMI intentionally. A former waste item is now a profit producer. It will take DuPont several years to recoup initial environmentally related investments, but operational savings and new revenue streams will make these efforts very profitable to DuPont in the long run. Dow Chemical also has devoted corporate resources to waste reduction through its "Waste Management Always Pays" program. The company publishes a list of 90 pollution reduction improvements suggested by employees. In one instance an employee's suggestion to install corrosion resistant pipes saved the company $890,000 a year and saved the environment from the discharge of a hydrochloric-caustic cleaner. Overall, the company estimates that six of its waste reduction programs have saved $28 million. Dow is the second largest chemical company, but was ranked 29th in total emissions by EPA in 1990, indicating that its waste reduction programs are effective.

All of these companies still have environmental problems, yet progress is being made. Were it not for the potentially high regulatory costs, it is doubtful they would have implemented any of these environmentally beneficial programs. After experiencing painful regulatory consequences, the chemical companies have re-examined the situation and decided to become proactive to enhance their corporate images and to put themselves on the cutting edge of technology in order to stay ahead of their competition. They have become active in the national discussion on environmental issues, and have discovered that they can save money by preventing pollution early rather than trying to cope with it later. If they have to spend money on the environment one way or another, companies would much prefer to invest in technology and services which will prove productive for years to come as opposed to sinking corporate dollars into fines and penalties.

Other industries are following the lead of the chemical industry. The oil business, for one, is just beginning to shift toward prevention, as companies are coming under increasing public scrutiny due to the large number of oil spills (one per day on average). Business opportunities exist for companies to create and shape markets "at the technological frontier in each phase of the oil industry—from exploration to transportation and utilization."[7] There is a wide variation in response from different companies. Amoco's environmental affairs and safety office has seen its staff balloon from 15 to 196 in just four years while Exxon reportedly has 10 fewer senior environmental experts than it did in the 1970s.

---

[7] Dan C. Boroughs, "Cleaning up the Environment," *U.S. News & World Report*, v.110, n.11, March 25, 1991, p.45.

Other companies can learn from the chemical industry's experience that a company that takes a leadership position on environmental issues may benefit from being the first to introduce new technology or products, and may be able to play a role in shaping regulation.

The Evolving Role of Government

As companies alter their practices, regulators are beginning to focus more on pollution prevention. For example, the EPA has supported the development of internal environmental auditing programs and has reduced fines for violations of environmental laws if companies commit to developing regular environmental audit programs. Such audits can be extremely beneficial. In one instance, Chevron and environmental groups in San Francisco were in conflict for two years over the issue of dumping toxic metals into the bay. Chevron finally agreed to do an audit. The results showed that more than 90 percent of the discharges came from easily preventable sources, so Chevron has reduced its dumping by 70-90 percent.

The EPA's support of environmental self-auditing is indicative of increased governmental efforts to find ways to use economic incentives and the profit motive inherent in our capitalist system to encourage business to make decisions that are good for the environment. By leaning more heavily on economic incentives rather than regulation, the government hopes business will have the motivation to keep looking for the most efficient ways of operating, rather than simply doing the minimum to reach prescribed standards. In so doing, progress toward new technological breakthroughs could emerge, benefitting both industry and the environment. The EPA recently published a report listing major ecological problems that lend themselves to market solutions. One approach is for government to set broad limits on the amount of pollution allowed for a region or an industry. Each firm is allotted their share of the total, quantified into units or allowances that can be bought and sold. Companies that can inexpensively reduce a pollutant can sell their allowances, thereby off-setting a portion of their capital expenses. Companies for whom costs for meeting the pollution standards would be prohibitive can instead buy allowances. This guarantees a lower level of pollution overall, but gives individual companies more flexibility.

Tax policy is another avenue open to government for effective change. Environmental taxes allow business and the public to better understand the true cost of a cleaner environment. Some economists are beginning to criticize economic systems that do not incorporate the costs of using natural resources or polluting the ecosystem. Jose Lutzenberger, special secretary for the environment of Brazil, has said such systems are based "in terms of an indirectional flow between two infinites. Infinite resources on one side and an infinite hold on the other for dumping our wastes."[8] Of course we know today that such thinking is unconditionally wrong. Tax policy is one way to set prices to better reflect the true cost of using environmental resources. Faced with these costs, companies will be more likely to value environmental resources in the same way they value labor and capital resources now. Industry will be economically motivated to strive for improved environmental productivity. The U.S. implemented its first "green tax" in 1989 on sales of ozone-destroying chemicals with the objective of giving business economic incentive to phase out CFCs by the year 2000. Environmentalists also support the idea of worldwide "carbon" taxes on the burning of gasoline, oil, and coal under a program that would be administered by the United Nations, with the proceeds going to a fund to protect the environment from the polluting effects of these fuels.

Tax policy could also be designed to reward companies for spending decisions that will benefit the environment. Tax credits could be given to firms that buy recycled equipment, use more recycled materials, or invest in businesses designed to help the

---

[8] Jose Lutzenberger, Address to PREPCOM, Nairobi, August 29, 1990.

environment. Some states have tax credit programs in place. A study by the Oregon Department of Energy found that among companies that received tax credits, 43 percent said they were a strong incentive to invest in recycling."[9]

Governmental economic policies that affect the environment are not new. However, they have usually produced negative effects by not valuing resources properly. Examples of the consequences of such policies can be seen around the world. In Eastern Europe and the states of the former Soviet Union, for example, whole economies have been built around artificially cheap natural resources which were squandered with polluting abandon. High coal consumption encouraged by low energy prices has resulted in terrible air pollution, and resources have been used up so rapidly that Poland, the fourth largest coal exporter in the world, may be a coal importer before the end of the decade. The World Bank estimates that 10 percent of Poland's GNP has been lost as a result of environmentally caused illness and because the country's water is so polluted it can't be used industrially. In what used to be known as East Germany, 80 percent of the rivers are contaminated and the air is polluted some 50 times above safe limits. Pollution in this region is estimated to cost $18 billion annually.

In our own country, the U.S. government has encouraged the mining and timber industries with tax breaks, depletion allowances, subsidies and price supports for decades. The result is that virgin production of such materials is cheaper than recycling, and recycled content products have difficulty competing in some cases. Proposals to levy advance disposal fees on purchases of virgin material are being brought forward. Says William Shiveman, recycling specialist for the R.W. Beck and Associates consulting group, "To achieve market development over the long term, industry must internalize the cost of

---

[9] Bill Breen, "Selling It: The Making of Markets for Recyclables," *Garbage*, Nov/Dec 1990, pp. 44-49.

disposal....Today's market system operates on the fictitious premise that resources are unlimited and dumps are free."[10]

The Bureau of Reclamation subsidizes irrigation water for farmers in the west so that they pay a tenth to a twentieth of the price cities must pay for their water. Farmers use 85 percent of the water in California, growing climatically ill-suited crops like rice and cotton and growing crops officially in surplus. They have no incentive to conserve. The Bureau of Reclamation spends billions annually to support this program. Meanwhile, the rest of the state is suffering economically and environmentally from the water shortage. Yet studies show that California has enough water for its needs if the resource was allocated more equitably.

Recently, at a United Nations conference, the head of a Swedish engineering firm, Bjorn Stigsar, said, "We treat nature like we treated workers a hundred years ago. We included then no cost for the health and security of workers in our calculations, and today we include no cost for the health and security of nature."[11] If government policy is structured properly, it can serve as a catalyst to create economic and environmental benefits. In fact, in the extreme, economic policies that ignore the environment have proved to be disastrous in the long run, as the above examples clearly show.

The Effect of the Green Movement on the Worldwide Competitiveness of American Business

Newly industrialized nations are competing with U.S. companies in the global marketplace, yet many have only a few environmental protection measures with which companies must comply. This creates two problems. First of all, their costs of

---

[10] Ibid..

[11] Catherine Johnson, Maurice Strong, Chairman, Strovest Holdings Inc. and Under Secretary General of the U.N. and Environmental Adviser to the Administrator of the U.N. Development Programme,"Our Common Future," *Canadian Business Review*, v.17, n.1, Spring 1990, p.8.

production do not include environmental costs, and secondly, they are dumping the same pollutants into the environment that western countries are trying at great expense to clean up. Critics have also accused business of conducting operations too dirty to be allowed at home in countries with fewer environmental regulations. Are these issues putting American business at a disadvantage?

The answer seems to be a qualified "yes" in the short term, but the disadvantage is narrowing significantly. Moreover, from a long term perspective, what's good for the environment is good for the economy. No business can achieve maximum profitability in a scenario such as that facing Eastern Europe. And some would argue that decisions about pollution are ethical ones that ought not to be decided through pure dollars and cents calculations anyway. Finally, as consumers become more aware of companies' actions vis-à-vis the environment, the evidence shows they prefer to patronize cleaner companies regardless of cost. This goodwill is difficult to quantify, yet it is a big benefit for any company.

A study by Dr. Jeffrey Leonard, a noted authority in the field of environment and business, found that in the late 1970s, a number of industrializing nations tried to use their lax environmental regulations to attract investment from developed countries, with some success. However, increasing environmental awareness is a global phenomenon, and these countries in more recent years are setting new rules. Indigenous populations are more likely to complain if they think a foreign company is polluting. Moreover, companies headquartered in more environmentally strict countries are beginning to lobby for their governments to impose "green tariffs" to compensate for production inequalities. The United Nations Environment Programme (UNEP) has discussed this possibility.

The playing field is leveling out. The United Nations is playing an increasingly active role in helping governments develop a framework for environmental cooperation. In 1972, the U.N. Conference on Human Environment put the environment on the map as a global issue and led to the creation of UNEP. UNEP led to a series of conventions and agreements on regional issues. In 1983, the U.N. established the World Commission on the Environment and Development. The Commission's task was to examine the relationship between the environment and economic development looking toward the year 2000 and beyond. The Commission issued the Brundtland Report which triggered new interest in the environment among world leaders. The next event of global significance was the Montreal Protocol, an international agreement calling for the reduction of CFCs. Discussions leading to the Montreal Protocol included representatives from 35 countries and from many transnational public interest groups, scientific organizations, and multinational companies. The agreement was unprecedented in its breadth of participation.

The most significant international environmental effort ever will take place in the summer of 1992 in Brazil, the United Nations Conference on Economic Development (UNCED). UNCED will involve participation from more than 100 heads of state, representatives from business, youth groups, scientists, and environmentalists and will address the issue of sustainable development: how the world can find ways of progressing economically and technologically without harming the environment. Discussing the meaning of sustainable development, Maurice Strong, chairman of the Canadian company, Strovest Holdings, and environmental advisor to the administrator of UNEP said:

> "In the field of economic policy, we have to ensure that growth continues. But, those who make economic policy have to realize that they are also making environmental policy. It is through the economic process that we affect the environment and the environment itself is a major resource for economic growth...Economic growth has been dominant at the expenses of the environment. We have to restore that balance."[12]

---

[12] Ibid.

Prevailing world opinion is shifting to strongly favor environmentally sensitive business practices. Companies all over the world will be subject to constraints which are more and more similar. The focus of future growth will be on adding more value to natural resources, a significant change from the focus of growth for the past 100 years, which has been on growth from increasing use of energy and raw materials.

In the area of energy efficiency, for example, research suggests that energy conservation efforts can pay for themselves within two or three years. Looking back at the 1980s, it appears that countries with the highest degree of energy efficiency, such as Japan and Germany, had much greater economic success than did nations with the least energy efficiency, such as Eastern Europe. Countries with market economies seemed to use resources more efficiently than did those with other economic systems.

New Opportunities for Growth

As part of their effort to capitalize on new areas of economic growth, American industry has put together a coalition of 21 blue chip companies called the Global Environmental Management Initiative (GEMI). GEMI's task is to devise a set of broad environmental principles for multinational companies to use as the basis for an international code of corporate environmental conduct, and to promote the use of management tools such as total quality management (TQM) in the environmental field. GEMI will monitor compliance of companies who decide to implement the GEMI code. GEMI is promoting TQM as a way for companies to conduct internal audits and identify ways of using resources more efficiently. Companies will increasingly think about the resource and waste implications of their product throughout the entire product cycle, from conception to production to disposal. The field of lifecycle analyses will be a growth area. Businesses are finding that there is no one answer to such questions as "What is the best packaging to use environmentally?" or "How can I heat my plant most efficiently?" Every decision will be different depending on a host of variables. As lifecycle analysis becomes a more exact science, a company's plant in San Francisco may make different environmentally responsible decisions than its plant in Dubuque.

The U.S. business community has organized GEMI, participated in international efforts, and re-examined business practices with an eye toward future growth. Whereas 75 percent of total expenditures on the environment are now devoted to cleanup and remediation, by the end of the 1990s up to 50 percent of environmental expenditures will be driven by non-regulatory factors such as global competition for efficient production technologies, economic gains from energy conservation, and evolving consumer preferences. Business recognizes those trends, and will produce many new innovations in production techniques, products, and services. Ongoing pressure from environmentalist organizations, consumers and investors, combined with government regulations and incentives, certainly will hasten such progress. However, once the structure is in place, market forces are ultimately the most effective tool in bringing about corporate change. David Nichol, president of a Canadian grocery chain, Loblaw, made this point emphatically when he recalled "...the many years when the Canadian government tried to persuade Procter & Gamble to introduce a phosphate-free detergent. When *we* started selling phosphate-free detergent, they got one on the market within six months."[13] As the *Economist* pointed out in a recent article, "For far-sighted companies, the environment may turn out to be the biggest opportunity for enterprise and invention the industrial world has ever seen."[14]

Today, federal government expenditures on the environment are only 10 percent of the total. As this figure has not grown as quickly as the overall expenditure, it is expected to be less than five percent by the end of the decade. Commercial industry will

---

[13] *Economist*, 9/8/90, "The Environment—Special Report."
[14] Ibid.

decidedly have the leading role. Dr. Leonard believes that overall expenditures on the environment will continue to increase at a rapid speed both here and abroad, so that by the year 2000, total expenditures could reach four percent of GNP.

The ideal environmentally-friendly product or service would be no more expensive than its polluting counterpart and just as easy to fit in to the average consumer's lifestyle. Thus, the corporate call to action is to build a better mousetrap. Those who do will profit indeed, while those who ignore the call will lose their customers. Let's look at some of the ways business is profiting from the greening of America.

Annual sales have boomed at a car repair shop in Tyson's Corner, Virginia, since a new owner changed the name from Tyson's Service Center to Ecotech Autoworks, and began marketing environmentally correct auto repairs. Revenues went from $200,000 to $500,000 within one year. Ecotech recycles antifreeze and freon gas from car air conditioners on site and sends auto parts to a rebuilder. The shop is heated by burning waste oil and even the waiting room floor is made from recycled tires.

Because surface and groundwater pollution can be caused by leakage from chemical fertilizers and agricultural pesticides, Calgene, Inc. is seeking to develop new pesticides and fertilizers that are safer and degrade more quickly. The company also is developing new strains of crops that are resistant to these herbicides. Its major success so far is the herbicide Bromoxynil which is used in Calgene's new strain of cotton plants.

California has broken new ground by mandating that beginning in 1998, two percent of all new cars sold in that state must be electric, rising to 10 percent by 2003. Several companies are working to produce products that will meet this requirement. Ford has announced two new cars that meet California's standards, new versions of the Ford Escort and Mercury Tracer. The cars will produce only half the polluting emissions permitted under California rules. General Motors displayed a prototype electric car in January 1990, called the *Impact*. AeroVironment Inc. developed and built the prototype. President Paul B. MacCready believes, "there's a so-so chance the internal combustion engine will go the way of the buggy whip by 2005."[15] Advances in the development of longer-lived batteries, and environmental pressure to increase demand to a level that would make production more cost effective, may make electric cars feasible transportation alternatives of the future. Southern California Edison, in cooperation with the Los Angeles Department of Water and Power, has announced plans to build a road that transfers electric power from underground cables to surface vehicles without physical contact. They are beginning with a $2 million demonstration project over 1200 feet of road.

In 38 states, municipalities will no longer pick up grass clippings, nor will they provide dump space. Homeowners have to figure out a way to dispose of clippings. Enter Simplicity Manufacturing which has developed and now markets two new walk-behind lawn mowers that mulch grass clippings as you go. With the mowers' twin blades, decomposition is accelerated and the clippings help fertilize the lawn.

Service companies have sprung up in the areas of waste measurements, environmental engineering and assessments, waste disposal and treatment, and recycling. Where there's a regulation, there's a service company to help other companies comply. ICF International in Fairfax, Virginia is one consulting firm that is benefitting early as companies begin planning for regulatory compliance.

Potential winners from the Clean Air Act range from producers of natural gas to corn farmers. Research-Cottrell, Cos. a division of Water Technologies Corp., makes scrubbers and other equipment used to clean up utility power plant emissions. It expects its workforce to increase from 700 to 1200 by 1992. In-

---

[15] Alan J. Miller, *Socially Responsible Investing*, N.Y. Institute of Finance 1991, 357 pages.

dustry officials believe the market for retrofitting existing boilers with scrubbers will exceed $10 billion.

Natec Resources, Inc., a Houston company, markets a process in which sodium bicarbonate, or baking soda, is injected into a coal-fired boiler's flue gas, transforming the sulfur dioxide into sodium sulfate. Sodium sulfate is a solid product that can be used in detergents and processes in paper production. Natec projects its revenues will skyrocket from $3-4 million in 1990 to about $200 million by 1995. The company attributes 80-85 percent of the growth to the clean air legislation.

Burlington Northern is offering incentives to utilities that conduct test movements of cleaner burning western coal on its railroad. The company expects that the Clean Air Act will boost its tonnage 10 percent in the next decade. A.T. Massey Coal Co., a subsidiary of Fluor Corp., is the largest producer of low sulfur coal in the eastern United States and is expecting a large increase in demand for its coal.

In the pursuit of lowering automobile emissions, Camet Co., an affiliate of W.R. Grace, introduced a new kind of catalytic converter in 1990 that promises to eliminate over 50 percent of exhaust pollutants. Corning Inc. produces diesel fuel and catalytic converter parts. The firm expects to receive a large share of an additional 200,000 to 600,000 orders a year for diesel fuel truck filters that the Clean Air Act is expected to generate by 1994. It also expects a pickup in European business as these nations enact tighter standards. Archer Daniels Midland and Atlantic Richfield produce additives to make gasoline burn cleaner. One additive, ethanol, is made from corn. There is debate over the environment efficiency of ethanol, but the National Corn Growers Association predicts that by mid-decade the Clean Air Act could increase demand for corn by 250 million bushels a year or more. Finally, Pacific Gas & Electric is opening nine publicly accessible natural gas stations in California this year. It has converted some of its fleet vehicles to natural gas and is helping to finance a fleet of 1,000 GM pickup trucks that will be natural gas powered.

Recycling in many forms presents exciting business opportunities as well. REsys Inc., in Salem, Oregon, makes a water reclamation system for use in photography labs. One early user in California reports that his six processors used up to 5,000 gallons a day, but since implementing the new system he uses only 700 gallons of water a year, and since the equipment keeps the water temperature at 90 to 100 degrees, it has reduced heating expenses as well.

Margaret Gainer established her own consulting firm, Gainer & Associates, in 1984 to assist communities in developing recycling services by showing small business entrepreneurs how to create local markets for locally collected recyclables. By concentrating on niche marketing in small towns, she is helping manufacturers succeed financially, in many cases providing new employment opportunities to depressed areas.

Plastics constitute seven percent of America's garbage by weight and 20 percent by volume. Plastics are among the most valuable materials in the garbage pile, and yet only one percent of plastics are currently being recycled. This number is expected to increase to 25 percent by the end of the decade as collection facilities and processes expand, and as technology is developed to make recycling more economical. Wellman Inc., the nation's largest recycler of plastic, manufactures finished goods such as fiberfill, carpeting, parking space bumpers, and even tennis ball fuzz from plastic waste. Environmentalists believe that secondary products only delay the day when plastic materials get dumped, and therefore encourage circular processes whereby a plastic bottle is made into another plastic bottle. The technology is not yet available to accomplish this, but several companies including Procter & Gamble, Sonoco, Lever Brothers, Coca-Cola, and Pepsico have announced a goal of up to 30 percent recycled content for their plastic products. There is no way they can achieve 30 percent now, due to lack of supply, but the goal still stands. Jackie Prince, staff scientist with the Environmental Defense Fund, says the bottle programs "could set a precedent for the fact that there may be technologies that can eliminate contaminants and enable a resin to be reused in a food application."[16]

Another area for technological breakthroughs is tire recycling. At present there is only a five percent recovery rate for used tires. None of the recycling methods have been attractive enough to keep up with newly dumped tires although several methods are being tried. Crumb rubber has been used in asphalt for roadbeds. It costs 50 percent more than concrete but has three times the lifespan. Oxford Energy in Westley, California, produces electricity to power 15,000 homes by burning tires within California's stringent air pollution guidelines. However, controversy over the incineration process has resulted in local opposition to new facilities the company wanted to set up in New York and Connecticut. Finally, a variety of small companies are experimenting with producing consumer goods, such as wallets, belts, and handbags from recycled tires.

We currently recycle 12 percent of our glass containers nationwide. Demand for waste glass is strong. Mixing waste glass with virgin materials to make new glass containers affords manufacturers energy savings. Glass can also replace up to 20 percent of the stone and sand used in a conventional asphalt mix to produce "glasphalt." Over the past four years, for example, New York City has used 30,000 tons of waste glass to pave 412 miles of roadways. There is more demand for waste glass than there is supply because many glass manufacturers have not invested in technology to keep waste glass contamination free in the recycling process. They say they will invest when they are sure recycling is not a fad, and are reasonably sure they will have a steady supply of waste glass to recycle from consumers.

---

[16] Ibid.

Aluminum is the most valuable recyclable. Demand and supply are strong. Imco Recycling, for example, is a highly successful aluminum recycling firm. Recycling aluminum containers saves about 90 percent of the energy required to produce the same product from virgin materials. The aluminum can recovery rate has gone from 15 percent in 1972 to 61 percent in 1990.

Government purchase programs requiring purchases of recycled products will be a big stimulus, as federal government purchases alone account for 20 percent of U.S. GNP. In addition, consumers are asking for more recycled and environmentally friendly products. Not only do most consumers say they are willing to pay more for a product made of recyclable or bio-degradable materials, 53 percent said they actually had *not* purchased a product due to environmental concerns. As long as the demand is there, so will there be opportunities for entrepreneurs.

New Employment Opportunities

The environmental movement produces not only new business opportunities, but new employment opportunities as well. Environmental consulting firms need environmental engineers, chemists, hydrologists, and geologists. Fortune 500 firms are using environmental compliance officers and public relations practitioners. In addition, environmental analysts are on staff to provide audits and site assessments, and corporate environmental litigators are available to argue past and present sins in court.

Many environmental experts will find new opportunities with firms not traditionally thought of as connected to the environment. Several real estate firms, insurance companies and law firms have environmental specialists, for example, and other firms make use of the growing selection of consultants. An increasing number of companies have director of environmental affairs positions, or even entire departments concerned with both technical and public relations issues. These positions were much more rare before the 1980s.

The environmental employment sector spans the range from attorney to Greenpeace activist, encompassing many educational disciplines. A quick glance at the employment ads in any major city's newspaper will show the growing variety of environmental employment opportunities. The sheer necessity of this field dictates an ever-expanding job market. Unlike the railroad industry or the junk bond market, the environment is not something that can be replaced with new technology or phased out by a more conservative public. While new technologies will emerge and public opinion will change with the years, the basic elements of a healthy planet and the desire to achieve that status will remain the same. Those environmental professionals who stay on the leading edge of the industry will likely have an exceptional chance for success.

The Effect of the Green Consumer

The green movement is the ultimate example of an effective grass roots effort. In 1991 a *Wall Street Journal*/NBC poll reported that 80 percent of Americans consider themselves environmentalists. Jon Grant, president and CEO of Quaker Oats Company of Canada, said the public expects business to be environmentally responsible. "Consumers will be calling the shots in the 1990s, and businesses that ignore their wishes do so at their peril."[17] The goal of environmental protection is shifting consumer tastes. The public wants to buy the services and products that use nature most frugally.

Retailers have been quick to respond. They have stocked environmentally friendly products and disseminated consumer information. Washington, D.C. has a supermarket that sells organically grown produce in large enough quantities to be very

---

[17] Pat Weisner, "The Business Issue of the '90s," *Colorado Business Magazine*, v.17, n.7, July 1990, p.8(1).

price competitive with local grocery store chains. New York City has a department store that sells only environmentally friendly products. Wal-Mart Stores Inc. and K-Mart Corp. have asked manufacturers to supply them with more recycled and recyclable products. They have set up recycling programs in communities and experimented with packaging.

Manufacturers are examining their production process for ways to become more environmentally friendly. When Esprit owner Susie Tompkins negotiated with her ex-husband to buy out his share of the company, one of his primary concerns was to keep the company environmentally sound. This she promised to do, so in reviewing company actions, she is asking questions such as, "How much are we manufacturing and how does that relate to renewable and nonrenewable resources?"[18] She says Esprit is using more enzymes and fewer chemical pollutants to clean up its manufacturing process.

Companies are also creating marketing and public relations campaigns to publicize various links of their products or services to the environment. Some firms structure strategic green corporate giving programs which give added PR mileage. Others have taken on the role of environmental promoters.

Gallo Wines, for instance, is involved in the Global Releaf program, an initiative of American Forests to replant trees around the world. The Body Shop uses posters, pamphlets and window displays in their store to air environmental messages. Ben & Jerry's Ice Cream supports organic farming methods. Patagonia, a maker of outdoor wear, highlights environmental activists in their catalogue and donates 10 percent of their pre-tax profits to environmental groups. Nike has an employee donation campaign to Earth Share, a fund that contributes to several environmental organizations; U.S. Sprint will donate five percent of your phone bill to this fund. Esprit is currently airing TV

---

[18] Ellie McGrath, "Esprit, the sequel," *Working Woman*, Sept. 1991, pp. 67-69.

commercials with the theme, "What would you do?", discussing various individuals' ideas about social issues, including how to save the planet. While these companies do not necessarily provide environmental products or services, they have aligned themselves with the environmental cause; good for business, good for PR purposes, good for the planet.

To assist companies in gaining recognition for their efforts, more and more environmental marketing consultants and public relations firms will appear. They will learn to make all green products look necessary and all necessary products look green. Faith Popcorn, author of *The Popcorn Report* and chairman of BrainReserve Inc., a trend forecasting firm, sees "cause marketing" as the wave of the future—a concept in which each purchase is influenced by social and environmental values and the sellers of the product or service donate a portion of their profits to a worthy cause. This concept is a part of the "save our society" trend she feels has taken firm root in today's culture, and is fueled by the passion of the "vigilante consumer."[19]

It takes just one corporate slip for consumers to stage a revolt. After the *Valdez* oil spill, almost 20,000 Exxon credit cards were cut into pieces and mailed back to the company. Exxon's name immediately appeared on many boycott lists. T-shirts emblazoned with anti-Exxon slogans were seen across the nation. During the month after the spill, the Wilderness Society gained 27,000 new members.

While corporate product managers clamor to cash in on the green revolution, some will make the fatal mistake of "greenwashing" an earth-threatening product. Mobil, the maker of the so-called biodegradable trash bags witnessed the wrath of the wronged "vigilante consumer" when they were called on the carpet for their false eco-claims. As the American public's environmental savvy increases, merely pasting on a "green label" won't con

---

[19] Faith Popcorn, *The Popcorn Report*, Doubleday, 1991, 666 Fifth Avenue, New York, NY 10103.

the masses. Claims must be substantiated and backed up by the experts.

In order to be a part of the "save our society" trend, many companies that have been polluters of the past are increasing their environmental PR effort in an attempt to rid themselves of the onerous "bad guy" status. They realize loss of consumer support can be devastating to their company's long-term profits. A bad environmental reputation will be the 90's version of the Scarlet Letter.

But empty gestures could end up being bad for business. Firms that mount environmentally oriented PR campaigns and then conduct business as usual may suffer a backlash in lost sales when the public finds out they have been misled. Companies that jump on the environmental bandwagon must realize they could be opening the doors to greater public scrutiny.

To assist consumers in judging the validity of companies' environmental claims, eco-labeling programs run by governments and non-profit groups are springing up in several countries around the world, including the U.S. Germany's program is the oldest; there the Blue Angel has been in use since 1978 and is currently affixed to over 300 products. Japan has had their Eco-Mark since 1989. It graces 850 products. Canada's Environmental Choice has been active since 1990. Sixty meals have been issued. These programs are all run by government agencies. In America, two independent organizations are developing standards for eco-labels: Green Seal and Green Cross. The Green Cross is an indication that a manufacturer meets minimum standards and is making truthful environmental claims. It is not intended as an environmental seal of approval. About 400 products now bear the Green Cross.

Green Seal's goals *are* to provide the consumer with an environmental stamp of approval by putting products through a shortened version of lifecycle analysis called an Environmental Impact Evaluation. The standards a product must meet to qualify for a Green Seal are more stringent than for a Green Cross. However, arriving at those standards is proving to be a complex process, and Green Seal has not approved any products yet.

The process of eco-labeling brings up many issues. Different research projects have come up with different conclusions about the most environmentally friendly packaging. Should only the best technology be rewarded, or is it sufficient to be better than a certain percentage of the competition? If standards vary from country to country manufacturers may have to vary operations, which could be quite expensive. Who should get standards anyway? For all the questions raised, the discussions instigated by eco-labeling efforts will encourage more thorough examination of the complexity of environmental choices, and will encourage leaders in government, business and environmental groups to think through their priorities. Hopefully it will open up areas of future cooperation.

The Effect of Green Investors

Ever since church groups first organized as investor shareholders in the 1960s around the issues of alcohol and tobacco, the influence of the socially responsible investment movement has grown. For most such investors the issue of corporate environmental responsibility is of great concern. In 1990 a coalition of investment advisors, religious leaders and representatives from environmental organizations put together the Valdez Principles, a list of ten principles designed to encourage companies to publish sufficient information about their activities and policies so that investors can make informed decisions. According to Joel Thomas, general counsel at the National Wildlife Federation, "If you want to further environmentally responsible investing, the most helpful thing you could do would be to encourage companies to sign the Valdez Principles and provide an annual report on their policies and activities." To date no publicly held company has signed the Principles.

Patrick Ramage, a public policy analyst with the environmental consulting firm of Mongoven, Biscoe and Duchin Inc., believes it unlikely that any major corporations will sign the Valdez Principles. The primary reason is that "the Valdez Principles were developed in a vacuum without any corporate participation." Also Ramage believes the meaning of the Principles is subject to interpretation, leaving the companies unclear as to what they are signing.

Environmentally concerned investors have had an impact through the Valdez Principles, although they are unsigned. Activist shareholders have initiated many resolutions calling for companies to sign the principles. Many of these resolutions received a relatively high percentage of shareholder support. In response, some companies have drafted environmental policy statements or conducted environmental audits. General Motors wrote its first environmental policy statement and introduced it in time for their annual meeting, since a Valdez resolution was to be discussed and voted on at that meeting. Waste Management Inc. issued a 160-page environmental audit that largely reflected the goals of the Valdez Principles. Eastman Kodak, Ford, American Express, and Gannett among others have agreed to answer the intensive questionnaire put out by the authors of the Principles. The Principles have been effective in raising the level of discussion on environmental issues at many companies.

In other areas too, concerned investors are making themselves known to American business. The recently elected treasurer of California, Kathleen Brown, campaigned on a promise to discourage the state's pension system from investing in companies with criminal pollution records. Stanford University has surveyed companies in which its endowment invests to determine their environmental policies. New York City Comptroller Elizabeth Holtzman has called investors' knowledge of a company's environmental record "a bottom line concern for stockholders."[20] Religious organizations with billions to invest have been lobbying businesses as activist, environmentally-concerned investors for years, sponsoring shareholder resolutions calling for major changes, and often meeting with top corporate executives who want to avoid messy public debates.

There is no doubt that investors who make their voices heard increase the public pressure on companies to become more sensitive to environmental issues.

Different Corporate Focus: Responsibility

The drastic corporate changes that were brought on by the 1990s environmental awareness, are changing the face of executive decision making in the decades to come. Environmental consciousness is becoming a basic management skill. To be successful, corporate leaders will find it ever more important to ensure that a company's environmental policies adhere to a variety of legal guidelines as well as to public expectations. Executives who fail in either of these realms will risk lowering the corporation's profitability. Executives who succeed will be able to proudly publicize the outstanding achievements of their pro-active efforts. Corporate public relations executives will be competing to get their clean environmental records in the news. In the 1990s the environmental crisis is presenting the business community with an incredible opportunity to create truly responsible companies which are both profitable enterprises and outstanding corporate citizens. It is up to all of us—environmentalists, consumers, investors, legislators, and business people—to do our part to make this possibility a reality.[21]

Karen McCullah also contributed to this chapter.

---

[20] Ibid.

[21] Saul Hansell, "It's Not Easy Being Green," *Institutional Invester*, January 1991, pp. 101-106.

Chapter 2

Effect of the Green Movement on Investors

Mark A. White
University of Virginia

Introduction

Developing concerns for preservation and protection of the environment over the past quarter century or so have created threats and opportunities for American businesses and the investment community. Recent Earth Day celebrations differed from earlier events by their inclusion of representatives from both large and small businesses, in addition to the usual complement of speakers from government agencies and environmental organizations. Throughout the country, indeed, throughout the world, hard questions concerning the environmental responsibility of corporations are increasingly being asked. This chapter outlines incidents and issues which have contributed to the growth of environmental concerns and explores the adverse impacts and investment opportunities arising from them. The role played by investors in directing capital flows away from potentially harmful activities and towards more environmentally benign alternatives will be addressed, with particular attention given to the financial performance of "green" investment funds.

Milestones

The beginning of today's environmental movement can be traced back to the writings of Henry David Thoreau, George Perkins Marsh and John Muir. Yellowstone National Park, the nation's first, was established in 1872 by an Act of Congress in partial response to the sentiments expressed by these citizens. In 1908, President Theodore Roosevelt, an ardent conservationist, sponsored the White House Conference of Governors on Natural Resources. Excepting creation of the National Park Service in 1916, the environmental movement languished until the Great Depression of the 1930s, when President Franklin Roosevelt's Civilian Conservation Corps (CCC) brought renewed attention to this area.

The 1940s saw publication of naturalist Aldo Leopold's *A Sand County Almanac*, a moving tribute to the natural beauty and ecological relationships among the sand dunes of his native Wisconsin. The beginning of the modern environmental movement roughly coincided with the 1962 publication of Rachel Carson's landmark work, *Silent Spring*, which chronicled dangers associated with the use of pesticides, particularly dichloro-diphenyl-tricloroethane (DDT). The book's title refers to DDT's tendency to cause fragility in the eggshells of birds, leading to increased mortality and the ultimate demise of many songbird species. Domestic use of DDT was banned in 1972, although it continues to be manufactured for application overseas.

Public awareness of environmental issues has been increased via a number of unfortunate accidents. The 1969 Santa Barbara oil spill led to passage of the National Environmental Policy Act (NEPA), and initiated planning for the first Earth Day celebration. In 1978, the supertanker *Amoco Cadiz* ran aground in the English Channel, spilling 69 million gallons of oil and damaging hundreds of miles of coastline. The world's largest spill occurred in February 1983, as 220 million gallons gushed into the Persian Gulf when an offshore oil well collapsed. By comparison, the March 1989 *Exxon Valdez* spill released approximately 11 million gallons of oil into Prince William Sound in Alaska.

Nuclear disasters at Three Mile Island (1979) and Chernobyl (1986) have dampened consumer and industry enthusiasm for the power source once promoted as "...too cheap to meter." Highly visible chemical catastrophes at Union Carbide's fertilizer operations in Bhopal, India (1984) and the Sandoz plant in Basel, Switzerland (1986) vie for attention with potentially more devastating long-term hazardous waste disposal practices at Love Canal, Times Beach and Virginia's James River.

Product safety concerns have further complicated matters. Over 150,000 claims have been filed against Manville Corporation, a major manufacturer of asbestos insulation which declared bankruptcy in 1982 as a result of its part in manufacturing what was once a standard construction component. The discovery that widely used chlorofluorocarbon (CFC) foam insulation, refrigerants and propellants contributed to depletion of the ozone layer caused Canada, Sweden and the United States to ban their use in aerosol sprays in 1978. Subsequently, DuPont Corporation, the world's largest producer of CFCs, has been working feverishly to develop substitutes in anticipation of their total prohibition by the year 2000. A 1989 television exposé on uses of the pesticide daminozide (Alar) significantly disrupted the operations of apple producers, wholesalers and retail outlets. These and other incidents have raised our nation's collective consciousness about environmental issues and have called into question our ability to wisely manage planetary resources. The following section highlights legislative attempts to correct environmental ills and establish rules governing the environmental conduct of individuals and corporations.

Environmental Legislation

Legislation intended to change current environmental practices and improve environmental quality was developed concurrently with the events discussed earlier. Many of these laws were milestones in their own right, for example, the National Environmental Policy Act (1969), the Clean Air Act (1970) and the Clean Water Act (1972). Although a complete discussion of environmental law is beyond the scope of this chapter, Table 1 lists major federal environmental legislation likely to be of concern to investors.

The 1980 Comprehensive Environmental Response, Compensation, and Liability Act (Superfund) and the 1986 Superfund Amendments and Reauthorization Act (SARA) have the greatest direct impact on investors. According to these acts, a firm may be held as a potentially responsible party (PRP) for cleaning up a hazardous waste site if it owns or manages a contaminated property, or is responsible for the generation, transport or storage of hazardous waste material, now or in the past. Because liability is joint and several, if one party is unable to pay its share of the cleanup, the EPA can recover remaining costs from the others, no matter how much or little they may have actually contributed to the property's current state. Although over 1200 sites are listed on the National Priority List (NPL) for *immediate* cleanup, only three have been fully restored to date. The remainder are mired in seemingly endless rounds of litigation and debate. More than $300 billion may be needed to clean up just the NPL sites, and it is quite possible that the Superfund Act may prove to be the most expensive piece of regulatory legislation ever enacted in the United States.

Depletion of the Ozone Layer and the Montreal Protocol

The nature and extent of our environmental problems have brought about unprecedented cooperation among the nations of our world. Realizing the seriousness of the ozone problem, in

Table 1.
Major U. S. Federal Environmental Legislation

Year	Legislation	Contents
1938, 1958	*Federal Food, Drug and Cosmetic Act*	establishment of Food and Drug Administration (FDA) to regulate food and drug additives; 1958 Delaney Clause prohibits sale of foods containing additives which cause cancer in humans or animals *in any amount*
1964	*Wilderness Act*	prohibited development of wilderness areas and established procedures for designation of new areas
1969	*National Environmental Policy Act (NEPA)*	landmark legislation declaring a national environmental policy and creating the Council on Environmental Quality (CEQ)
1970, 1977, 1990	*Clean Air Act*	formation of the Environmental Protection Agency (EPA) to oversee enforcement of air quality standards
1972, 1988	*Federal Insecticide, Fungicide and Rodenticide Act (FIFRA)*	requires registration of all pesticides, applicant certification and premarket testing
1972, 1977, 1981, 1987	*Clean Water Act*	established effluent limitations and water quality standards
1973	*Endangered Species Act*	regulations for the protection of endangered or threatened species
1976, 1984	*Resource Conservation and Recovery Act (RCRA)*	regulates the generation, transport, storage, treatment and disposal of hazardous wastes
1976	*Toxic Substances Control Act*	charges EPA with recordkeeping and assessing risks of new chemicals
1980	*Comprehensive Environmental Response, Compensation, and Liability Act (Superfund)*	imposes liability on owners, transporters and generators of hazardous waste materials; established fund to assist in cleanup costs
1986	*Superfund Amendments and Reauthorization Act (SARA)*	Title III, aka the Emergency Planning and Community Right-to-Know Act requires industry to publicly disclose chemicals and toxic hazards in their operations

1987, thirty nations ratified the Montreal Protocol, a document proposing to cut CFC production in half by the year 2000. In January 1989, thirteen nations, including the United States, announced they would ban *all* production and use of CFCs by the year 2000. Two months later, an agreement in Helsinki signed by 89 nations reiterated these goals and established a global fund to aid less-developed nations in accomplishing this task. While no federal legislation has yet resulted from these agreements, several municipalities (e.g. Irvine, Berkeley, Tempe and Newark) have passed legislation prohibiting certain uses of CFCs.

Adverse Impacts of Growing Environmentalism

In addition to the expense of complying with burgeoning environmental regulations, businesses must deal with increased consumer environmental literacy and demands for "greener" products. Failure to meet these needs or attempts to "greenwash" the American public can lead to negative publicity, product boycotts and hostile reactions such as protest marches, tree spiking, and even oil-covered rocks mailed to one's corporate headquarters.

The issue of "dolphin-safe" tuna provides a good example of the power of consumer attitudes. In the eastern tropical Pacific fishery, from the coast of California down to Chile, yellowfin tuna often school directly below dolphins. More than 100,000 dolphins are killed annually by fisherman using helicopters and speedboats to drive both species into their encircling nets. Dolphins also become entangled in the 40-mile long driftnets used to catch albacore and other tuna species. Earth Island Institute, a conservation group, mounted a campaign to save the dolphins and called for a boycott of the major tuna-processing firms. Three major distributors (Heinz, Van Camp and Unicord) responded by pledging to stop the purchase, processing or sale of tuna caught at the expense of dolphins. However, in 1990, Earth Island Institute took out a full-page advertisement in the *New York Times* denouncing Bumble Bee brand tuna and its parent company, Unicord, for breaking its promise. The ad's copy read, "To save dolphins from being killed in tuna nets, you can buy StarKist or

Chicken of the Sea. But don't buy Bumble Bee!" Two days later, Unicord responded with an advertisement attacking Earth Island Institute for false and misleading statements. The "tuna wars" exemplify the environmental movement's growing sophistication and highlights the danger of ignoring consumer attitudes.

Mobil Corporation's decision to market degradable Hefty trash bags is another illustration of an environmental strategy gone awry. In December 1989, shortly after the bags' introduction, six environmental groups called for a boycott of all allegedly "degradable" plastics, claiming that the bags did not fully break down under normal landfill conditions. Attorneys general from seven states sued Mobil for deceptive advertising practices in June 1990, and Mobil has since removed the word "degradable" from its packaging.

Disposable diapers are also a concern. A $3.5 billion business, they are the third largest component of household waste streams, after newspapers and beverage containers. They account for about two percent of solid waste deposited in landfills. Disposables comprise about 85 percent of the diaper market, due to their greater convenience and in spite of higher costs and increased sanitation risks. Citizens and environmental groups concerned over the growing lack of landfill space are pressuring hospitals, day care centers and parents to use more environmentally benign alternatives. Manufacturers' claims that their products are "degradable" or "recyclable" add to the controversy. Procter & Gamble, the nation's largest manufacturer of disposable diapers (Pampers and Luvs), has funded two projects examining alternative methods of waste disposal. In Seattle, used diapers are collected in a curbside recycling program and reprocessed into flowerpots, drywall backing and computer paper. A composting project in Minnesota turns soiled diapers into humus for agricultural use.

McDonalds Corporation has handled its environmental problems somewhat differently. Criticized for its use of non-degradable polystyrene "clamshell" hamburger containers, the fast-food restaurant chain enlisted the aid of a respected environmental group, the Environmental Defense Fund (EDF), to develop alternative policies that are viewed as more friendly to the environment. A joint task force consisting of representatives from both organizations developed a set of recommendations proposing to reduce solid wastes by 95 percent by substituting recycled and recyclable materials for virgin products where practical. Many of these recommendations have already been implemented and have enhanced the firm's environmental image.

Finally, growing environmental concerns have fostered the development of several organizations which provide information and rankings on firms' commitment to environmental responsibility. Franklin Research and Development, the Investor Responsibility Research Center and the Interfaith Center for Corporate Responsibility are examples. *Shopping for a Better World*, published recently by the Council on Economic Priorities, rates companies' performance on a number of social issues, including environmental responsibility, treatment of women and minorities, employee benefits and involvement in South Africa. This book and others with titles like *The Green Consumer, How to Make the World a Better Place*, and *The Green Lifestyle Handbook*, suggest that consumers can make a difference by purchasing from companies with good environmental records and eschewing products from known polluters or environmental scofflaws. Irresponsible companies and their products risk being branded as uncaring and undesirable, although significant opportunities exist for concerned businesses which demonstrate higher standards of environmental responsibility. Ben and Jerry's, a Vermont-based manufacturer of premium ice cream and Ringer Corporation, a Minnesota firm specializing in natural/organic lawn care supplies, are firms which are successful and yet maintain high environmental standards within their operations.

Investment Opportunities

Areas for investment growth in the environmental services industry include waste management and pollution control, energy efficient technologies and alternative energy sources. Additional opportunities exist for smaller firms to distinguish themselves by providing environmentally desirable alternatives to current consumer products. For instance, The Body Shop, a British firm specializing in natural cosmetic products not tested on animals, has expanded at a rapid rate since its founding in 1976. Cultural Survival Enterprises, a cooperative formed in 1990 to facilitate a greater sharing of the profits from rainforest products with indigenous tribes, markets "Rainforest Crunch," a confection of Brazil nuts, cashews and other renewable rainforest resources. The project's goal is to provide local residents with incomes sufficiently high to induce them to harvest, rather than burn, tropical rainforests. Shaman Pharmaceuticals, a California firm, hopes to identify and bring to market useful medicines derived from some of the 250,000 known plant species. Nearly 25 percent of all prescription drugs are derived from plants, including quinine, digitalis, morphine and codeine.

Waste Management and Pollution Control

Tremendous opportunities exist for technological improvements to our current systems for waste disposal. According to the Environmental Protection Agency, 80 percent of the country's landfills will close within the next 18 years, and new sites are difficult to develop due to the NIMBY ("Not In My BackYard") syndrome. Alternative technologies—incineration, composting and recycling—may provide solutions. For example, a modern waste-to-energy plant in Rochester, Massachusetts transforms municipal solid waste (MSW) into processed-refuse fuel which is used to heat water and produce steam. The steam drives a turbine, generating 52 megawatts of energy. Over one hundred such plants are scattered throughout the country, earning money from tipping fees and the sale of electricity. Disposal of the remaining ash is problematic, although some advances have been made to recycle it into construction blocks, roadbed material and landfill cover.

Composting, or biological decomposition of organic wastes, is an older technology which has recently regained its popularity. Composting can reduce the volume of solid wastes by as much as 50 percent. Separating organic wastes from the municipal solid waste stream reduces metals contamination, lowers costs and yields a higher-quality product. Mixed MSW systems are more expensive, but treat the entire waste stream. As of 1988, five mixed MSW composting facilities were operative in the United States.

Recycling is perhaps the most visible alternative waste management technique. Markets exist for the recycling of glass, aluminum, paper, plastics, iron and steel. More specialized programs recycle tires, used oil, batteries and CFCs. Consumer and industry responses have been overwhelming, resulting in a glut of recycled materials and correspondingly low prices. The United States is the world's largest exporter of recycled paper. The recycling of plastics, particularly polyethylene terapthalate (PET) soda bottles and high-density polyethylene (HDPE) milk jugs, is well-established and growing. High prices for virgin resins, at-capacity production and increased legislative initiatives indicate a favorable outlook for continued growth.

Other opportunities within the waste management and pollution prevention industries include the development of cleaner technologies and remediation of hazardous waste sites. 3M Corporation, widely known for its "Pollution Prevention Pays" program, has discovered methods for capitalizing on its experiences and now offers environmental consulting services to other companies. The vast number of Superfund sites in need of cleanup has created a new growth industry in environmental remediation.

Energy Efficient Technologies and Alternative Energy Sources

Environmentalists frequently blame our planetary problems on either of two fundamental causes: overpopulation and inefficient energy usage. Investment opportunities abound in the development and application of energy efficient technologies. To cite just one example, a solution promoted by the Lawrence Berkeley Lab (LBL) recommends painting building walls white and planting trees around them. This would reduce energy cooling needs to one one-hundredth of their current levels, decrease the amount of carbon dioxide released from the burning of fossil fuels *and* save money. In LBL's words,

> "Investments in improved efficiency would provide U.S. industry with a better competitive position in world markets and free up more than $100 billion annually for capital investments in other U.S. industries. The poor would benefit from lower energy costs and additional jobs. Reduced emissions of carbon dioxide and other pollutants would lessen environmental damage and reduce the impact of global warming."[1]

Most countries could realize a 10 to 20 percent reduction in energy consumption if they adopted the most efficient energy technologies already on the market, according to a recent survey in *The Economist.*

Alternative energy sources include wind power, geothermal power, hydropower and solar energy. While the first three are suitable only in certain areas, photovoltaic power (the direct conversion of sunlight into electricity) holds significant promise.

---

[1] Peter Asmus and Bruce Piasecki, *In Search of Environmental Excellence: Moving Beyond Blame,* (New York: Simon & Schuster, Inc, 1990) p. 92.

ARCO Solar, now a division of the German firm Siemens AG, is a leader in this industry. To date, the primary impediment has been costs, although these continue to decline and are expected to be competitive with other forms of energy by the end of the century. Another avenue for research concerns solar-powered vehicles. Rising petroleum costs and global warming concerns place a premium on the development of cleaner modes of transportation.

Opportunities for investors to profit from the research, development and production of energy-efficient technologies, environmentally friendly products and innovative waste management techniques are legion. Significant rewards await those organizations that develop imaginative solutions to our current set of environmental perils. The next section discusses the performance of several investment funds dedicated to the pursuit of "green" returns.

Environmentally Oriented Mutual Funds

Environmental investing is a subset of a broader category known as socially responsible investing or "ethical investing." Socially responsible investing dates back to the late 1920s, when many religious institutions avoided investing in alcohol, tobacco and gambling activities—the so-called "sin stocks." The Pax World Fund and the Dreyfus Third Century Fund, founded in the early 1970s, were designed as vehicles for investors desiring higher moral standards in the composition of their portfolios. Socially responsible funds invest in firms with exemplary records of employee relations, equal opportunity practices, community development, advancement of women and minorities, product safety and environmental responsibility. Within the past three years, at least six new mutual funds have been launched to specifically capitalize on growing environmental concerns. There is, however, no consensus on what exactly constitutes an "environmental" fund.

One group of funds includes firms involved in the environmental services and hazardous waste disposal industries, for example, Waste Management and Browning-Ferris Industries. Critics point to the historically poor environmental records of these companies—each has paid over $15 million in fines and settlements for environmental and criminal violations—and argue that fund managers should use firms' own pollution records in screening.

Another group of funds selects investments based on a company's environmental record. Firms which recycle, control pollution, promote alternative energy and alternative production processes and voluntarily disclose information on their environmental performance are sought after for portfolio inclusion. Unfortunately, investors may find it difficult to identify a fund's composition solely from its prospectus. Advisory services have emerged to help investors with their selection decisions.

In addition to selection criteria, investors should be concerned with financial performance. Contrary to recent reports by the popular press, environmental mutual funds substantially underperformed the market on a risk-adjusted basis during the period from June 1990 to June 1991. Table 2 presents the recent risk and return characteristics for several of these funds.

As a group, environmentally oriented funds are newer, smaller and more risky than socially responsible funds. The market as a whole turned in a lackluster performance during the study period, but the majority of environmental funds actually *lost* money—both adjusted and unadjusted for risk. By comparison, the Domini Social Index, a broad-based group of 400 socially responsible stocks developed by the investment firm of Kinder Lydenberg Domini, outperformed the S&P 500 over this period.

The dismal performance of environmentally oriented mutual funds may be attributed to a restricted investment set and/or poor managerial performance. Early attempts to cash in on the green

Table 2. Mutual Fund Risk and Return (6/30/90 - 6/28/91; weekly)

Name	When Founded	Net Assets (millions)	Mean Return	Standard Deviation	Total Return	Diff'tial Return S&P 500	Diff'tial Return DSI
Environmental Funds							
New Alternatives Fund	Sep 82	$19.6	0.04%	2.50%	0.55%	-1.32%	-2.41%
SFT Environmental Awareness Fund	Nov 88	$1.2	-0.33%	3.78%	-18.69%	-18.13%	-19.79%
Fidelity Select Portfolios / Environmental Services	Jun 89	$102.2	-0.13%	2.90%	-8.69%	-9.80%	-11.06%
Schield Progressive Environmental Fund	Feb 90	$3.9	-0.20%	4.83%	-13.49%	-10.93%	-13.05%
Oppenheimer Global Environmental Fund	Mar 90	$61.0	-0.28%	2.29%	-14.68%	-16.94%	-17.95%
Kemper Environmental Services Fund	Apr 90	$68.9	-0.03%	2.75%	-3.34%	-4.75%	-5.95%
Freedom Investment Trust III / Environmental Fund	Jun 90	$53.5	-0.25%	2.39%	-13.71%	-15.78%	-16.83%
AVERAGE			-0.17%	3.06%	-10.30%	-11.09%	-12.43%
Socially-Responsible Funds							
Pax World Fund	Aug 71	$145.1	0.07%	2.07%	2.70%	0.02%	-0.88%
Dreyfus Third Century Fund	Mar 72	$280.5	0.10%	2.78%	3.14%	1.81%	0.59%
Calvert Social Investment Fund / Managed Growth	Nov 82	$287.4	0.00%	1.22%	-0.27%	-4.56%	-5.10%
Parnassus Fund	May 85	$27.4	0.05%	3.28%	0.00%	-0.39%	-1.82%
Calvert-Ariel / Growth Fund	Sep 86	$249.0	-0.01%	2.65%	-2.51%	-4.09%	-5.25%
Calvert Social Investment Fund / Equity Portfolio	Aug 87	$31.9	0.05%	1.86%	1.85%	-1.23%	-2.04%
AVERAGE			0.04%	2.31%	0.82%	-1.41%	-2.42%
Benchmark Portfolios							
S&P 500 Index (SP)			-0.06%	2.24%	2.37%	0.00%	-0.98%
Domini Social Index (DSI)			-0.05%	2.42%	3.07%	1.06%	0.00%

Source: M. A. White, "Green Investing: The Recent Investment Performance of Environmentally-Oriented Mutual Funds," Working Paper, McIntire School of Commerce, University of Virginia, July 1991.

movement may also have driven prices up to unrealistic and consequently unsustainable levels. The results of this relatively short study period indicate that investors in green mutual funds earned risk-adjusted returns substantially below the market. From this evidence, a better strategy might have been to have invested in a more broad based fund. After earning average or superior returns, a larger (tax-deductible) donation could then have been made to one's favorite environmental organization at the end of the year.

Debt-For-Nature Swaps

Two rather unorthodox financial markets have developed in response to the green movement and its search for alternative methods of preventing further environmental degradation. Debt-for-nature swaps involve the purchase and subsequent forgiveness of less-developed country (LDC) debt in return for governmental guarantees to protect sensitive ecosystems. The advantage of these transactions is that they provide funds for long-term conservation management without transfer of land ownership or foreign exchange. Because many LDC debt issues are in technical default, foreign conservation agencies can often purchase the debt at a steep discount and realize greater leverage on their monies when it is redeemed (at face value) for promises of environmental stewardship.

Over a dozen debt-for-nature swaps have been arranged to date. In July 1987, Conservation International paid $100,000 for $650,000 (face value) of Bolivian debt, then swapped it for a guarantee to establish a $250,000 management fund and protect 3.7 million acres of endangered habitat. The World Wildlife Fund contracted to purchase up to $10 million of Ecuadorian debt at a steep discount from various U.S. banks in December 1987. The debt is to be converted into local currency bonds paying interest to Fundacion Natura, an Ecuadorian environmental organization. Monies are used to fund conservation and education projects.

Unfortunately, the usefulness of debt-for-nature swaps in providing environmental protection funds to developing countries is, for the most part, restricted to Central and South America. Other countries' debts are owed to the World Bank or the International Monetary Fund. Private parties are generally much more willing to negotiate repayment terms.

Marketable Emissions Permits

The free market's answer to environmental problems is to use the price mechanism to reveal individuals' preferences for clean air, water and habitat. Several firms have traded hydrocarbon emission-reduction credits (ERCs) among themselves during the past ten years or so. Essentially, an ERC provides a producer with the right to release a certain amount of pollutants into the atmosphere, and is issued to a company on the basis of current production practices. If the firm later decides to install pollution prevention equipment which reduces its emissions, it may sell its excess ERCs on the open market to firms unable to meet environmental regulations or wishing to increase capacity. A Washington–based firm, Aer*X, serves as the major broker of ERCs.

The Clean Air Act Amendments of 1990 expanded this program to include permits for sulfur dioxide (SO_2) emissions, a major contributor to acid rain. As SO_2 standards are tightened, firms may choose to install smokestack scrubbers, use low-sulfur coal, shut down aging plants or purchase additional emissions permits. Investors will be able to participate in this market in 1993, when the Chicago Mercantile Exchange proposes to add futures contracts on SO_2 emissions permits to its stable of tradable commodities.

Shareholder Resolutions and the Valdez Principles

Shareholder resolutions have become an increasingly popular tool for effecting social and environmental change. The first shareholder resolution motivated by social concerns was filed in

1969 with Dow Chemical in protest against the production of napalm, a chemical defoliant used extensively in the Vietnam War. Numerous requests for better treatment of the environment followed accidents at Three Mile Island and Bhopal, India. Over 50 shareholder proposals dealing with the environment were submitted to corporations during 1990 according to the Investor Responsibility Research Center (IRRC), an organization which tracks this activity. The proxy process provides a valuable arena for focusing debate on corporate environmental responsibility.

The most visible evidence of shareholders' environmental agenda has been the *Valdez Principles.* Developed in 1989 by the Coalition for Environmentally Responsible Economies (known as CERES, after the Greek goddess of agriculture), these ten principles attempt to define guidelines for responsible corporate behavior regarding the environment, much as the Sullivan Principles were used to affect corporate investments in South Africa. Joan Bavaria, a founding member of the Social Investment Forum and now president of Franklin Research and Development Corporation, was the leading proponent behind their construction. Other influential participants were Elizabeth Holtzman and Gray Davis, representing the New York City and California employees' pension funds, and Denis Hayes, organizer of the 1970 and 1990 Earth Day events. Since pension funds own 40 percent of the common stock of American companies and control over $2.5 trillion in assets, it is extremely significant that the heads of two of our nation's largest pension funds helped to draft this set of principles. The Valdez Principles are listed in Table 3.

Table 3.
The Valdez Principles

1. *Protection of the Biosphere:* We will minimize and strive to eliminate the release of any pollutant that may cause environmental damage to the air, water, or earth or its inhabitants. We will safeguard habitats in rivers, lakes, wetlands, coastal zones and oceans and will minimize contributions to the greenhouse effect, depletion of the ozone layer, acid rain or smog.

2. *Sustainable Use of Natural Resources:* We will make sustainable use of renewable natural resources, such as water, soils and forests. We will conserve nonrenewable resources through efficient use and careful planning. We will protect wildlife habitat, open spaces and wilderness, while preserving biodiversity.

3. *Reduction and Disposal of Waste:* We will minimize the creation of waste, especially hazardous waste, and wherever possible recycle materials. We will dispose of all waste through safe and responsible methods.

4. *Wise Use of Energy:* We will make every effort to use environmentally safe and sustainable energy sources to meet our needs. We will invest in improved energy efficiency and conservation in our operations. We will maximize the energy efficiency of products we produce or sell.

5. *Risk Reduction:* We will minimize the environmental, health and safety risks to our employees and the communities in which we operate by employing safe technologies and operating procedures and by being constantly prepared for emergencies.

6. *Marketing of Safe Products and Services:* We will sell products or services that minimize adverse environmental impacts and that are safe as consumers commonly use them. We will inform consumers of the environmental impacts of our products or services.

7. *Damage Compensation:* We will take responsibility for any harm we cause to the environment by making every effort to fully restore the environment and to compensate those persons who are adversely affected.

Table 3. continued

8. *Disclosure:* We will disclose to our employees and to the public incidents relating to our operations that cause environmental harm or pose health or safety hazards. We will disclose potential environmental, health or safety hazards posed by our operations, and we will not take any action against employees who report any condition that creates a danger to the environment or poses health and safety hazards.

9. *Environmental Directors and Managers:* At least one member of the Board of Directors will be a person qualified to represent environmental interests. We will commit management resources to implement these principles, including the funding of an office of vice president for environmental affairs or an equivalent executive position, reporting directly to the CEO, to monitor and report upon our implementation efforts.

10. *Assessment and Annual Audit:* We will conduct and make public an annual self-evaluation of our progress in implementing these principles and in complying with all applicable laws and regulations throughout our worldwide operations. We will work toward the timely creation of independent environmental audit procedures which we will complete annually and make available to the public.

Source: Coalition for Environmentally Responsible Economies (CERES)

Thus far, no major corporation has signed off on the complete set of principles, although a number have adopted substantial portions. The last four principles are the most difficult for corporations to agree to. Corporations are understandably reluctant to sign agreements which may be used against them in litigation, especially ones which promise to "...fully restore the environment and to compensate those persons who are adversely affected." Disclosure of environmental hazards and debate over what constitutes a "qualified" environmental representative are also points of contention. Principle 10 causes trepidation owing to the lack of standardized auditing practices for environmental matters and questions over who should be setting compliance standards. Nonetheless, the Valdez Principles are a powerful example of how shareholders can exert considerable influence over the environmental management of our nation's largest corporations.

Environmental and Financial Performance

The opening lectures of any standard financial management course begin with the notion that financial managers should strive to maximize shareholder wealth. This goal is based on the belief that shareholders, as owners of the corporation, enjoy a preeminent position with regard to the disposition of a firm's assets and income. The doctrine of shareholder supremacy is *not* shared by certain other disciplines, notably marketing, which tends to espouse the goal of *stakeholder* satisfaction, where stakeholders are defined as those individuals and groups who have a "stake" in the firm. These might include a firm's management, labor, customers, suppliers, community, government, environment and yes, shareholders, too. Inasmuch as current theories fail to provide objective, consistent criteria for financial decision making, stakeholder concerns are unlikely to supplant shareholder wealth maximization as a goal for financial managers, however. Consider the following quote from an introductory text:

> Does this mean that firms should not exercise social responsibility in regard to pollution control? The answer is no—but certain cost increasing activities may have to be mandatory rather than voluntary, at least initially, to ensure that the burden falls equally over all business firms.[2]

The doctrine of shareholder wealth maximization provides guidance on how to best allocate a fixed pool of resources. Using Lester Thurow's terminology, management is engaged in a "zero-sum game." Dollars used to provide on-site child care or to

---

[2] Robert S. Harris and John J. Pringle., *Introductory Corporate Finance*. (Glenview, IL: Scott, Foresman and Company, 1989),pp. 5-6.

achieve greater pay equity for women and minority employees are dollars not ending up in shareholders' pockets. Similarly, monies spent on "unnecessary" minimization of environmental hazards (i.e. action not required by law) are indirect contributions by the firm's owners. Faced with decisions of an ethical or moral nature, corporations can absolve themselves of responsibility by maximizing the wealth of shareholders and allowing *them* to choose how to allocate profits.

This argument has been criticized along two lines. First, absolving corporations of moral responsibility by transferring difficult decision making to their shareholders seems unjust and unrecognizing of the immense power wielded by mega–corporations, a number of which exceed the size of many nations. Second, it has been argued that investments in better working conditions, equal opportunity programs and community affairs benefit companies and their shareholders in the long run.

Empirical studies examining the relationship between a firm's record of environmental responsibility and its financial performance have shown mixed results. Early studies reported a positive relationship between a firm's environmental record (as reported by the Council on Economic Priorities, or CEP) and its financial performance, although others have reached indefinite conclusions regarding the value of a good environmental record.[3] Using data from CEP's *The Better World Investment Guide*, firms were classified on the basis of their environmental reputation as either "green" or "brown." Brown firms significantly underperformed industry averages for several key financial variables. Green firms slightly outperformed industry averages, although not significantly. These preliminary findings suggest

---

[3] See Arieh Ullmann,"Data in Search of a Theory: A Critical Examination of the Relationships Among Social Performance, Social Disclosure, and Economic Performance of U.S. Firms," *Academy of Management Review.* July 1985, pp. 540-557.

that while being "green" is not associated with substantial financial premiums, brown firms provide inferior performance.

Summary

The 1990s have been called the "Decade of the Environment." Responding to calls for greener products, better pollution prevention practices and less wasteful energy technologies, businesses are faced with opportunities and threats. Firms which ignore the environmental movement do so at their own peril, as empirical evidence suggests that "brown" firms are penalized for their environmental irresponsibility. Conversely, investors identifying companies engaged in the development of superior environmentally friendly products and services should earn superior returns as demand increases due to heightened public awareness and ever-more-stringent regulations.

Bibliography

"A Cleaner Environment: Where to Invest." *Changing Times* (February 1990) pp. 32-38.

Alperson, Myra, Alice Tepper Marlin, Jonathan Schorsch and Rosalyn Will. *The Better World Investment Guide.* New York: Prentice-Hall, 1991.

Attorneys General of California, Florida, Massachusetts, Minnesota, Missouri, New York, Tennessee, Texas, Utah, Washington and Wisconsin, *The Green Report II: Recommendations for Responsible Environmental Advertising,* May 1991.

Block, Walter E., Ed. *Economics and the Environment: A Reconciliation.* Canada: The Fraser Institute, 1990.

Bloom, Gordon F. and Michael S. Scott Morton. "Hazardous Waste Is Every Manager's Problem." *Sloan Management Review* (Summer 1991) pp. 75-84.

Blumberg, Louis and Robert Gottlieb. *War On Waste: Can America Win Its Battle With Garbage?* Washington, DC: Island Press, 1989.

Bruyn, Severyn T. *The Field of Social Investment.* Cambridge: Cambridge University Press, 1987.

Cairncross, Frances. *Costing the Earth.* London: Business Books, Ltd., 1991.

Carson, Patrick and Julia Moulden. *Green is Gold.* Toronto: Harper Business, 1991).

"Cool It: A Survey of Energy and the Environment." *The Economist* 31 (August 1991).

Council on Economic Priorities. *Shopping for a Better World, 1991 Edition.* New York: Ballantine Books, 1990.

Crawford, Mark. "Green Futures on Wall Street." *New Scientist* 5 (January 1991) pp. 38-40.

Cross, Frank B. "The Weaning of the Green: Environmentalism Comes of Age in the 1990s." *Business Horizons* (September/October 1990) pp. 40-46.

Davis, John. *Greening Business: Managing for Sustainable Development.* Cambridge, MA: Basil Blackwell, 1991.

Deal, Michael. "Shareholders and the Environmental Agenda." *Institutional Shareholder Services, Inc. Special Report,* 28 (January 1991).

Elkington, John, Julia Hailes and Joel Makower. *The Green Consumer.* New York: Penguin Books, 1990.

Engle, Claude. "Getting in on the Bottom Line." *Environmental Action* (March/April) 1990, pp. 20-23.

Gottschalk Jr., Earl C. "Investments Promoted as Ecologically Clean Pop Up Like Weeds." *The Wall Street Journal* (10 April 1990) E1, 18.

Plant Christopher and Judith Plant, eds.*Green Business: Hope or Hoax?,* Philadelphia: New Society Publishers, 1991.

"The Greening of Corporate America." *Business Week* 23 (April 1990) pp. 96-103.

Hirschhorn, Joel S. and Kirsten U. Oldenburg. *Prosperity Without Pollution.* New York: Van Nostrand Reinhold, 1991.

Kirkpatrick, David. "Environmentalism: The New Crusade." *Fortune,* 12 (February 1990) pp. 44-52.

Kleiner, Art. "Brundtland's Legacy: Can Corporations Really Practice Environmentalism While Fattening Their Profit Margins?" *Garbage* (September/October 1990) pp. 58-62.

Landler, Mark. "Suddenly, Green Marketers are Seeing Red Flags." *Business Week* 25 (February 1991) pp. 74-76.

Managing Planet Earth: Readings From Scientific American. New York: W. H. Freeman, 1990.

Naar, Jon. *Design for a Livable Planet.* New York: Harper & Row, 1990.

Piasecki, Bruce and Peter Asmus. *In Search of Environmental Excellence: Moving Beyond Blame.* New York: Simon and Schuster, 1990.

Plant, Christopher and Judith Plant, eds. *Green Business: Hope or Hoax?* Philadelphia, PA: New Society Publishers, 1991.

Post, James E. "Managing As If The Earth Mattered." *Business Horizons* (July/August 1991) pp. 32-38.

Rose, Ronit Addis. "Environmental Investing." *Garbage,* September/October 1990, pp. 48-53.

Wang, Penelope. "Finish First." *Money* (June 1991) pp. 130-138.

Von Moltke, Konrad and Paul J. DeLong. "Negotiating in the Global Arena: Debt for Nature Swaps." *Resolve* No. 22 (1990) pp. 1-10.

Chapter 3

Corporate Environmental Liability: Criminal Sanctions, Government Civil Penalties, and Civil Suits

Gabriele G. Crognale
Science Applications International Corporation

Overview

Enforcement is the "teeth" behind the "command-and-control" approach that has been EPA's trademark for compliance. EPA's enforcement division has added more teeth to its "bite" with the issuance of the revised RCRA Civil Penalty Policy, or RCPP, in October 1990. With this policy, EPA has achieved the first milestone in its attempt to better target its audience for more effective results.

As stated in EPA's RCRA Implementation Study (RIS)[1]

An effective enforcement program must detect violations, compel their correction, ensure that compliance is

---

[1] EPA/OSWER study, "The Nation's Hazardous Waste Management Program at a Crossroads" (EPA/530-SW-90-069), July 1990, p.57.

achieved in a timely manner, and deter other violations. The RCRA enforcement program will obtain substantial voluntary compliance only if the regulated community perceives that there is a greater risk and cost in violating a requirement than in complying with it.

In 1991, EPA announced that it had beefed up its enforcement strategy and planned to hit RCRA violators, probably the recalcitrant or high priority (HPV)[2] ones, even harder than before.[3]

Thus, 1991 was the year in which EPA took a long, hard look at itself and decided to make enforcement one of its top priorities. The RCPP is an enforcement enhancement tool devised by EPA after the agency got the message that many violators considered the fines nothing more than the cost of doing business.[4]

In light of EPA's "refocused" direction, Bruce Diamond, the director of the Office of Solid Waste, stated that both EPA and the states are seeking higher penalties in enforcement actions.[5] In addition, based on apparent staffing increases at NEIC[6] regional offices, it would not be surprising to see an increase in criminal investigations and actions as well.

With this overall increase in enforcement staffing, as well as an increase in the number of states (presently, all but two or

---

[2] HPV, high priority violator, is an EPA term for those violators found to be either consistently out of compliance (recalcitrant), or found to be in violation of RCRA requirements where there is a high probability that such a violation, if left as is, could threaten human health or the environment. (Reference: EPA's Enforcement Response Policy.)

[3] Hazel Bradford, "EPA's RCRA Program Gets Tough, *Engineering News Record,* July 22, 1991, p.8; BNA's *Environment Reporter,* July 12, 1991, p.602.

[4] There is a detailed discussion of penalties and compliance-mandated corporate expenditures later in the book. See Chapter 8 on the Allocation of Corporate Resources for Environmental Compliance.

[5] Ibid.

[6] National Enforcement Investigations Center, Denver, Colorado, EPA's Criminal Enforcement Branch.

three)[7] that EPA has authorized to administer the RCRA base program,[8] it would not be surprising to also see inspectors shift their focus more towards generators and "non-notifiers"[9], instead of just TSDFs (transfer/storage/disposal facilities). At least one EPA region along with several state agencies as have echoed this prediction, that those companies will be the next targets.

In a clear, concise way, EPA has proven itself to be a formidable agency to be reckoned with, and the message that has permeated the "regulated community" is that the "Pollution Police" mean business, and it will be costly for those violators who do not acknowledge the intent of EPA's enforcement thrust.

Enforcement Tools That Are Commonly Used

EPA has been empowered by Congress with a wide array of formidable enforcement tools to insure the protection of human health and the environment. Under the provisions of RCRA, HSWA, UST and CERCLA, EPA has the authority to issue specific administrative orders (either consent or unilateral) to compel a violator to do one or all of the following: study the impacts of contamination (the RCRA facility assessment, or RFA); evaluate the corrective action alternatives (the RCRA facility investigation or RFI); or undergo corrective action as a result of one or more EPA corrective action orders.[10]

---

[7] EPA/530-SW-90-069, Chapter 3.

[8] Ibid. This does not include administering the Corrective Action program under HSWA (Hazardous and Solid Waste Amendments). According to information presented in Chapter 3 of EPA/530-SW-90-069, only 6 states were fully authorized.

[9] Those companies that have not notified EPA that they deal with RCRA-regulated materials.

[10] Authorized under Sections 3004(u), 3008(h), and 7003(u) of RCRA and Section 106 of CERCLA. (EPA also has the authority to administer penalties under the Clean Water Act and the Toxic Substances Control Act.)

In most cases, the corrective action order also has a penalty component, which is allowed under Section 3008(a). In the event a facility is unwilling to undergo any of the above corrective action orders, which can be written as a consent order, EPA then has the authority, under Section 3008(h) to refer such enforcement actions to the Department of Justice (DOJ). Prior to referral, the next step in negotiations would be to present the case before an Administrative Law Judge (ALJ).

If targeted violators are suspected of a criminal activity, EPA also has the authority to pursue criminal prosecution under Section 3008(c) of RCRA. Another aspect that EPA considers in issuing enforcement actions are the goals and objectives that are given to the regional offices by EPA Headquarters. The corner-stone document is the agency's Enforcement Response Policy (ERP) which is an EPA/OSWER (EPA's Office of Solid Waste and Emergency Response) policy directive issued to provide guidance to enforcement personnel for consistency in all regional enforcement responses. Specifically, the ERP provides guidance on what constitutes a timely and appropriate enforcement response; what the difference is between an HPV (high priority violator), Class I and Class II violation; what the appropriate enforcement response is—Notice of Violation (NOV), Administrative Order (AO) or referral; what timely and appropriate response considerations are; and what the overall priorities are.

Other guidance documents include policy memoranda and Agency Operating Guidance on various enforcement topics that may require further clarification, and/or explanation of questions raised by a regional office on a specific enforcement item.

The underlying goal of RCRA, which any corporate executive must remember, is the protection of human health and the environment. The goals and objectives highlighted above are designed to focus on RCRA's goal using a plan that provides national direction and a framework for assigning priorities to implement RCRA. This plan is called the RCRA Implementation Plan (RIP). It is revised each year to address EPA's priorities. For several years now, the highest priority activity has been to ensure that all environmentally significant handlers (TSDs, "closure" of land disposal facilities and others) were identified and adequately addressed through permits, closure/post-closure, corrective action orders, CERCLA action, or other appropriate action.[11] More specifically, the FY 89 RIP established priorities to include: inspections, enforcement to compel handlers to return to compliance, corrective action, and closure.

There seems to have been no real change in the direction of the RIPs in FY90 and FY91. The current enforcement approach, which has appeared to gain some momentum, is to assess higher penalties. Also, with waste minimization and pollution prevention becoming a more active EPA concern, and multi-media inspections[12] becoming more structured, there is a very real possibility that these two areas will also become key recuring topics for the RIP in coming fiscal years.

The Targeted Company

It is not surprising, then, with this formidable battery of enforcement tools, policies and databases (which will be discussed later), that a facility targeted for an enforcement action faces a potentially long, protracted legal battle if it either decides to ignore the inspector's visit, or scoffs at the enforcement action and decides to dig in its heels. This in no way implies that a company should not fight if it firmly believes in its position and believes that EPA or the state is wrong, unless, of course, the

---

[11] The FY89 RCRA Implementation Plan.

[12] In summer 1991, EPA issued a multi-media inspection checklist that provides instructions for a wide range of programs including: asbestos, CAA, EPCRA, FIFRA, RCRA, Pollution Prevention, TSCA, UST and Water/NPDES.

outcome has the potential to become a "Pyrric Victory" for the company, where the battle is won, but at a financial loss.

One exception is the Envirite Corporation, a hazardous waste storage and treatment facility, that discovered through its Freedom of Information Act (FOIA) request that analysis performed by EPA on split samples taken of its treated wastes had been found to be interpreted incorrectly. That company was subsequently granted a request by a federal judge to re-open the case.[13]

This particular case is more the exception, where results of follow-up analytical tests that could have been a factor during settlement negotiations were apparently withheld. Typically, the majority of violations noted on orders are for obvious violations. Respondents usually challenge the EPA when the interpretation of violations is not clearly defined, for example groundwater contamination and deficiencies in existing groundwater monitoring programs; who the responsible parties are if the contaminated area covers different facilities; and alleged missing documents which may have been misplaced at the time of the inspection.

Differences with EPA may also arise over the assessment of penalties, where, because of the penalty matrix used for calculating the penalties, there is much room for interpretation on the part of the EPA people involved.

An EPA Administrative order can be an exacting undertaking for the targeted company, where its severity may be dependant upon several factors. Examples of this may include: the gravity of the violations encountered; the willingness of the respondent (violator) to work with EPA on the consent order; the size of the facility; the competency of the facility manager and support

---

[13] *Hazardous Materials Intelligence Reporter*, vol. XII, no. 16, 19 April 1991, p.1.

technical and legal staff; and the competency and reciprocal willingness on the part of EPA personnel directly involved.

Of course, it is not easy to determine which targeted facility will encounter any or all of the above scenarios, with each case having its own special problems. Case studies can provide a flavor for possible scenarios which may be encountered.

For example, it is a prudent company executive that decides to retain the best possible technical and legal consultants to assist in the facility's defense, not just for litigation, but, as shall be seen, for guiding the facility through corrective action. The important point here is that if EPA has targeted a facility, it is prepared to battle to the end. It would then be in the company's best interest to be equally prepared.

Criteria For Selecting A Target Company

This next discussion will focus on how a particular facility or company is targeted by EPA. If a facility fears that it will be targeted, it may wish to re-evaluate or audit its internal compliance program (referring to the RCRA program, specifically) to assess its compliance status. The better its compliance status, the less likely it may become an enforcement target should the facility receive a surprise RCRA, or possibly a multi-media, inspection.

A hypothetical case would go like this. Suppose that the company is listed on EPA's data base (HWDMS)[14] as a storage TSD. The facility manager has also received and responded to a Section 3007 informational request letter under RCRA to identify the solid waste management units (SWMUs) on-site since it has lost interim status as a TSD (as of 11/08/85). Subsequently, the facility is now required to either undergo closure, or submit a

---

[14] Hazardous Waste Data Management System, soon to be replaced with RCRIS (Resource Conservation and Recovery Information System).

Part B application to continue to operate as a TSD. In addition, if any of the SWMUs have had releases and could threaten human health or the environment, corrective action will also be required as part of the permit.

At some point, since the RIP places the highest priority on environmentally significant handlers, and a storage TSD with SWMUs with releases into the groundwater fits that category well, it will most likely be inspected at least once in each year. During the inspection, the inspector finds various violations related to groundwater monitoring, closure, reporting requirements deficiencies, deficient contingency plans, personnel training, manifests, drum labeling and land ban violations, and assigns a fair number of HPV and Class I violations to these observations.

Based on this hypothetical situation, the facility would more than likely be issued an Administrative order with penalties to return to compliance. Whether the order would include corrective action would depend on the extent of documented groundwater and/or soil contamination, or the potential for such contamination. The responsibility would then rest with the owner/operator to submit any required information in response to the order to either refute or substantiate the findings of the order and perform the required work.

It is a safe bet to presume that neither EPA nor the states will allow a facility, once identified, to manage its hazardous waste management program in such a way that threatens human health or the environment. The farther removed from that threat that facility is, the less likely it will become an enforcement target.

Companies That Receive Enforcement Actions

Suppose that the same hypothetical company had operated its hazardous waste management program somewhat loosely over the years, and furthermore, had paid only token attention to state enforcement actions or EPA NOVs (Notice of Violation).

The next step would be for the state to refer the case to EPA for action, or if it is an EPA lead, EPA would then escalate the enforcement action to an AO (Administrative order). EPA would then assign a case manager to review the case, conduct an inspection and produce an updated inspection report with observations. That inspection would become the basis for the AO, which could be written as a consent or unilateral order. Once the order has been issued, the respondent has the opportunity consenting to the order and the assessed penalties, or preparing to battle it out with EPA. If EPA is not satisfied with the actions taken, they then have the authority to refer the case to the Department of Justice. If it proceeds that far, there is no longer room for consent, since the decision would then be handed down unilaterally from the judge hearing the case. However, a judge may decide for either party, depending upon the evidence provided.

To avoid enforcement action altogether, the logical step for the company would be to try to avoid all this by maintaining a more compliant stance. While not an easy task to accomplish, there are some measures that can be taken by the facility to put it into a more compliant state with the regulators, thus, possibly avoiding an order. Specifically, the facility should try to manage all containers of hazardous waste appropriately; all hazardous waste records should be kept up-to-date and in order; all applicable forms, such as land ban and exporting forms, should be maintained, as well as other pertinent documents. For those facilities with on-site groundwater monitoring wells, the wells should be properly maintained and all analytical data kept up to date.

If nothing else, such proactive measures taken by the facility could help to mitigate the assessed penalties if an order were to be issued.

Section 3008(a) of RCRA is the authority allowing for the administrative complaint framework and the assessment of penalties up to $25,000 per day for each day of non-compliance. The penalty policy, now the revised RCPP, is the tool that EPA uses to calculate penalties against a violator.

To fine tune the penalty, each of the components (gravity-based and multi-day) are analyzed through a matrix that gauges the potential for harm and the extent of deviation from the regulations. Both matrices decrease in scale from major to minor, from a maximum of $25,000 to a minimum of $100 for the gravity-based component; and, a maximum of $5000 to a minimum of $100 for the multi-day component. Mitigative measures that the inspector and/or attorney factors into the penalty matrix include such items as: size of the sample universe from which the violation was noted; relative threat to human health or the environment based on land/water usage; whether the facility really tried to stay in compliance and failed; and other subjective considerations that the inspector would discuss with the case attorney and/or supervisor prior to inclusion.

As in any other dealing, business, legal or otherwise, the secret to successful negotiations is the ability of one party to successfully demonstrate to the other the rationale behind the subject matter being presented. It is no different when dealing with the EPA, whether it's an Administrative order or a Notice of Violation.

It is the responsibility of the respondent to the order to successfully demonstrate to EPA's inspectors and attorneys their situation, especially if they feel the order was in error. The success of this argument hinges upon several factors, some of which are intangible, such as: the severity of the violations, the facility's enforcement history, the attitudes of all parties, the public perception of the company, the evidence presented from both sides, the track record of similar enforcement cases, and a host of other factors. Ultimately, the facility or corporate executives must decide whether it is prudent to enter into a protracted legal battle (the clock is always running there), or try to negotiate a settlement to cut costs and just go on. This decision rests with the executives and is generally influenced by what their attorney advises.

The option of going forward to a civil referral should only be used in those cases where the company feels very strongly about the case, has substantial evidence to defend itself, is so advised by its counsel, and has the deep pockets to do so.

One case that exemplifies this scenario from a defense standpoint is the Envirite Corporation, referred to earlier. According to the news source (Footnote 14), the company was allowed to reopen the case and collect the $60,000 fine back from EPA.

This is pointed out as an example of a case that may eventually conclude in favor of the company. One should keep in perspective, though, that establishing rapport with the agency is also important, especially since the bigger costs usually lie in the corrective action process. Furthermore, a facility should not focus solely on the penalty imposed by the order, but look further into any subsequent costs, especially if soil or groundwater contamination may be present. As noted in several enforcement actions, the real costs lie in the unseen, although suspected, violations that involve groundwater and soil contamination from past disposal practices or systematic leaks and other unseen discharges from floor drains, underground waste or product storage tanks, and septic fields, to name a few.

Using ballpark figures for unit costs associated with groundwater sampling as an illustration, it is not difficult to foresee the costs associated with these RFAs/RFIs reaching upwards of $10 million, and stretching out over several years. These costs typically include: soil borings at $8-$10 per foot, casing (PVC to stainless steel) at $5-$50 per foot, groundwater monitoring (Appendix IX parameters as the most costly) at $1500-$2000 per test, etc.[15] These costs may become one consideration the company executives might want to consider seriously during settlement negotiations. The big picture should not be obscured by the immediate situation, and arguments up front may compromise the facility further down the road where substantial dollar costs may await.

Selected Case Studies

One very good example of corrective action that was negotiated effectively was the consent order issued to Monsanto at its Springfield, Massachusetts, facility in 1983-84.[16]

The facility had begun initial studies in 1981 to assess the extent of contamination of groundwater from their waste disposal areas (SWMUs). The facility encompasses 328 acres and is located in a river valley and bounded by the Chicopee River. The first groundwater monitoring wells installed on-site had detected volatile organics like benzene, toluene and xylene, and, as a result, caused EPA to issue a Section 3013 Unilateral Order. The state had also issued a 21E Order under new state Superfund authority. Both orders required the submittal of a Remedial Investigation Plan by the facility. During 1983 and 1984, many meetings were held between the three parties to hammer out the draft plan, which was crucial, since it then set the tone for oversight of the project by the regulators. A positive outcome of these meetings was EPA's changing of the action to a consent order from a unilateral order.

---

[15] 1991 estimated range of prices, based on discussions with geohydrologists and drilling contractors.

[16] George Furst, "RCRA Corrective Action at a Large Chemical Manufacturing Facility; Process and Results," Proceedings of the National Conference on Hazardous Waste and Hazardous Materials, HMCRI Conference, Washington, D.C., March 1987.

After joint approval of the plan, which utilized a phased approach (that is, corrective action work over separate stages, such as preliminary borings, location of monitoring wells, sampling parameters, etc.), the work was begun. As new information was gathered, it was used modify the geohydrological studies which dictated the location of future monitoring wells. In addition, constant field decisions were a critical component of the project, allowing it to move ahead smoothly and on schedule.

Briefly, Phase I consisted of the collection and review of existing information regarding prior waste disposal practices, and a review of all relevant company documents.

A 50-foot grid was established in the study area to facilitate locating seismic and magnetometry lines and future sampling locations. This grid was also instrumental in referencing sampling locations over large open areas and as a basis for computer data management.

The Phase II work, begun immediately afterwards, consisted of taking soil borings (well depths ranged from 110 feet to 130 feet). In addition, areas where the magnetometry scans had detected high metal readings were further scanned with earth-penetrating radar to pinpoint locations where drums or demolition debris could be found. During this phase, field screening techniques were established to allow the development of a more accurate conceptual site model.

Phase III, which was being initiated at the time of this study, concentrated on the remedial options for the study area, and included the preparation of a "corrective measures study" pursuant to the order and the setting of media protection standards to be met by corrective measures implementation.

Retrospective comments by the author included these key components:

- If a facility is ordered to conduct an investigation that may be contrary to established standards, consequences may arise, such as communications breakdown, or a slow down in the project schedule.

- Treat the facility personnel with diplomacy and dignity. Requests made clearly should aid working relations.

- Maintain constant communication.

- Let the data guide the project, that is, as new investigative data surfaces, use that to guide the direction of the study.

This is one example of the types of RCRA corrective action process that many interim status facilities regulated under RCRA may yet have to face, or may have experienced in one form or another. Of those that experienced such action, some facilities may have undergone "closure" procedures or applied for a Part B permit, as noted earlier. The point is that Corrective Action is very complex and it requires constant agency/facility communication as well as experienced technical judgement to make it work; otherwise, one could be facing a real regulatory nightmare.

A similar Corrective Action process that was initiated as a result of documented groundwater contamination also incorporated a phased approach to arrive at the requirements of the Section 3013 Order. That order required the facility to determine rate, degree and extent of contamination of the underlying groundwater and soils.

Its similarity to the previous case evolved from the congenial working relationship, although trying at times, established between EPA personnel and the facility and their consultant. Constant field oversight and field decisions during problematic moments allowed for work to proceed at or near schedule. Potential logistical snags were also avoided by EPA's recommendations that the facility's consultants initiate off-site contacts as soon as possible, and EPA's early attempts to include the municipal officials in the loop.

In this case, the facility's documentation of volatile organic compounds in their monitoring wells prompted EPA to request assistance from the town's health official to sample private wells downgradient of the facility. The town official was very pleased that EPA had asked for his assistance.

Several years later the town's engineer allowed a quick turnaround time for approval of the facility's request to drill on town easements of the private property. Some of that negotiating was facilitated by EPA having established favorable professional and community ties with the town.

The technical work on-site was also aided tremendously by the ability of the EPA technical team and the facility's consultants to understand each other's viewpoints and concerns. They were also able to resolve technical differences, and with the phased approach, were able to refine changes in approving well locations (cluster or individual), and approving locations for conducting pump tests to check for possible underlying aquifer contamination.

The lesson learned here is that it is very important to open communication early with all the parties concerned, and to resolve rationally and technically both the agency's concerns and those of the facility.

Another good example of an enforcement action that produced a visible change in a company's compliance program was a state (Department of Environmental Quality Engineering, or DEQE) Consent Agreement issued to a heavy machine manufacturer in Massachusetts.

Based on information contained in the state and EPA files, DEQE (now DEP—Department of Environmental Protection) inspectors noted approximately 70 RCRA violations that included such items as: accumulation date violations; unauthorized storage areas; releases into the environment from container leakage (which is also container mismanagement); and disposal of contaminated speedi-dry in the garbage/dumpsters.

As a result of this consent agreement, the company agreed to pay a $190,000 fine and clean up their hazardous waste management areas. Since that consent agreement, the facility has not only made a concerted effort to stay in compliance, but is striving diligently to stay ahead of compliance, based on the most recent (August 1991) information in EPA's HWDMS data base.

As emphasized earlier in this chapter (and in Chapter 8), when a company is "dinged" with a serious and potentially costly enforcement action, the corporate management must quickly learn that the federal and state agencies mean business.[17] Further case studies will focus on several examples of criminal enforcement, highlighting examples of the more damaging individual and corporate penalties, which can include the possibility of incarceration.

Another example of a corrective action that was negotiated effectively is the Canob Park[18] case involving Mobil and Exxon. Underground storage tanks at two of their gas stations had gasoline releases which subsequently contaminated a small residential development of 250-300 people.

---

[17] In FY 1990, EPA referred 375 civil cases and 65 criminal cases to the U.S. Department of Justice. See *Hazardous Materials Intelligence Report*, vol. XI, no.48, 30 November 1990, p.1.

[18] Steve Fradkoff, "Case Studies—Lessons Learned, Canob Park, Rhode Island," Underground Fuel Tanks Regulatory & Remedial Outlook, Arlington, VA, July 1984. Co-sponsored by Inside EPA and The Center for Energy & Environmental Management.

This Administrative order was issued under Section 7003(u) of RCRA in September 1983, after cessation of voluntary remedial actions by the two companies.

Prior to the issuance of the AO, the residents of Canob Park, as early as 1970, complained to the State of Rhode Island about gasoline contamination in their wells. In 1981, a Rhode Island congressional delegation brought this problem to EPA's attention. That led the EPA to mobilize its FIT (Field Investigation Team) to investigate further. Concurrently, Mobil had removed three of its underground tanks and had found no leaks or signs of product leakage in the excavation holes, according to the FIT.

Based on available data and FIT's subsequent studies, EPA believed that both Exxon and Mobil were responsible for the gasoline contamination, and requested the companies to meet with EPA in October 1982. These negotiations continued until May 1983, when both companies halted negotiations. As a result, EPA then issued the 7003 Order to both companies.

The order required the companies to:

1. Review all existing private groundwater well data for gasoline contamination;

2. Submit a proposal for additional well sampling and analysis, and conduct sampling and analysis;

3. Supply bottled water and submit a proposal for the installation, and operation and maintenance of a groundwater interceptor system;

4. Submit a proposal for the removal and disposal of contaminated soil.

After the consent orders were signed and the unilateral orders vacated, both companies approached EPA and negotiations resumed. Both companies, along with the State of Rhode Island, agreed to share the costs of a community water system, and both Mobil and Exxon agreed to sample the wells and supply bottled water to homes with contaminated wells; in addition each agreed to place one-third the cost of the new community water system into an escrow account.

As a result of the consent orders, both companies have made their contributions to the water systems, supplied bottled water, and Exxon has also submitted a study to the EPA that determined a negative impact on downgradient surface water as the result of not treating contaminated groundwater in the aquifer. That study was submitted to EPA in January 1984 and EPA concurred with its findings.

As evidenced by this case study, the resolution of contamination problems caused by underground leaking storage tanks (or any other sudden or non-sudden release underground or on the surface) is not something that can be resolved quickly. Each occurrence needs to be evaluated on a case-by-case basis and brings with it a unique set of circumstances, whether a RCRA corrective action, UST or CERCLA remediation. Prior enforcement actions and their outcomes are reference points for future work, and are not necessarily the same in each instance.

The next case studies involve criminal prosecutions that also highlight individual incarceration as a component of the penalty. The information on these cases was gleaned from public sources as noted.

The first case involves a paper manufacturer[19] accused of illegally storing and treating hazardous waste and making false statements to regulators. The infractions are alleged to have occurred at the company's paper mill in Maine.

---

[19] *Wall Street Journal*, July 3, 1991, p.B3.

According to the news story, the company mixed flammable waste solvents with waste oil and disposed of them in power boilers and knowingly made false statements on permit applications and compliance reports to the state and EPA. EPA subsequently fined the company $2.2 million.[20]

In another criminal action, a heavy machinery manufacturer pled guilty to six felony violations of RCRA for illegally dumping a cleaning solution consisting of perchloroethylene and 1,1,1-trichloroethane at its plant in Connecticut.[21]

In a case involving the Clean Water Act, an executive of a defense contractor was sentenced to a 26-month prison term, with two years' probation, and a fine of $400,000 on four counts of illegally dumping toxic metals and acids from its facility in Massachusetts into the local sewer system.[22] This was the first conviction in a "knowing endangerment" case under the Clean Water Act (CWA).

According to a 1988 investigation by EPA and the Federal Bureau of Investigation (FBI)[23], the company ordered employees to drop nickel plating and nitric acid solutions down sinks at the facility. These solutions contained illegally high concentrations of nickel and acid, as specified in the CWA.

This was one case that depicted the cooperation between EPA and the FBI in their aggressive investigations of environmental crimes.

These are just a few of the criminal investigations that have been successfully prosecuted. Given the present civil and criminal

---

[20] *EPA Environmental News* press release, January 16, 1992.

[21] *Chemical & Engineering News*, May 20, 1991, p.17.

[22] *Hazardous Materials Intelligence Reporter*, vol. XI, no. 46, 16 November 1990, p.4.

[23] Ibid.

enforcement climate, there is a very good likelihood that the trend will continue, at least until EPA is convinced that the companies in EPA's "regulated community" have learned that it does not pay to pollute the environment or harm people.

Also taking note of this stepped-up enforcement by EPA are our Canadian neighbors, where the justice system is beginning to catch up with public outcry for tough action against companies and executives causing environmental damage. A handful of cases scheduled to appear before the courts could mean jail terms for those convicted of environmental crimes. The environmental officials in several provinces are sending out a signal (like EPA) that not only companies but also individuals responsible for pollution face tough legal action in Canada.[24]

The next section will discuss where enforcement may be headed in the foreseeable future and what it will entail.

Future Enforcement Trends

As noted earlier in the 1990 RCRA Implementation Study, EPA is authorizing more states to administer the corrective action program to assist EPA in conducting more frequent and complex corrective action work since this universe of facilities is very large (See Footnote 7). According to EPA figures, there are approximately 4700 facilities that contain over 80,000 SWMUs that will require corrective action.[25] The thrust of corrective action focuses on facilities issued a RCRA permit after November 8, 1984, which must investigate[26] and clean up contamination at or from the facility, including releases from past disposal; facilities under interim status (40 CFR Part 265); and those facili-

---

[24] Don Hogarth, "'Envirocops' step up war on polluters," *Financial Post*, August 26, 1991.

[25] Chapter 7 of EPA/530-SW-90-069.

[26] Ibid., required under the Hazardous & Solid Waste Amendments of RCRA.

ties that should have had interim status. In addition, with the passage of (Proposed Rule) Subpart S of RCRA,[27] corrective action of SWMUs will be further delineated by CAMUs (Corrective Action Management Units), which could include areas that experienced routine and systematic releases from processes. Among the controversial aspects of Subpart S are the cleanup goals for identified contamination levels, the so-called "action levels", and the "Economic Impact"[28] Subpart S will have on industry. Both the HSWA and Subpart S requirements will be formidable enforcement tasks to accomplish. For these reasons, EPA appears to have accelerated the state authorizations, along with increased inspector training, as a means to manage this tremendous workload.

In addition to the field workforce, EPA has relied on and will continue to rely on quantitative and analytical tracking data bases, such as the GIS (Geographical Information System), HWDMS and RCRIS. The latter is an enhanced version of HWDMS.

GIS has been implemented to accurately pinpoint where the significant environmental polluters are in relation to environmental receptors, such as surface and groundwater drinking supplies, and to facilitate ranking these facilities for expedient enforcement actions.

HWDMS and RCRIS are the main analytical database used by EPA to track compliance actions, penalty payments, timely and appropriate enforcement, and HPVs, in an effort to discover significant environmental violators and to facilitate ranking these facilities for expedient enforcement actions. It is antici-

---

[27] "Corrective Action For Solid Waste Management Units at Hazardous Waste Management Facilities; Proposed Rule," 55 *Fed.eral Register*. 30804, (July 27, 1990).

[28] EPA is mandated by Executive Order 12291 to perform a Regulatory Impact Analysis prior to the passage of the proposed rule.

pated that RCRIS will possibly begin to incorporate GIS and a modified version of Superfund's Hazard Ranking System (HRS), into its tracking system. If so, the combined effort will be a formidable enforcement enhancement tool to complement the RCPP.

Moving forward in this endeavor, EPA has been streamlining multi-media inspections as an effective enforcement enhancement cross-reference. The Multi-Media Checklist was introduced in late summer 1991 to assist the inspectors of the various programs. It provides them with a means of referring violations noted in other programs, and will also aid enforcement overall. Branching out, EPA has also joined forces with OSHA by developing a similar cross-sharing information database. Having perceived the regulated community as having a "Doubting Thomas" mentality, EPA decided in October 1990 to revise its penalty policy to dispel those rumors once and for all. One need only look at the various environmental "news services" and increased penalties to see the effects of the RCPP in action. Compared to previous enforcement actions the point comes home very quickly.

As noted in the criminal case studies presented earlier, EPA's Criminal Unit has beefed-up its forces and is not letting up in its pursuit of environmental criminals. Jail terms are also something that can befall the environmental criminal.

Finally, it will not be too long before EPA focuses its enforcement attention on the rest of the regulated community. This will include the generators, transporters, and the non-notifiers. It would be prudent for these companies to get their houses in order as well, if it hasn't happened already.

Tips for a Company to Protect Itself

The overall theme in the previous presentation has been one of what to expect when a company is "caught with their pants down", so to speak. In Chapter 8 there is detailed discussion about what a company can attempt to do to stay in compliance, and hence, away from enforcement actions. The purpose in this section is to provide a slightly different perspective with "bulleted" tips to assist the reader.

E.G. Fiesinger of Monsanto has urged companies to take proactive stances with government agencies to avoid big fines.[29] To be proactive, a firm's environmental compliance staff must establish a credible presence with environmental agencies, network, become experts on various environmental topics, and learn how to communicate effectively.

Before any of this can be accomplished, corporate management must be committed to allowing their personnel sufficient time to develop these qualities. If management won't make this commitment, then they can forget trying to be proactive. Furthermore, the firm must establish a solidly credible presence with regulators. This can take time to develop. Fiesinger also suggests joining professional organizations to communicate and share concerns with other firms (networking).[30]

The following tips are provided to help the reader design a successful environmental management program.

- EPA regularly sponsors workshops and seminars, many of which are available to the public. For further information, contact one of the regional offices for a listing of available workshops, dates and locations.

- EPA's hotlines are a valuable source of regulatory information, from interpretation of the regulations to

---

[29] "Dealing With Environmental Regulations and Agencies—An Industry Perspective." Presented at AWMA's annual meeting, Vancouver, B.C., June 1991; BNA's *Environment Reporter*, July 19, 1991, p.648.

[30] See notes 8, 12 & 18 in Chapter 8. See also *Environmental Protection Magazine*, April/May 1991, p.41.

sources of handbooks, training brochures, and general assistance. Listed below are several frequently called numbers:

RCRA/Superfund Hotline	800-424-9346
TSCA Hotline	800-835-6700
EPCRA/SARA Hotline	800-535-0202

- The availability of networking or Roundtable Discussions varies by geographical location, depending on the corporate culture and/or openness of inter-corporate facilities.

- Private organizations, such as Government Institutes and the National Association for Environmental Management (NAEM), often conduct roundtable meetings. These events bring together environmental experts from a wide range of industries to exchange ideas in a nonthreatening environment.

- The proper maintenance of up-to-date records cannot be stressed enough. Contact the regional EPA or state office (anonymously, if you wish) for assistance, if appropriate.

- Employees are the main line of compliance. Their responsibility to obey the laws and protect the environment should be emphasized as much as possible.

- One of the surest ways to gauge a company's compliance status is to perform periodic corporate or in-house environmental audits.

Financial Management and the Risk of Non-Compliance

As presented, corporate liability is directly related to the extent of regulatory non-compliance. To minimize that liability, the prudent corporate executive should implement programs to ensure the minimization of risk. This chapter has highlighted those forces that adversely affect corporate liability, while Chapter 8 will focus on steps to effectively allocate corporate resources for environmental compliance, thus aiding in minimizing corporate liability.

A management consulting firm conducted a survey[31] of the environmental compliance programs of major U.S. corporations. That survey concluded that expenditures were as much as 65 percent of net income, and that environmental issues were being viewed as extremely important.

In addition, since EPA interpreted prior corporate willingness to pay fines as part of doing business and responded with a revised penalty policy to deter future violators, it seems very appropriate that corporations should move voluntarily into compliance before they are forced into it by an enforcement action.

Furthermore, with the emergence of "green awareness" issues, there is an underlying push to keep both customers and the public satisfied, especially if a company's product success hangs in the balance. Such public concern agencies as Greenpeace, National Toxics Campaign Fund, Sierra Club and others, are always looking for controversial issues to bring to the public's attention.

Lastly, since most of corporate America is publicly owned, there is a growing trend among shareholder groups, like pension funds, to become more vocal about environmental issues. It is not uncommon to see this emerge during corporate annual meetings, where ballots and questions are raised concerning environmental issues.[32] There are also mutual fund investment corporations,

---

[31] "Corporate Spending Rises," *Engineering News Record*, June 3, 1991, p.11.

[32] Frank Allen, "Shareholder Resolutions Mushroom Since Valdez," *Wall Street Journal*, March 25, 1991, p.B1. Approximately 54 corporations were noted, including IBM, Kodak, GE, GM and McDonalds.

such as Franklin Research & Development, that invest their clients' funds into companies based on several factors, including environmentally-sound business practices.[33]

These concerns all seem to point to a growing trend regarding corporate expenses, and how much money should be directed towards enhancing a corporation's environmental compliance level and its "green" image.

Company public affairs offices can play a key role in helping to disseminate information to the public. After all, if a corporation wishes to be truly seen as an environmental do-gooder, one way to ensure that would be to maintain as much of an open door policy as possible with the public.

Steve Fradkoff, formerly with EPA, provided the technical review on the material in this chapter. In addition, Steve Fradkoff and George Furst, also formerly with EPA, provided the technical material on the case studies presented herein.

---

[33] Karen Heller, "Public Outreach: The Stakes Are High," *Chemical Week*, July 17, 1991, p.84.

Chapter 4

Environmental Liability in Real Estate Transactions

Daniel M. Steinway and Neil A. Belson
Anderson Kill Olick & Oshinsky

Introduction

Environmental considerations have come to play an increasingly important role in commercial real estate acquisitions and divestitures. Current environmental laws allow a buyer that unwittingly acquires a contaminated property to be held liable for the costs of cleaning up the property—costs which sometimes total many millions of dollars—even though the buyer is not responsible for the environmental problems on the site.

Although it is not possible to totally eliminate the risk of inadvertently assuming environmental liabilities arising from the cleanup of contaminated properties, a purchaser of real estate can take several measures to reduce the chances that such liabilities will occur. This chapter examines different ways in which a company risks assuming environmental liabilities in various types of real estate transactions, and then examines potential alternatives for effectively managing these risks, including contractual allocations of liability and pre-acquisition environmental audits.

The Risks of Assuming Environmental Liability Through Real Estate Transactions

Enactment of the Comprehensive Environmental Response, Compensation, and Liability Act (CERCLA)

The single most important reason for the increased focus on environmental matters in real estate transactions is the enactment, in 1980, of the federal Comprehensive Environmental Response, Compensation, and Liability Act ("CERCLA" or "Superfund"). Congress enacted CERCLA in the wake of the Love Canal disaster in New York primarily in order to provide for the cleanup of the nation's abandoned toxic waste disposal sites.

CERCLA specifies that four different classes of parties may be liable for the costs of responding to a release or threatened release of a hazardous substance from a waste site or "facility":[1] (1) the present owners and operators of a facility, (2) any parties who previously owned or operated a facility at the time that hazardous substances were being disposed of at the facility, (3) any parties who by contract, agreement, or otherwise arranged for the disposal or treatment, or arranged with a transporter for transport for disposal or treatment, of hazardous substances at a facility owned or operated by another party, and (4) any parties who transported hazardous substances to a facility.[2]

---

[1] CERCLA defines "facility" very broadly, to include "(A) any building, structure, installation, equipment, pipe or pipeline . . .,well, pit, pond, lagoon, impoundment, ditch, landfill, storage container, motor vehicle, rolling stock, or aircraft, or (B) any site or area where a hazardous substance has been deposited, stored, disposed of, or placed, or otherwise come to be located; but [not including] any consumer product in consumer use or any vessel." 42 U.S.C. § 9601(9).

[2] 42 U.S.C. § 9607(a).

There are only three narrow statutory defenses to CERCLA liability: that the release or threatened release was caused by 1) an act of God, 2) an act of war, or 3) an act or omission by a third party which is neither an employee or an agent of the defendant, and whose act or omission did not occur in connection with a contractual relationship with the defendant. To assert this last defense, which is often referred to as the defense, a defendant in a CERCLA action must establish that it had exercised due care with respect to the hazardous substance concerned, and that it had taken the necessary precautions against foreseeable acts or omissions of third parties.[3]

Most judicial decisions have interpreted the scope of CERCLA liability very broadly. Courts have been unanimous in holding that CERCLA is a strict liability statute: that is, a party is liable if it falls into any of the four categories of liable parties specified above, regardless of whether it actually caused the environmental contamination.[4] Courts also have generally held that liability under CERCLA is joint and several: any potentially liable party can be held accountable for the entire cost of the cleanup,[5] although any party held liable under CERCLA has the right to sue other potentially liable parties to compel them to contribute their proportionate share to the cleanup.[6]

Corporate Successor Liability Under CERCLA

In interpreting CERCLA, both the U.S. Environmental Protection Agency (EPA) and many courts have attempted to expand the net of CERCLA liability to cover a broad range of potentially

---

[3] 42 U.S.C. § 9607(b).

[4] See, e.g., *New York v. Shore Realty Corp.*, 759 F.2d 1032, 1042 (2d Cir. 1985) ("Shore Realty"); *United States v. Northeastern Pharmaceutical and Chem. Co.*, 579 F.Supp. 823, 843-844 (W.D. Mo. 1984) ("NEPACCO").

[5] See, e.g., NEPACCO, 579 F.Supp. at 844-45; *United States v. Monsanto*, 858 F.2d 160, 171-73 (4th Cir. 1988), cert. denied, 490 U.S. 1106 ("Monsanto").

[6] 42 U.S.C. § 113(f)(1); see also Monsanto, 858 F.2d at 173.

responsible parties. In many recent cases, the courts have expanded this net of CERCLA to hold even secondary parties such as corporate successors, liable for the environmental problems that were previously caused by their predecessors.[7]

For purposes of CERCLA liability, EPA also has taken the position that a corporation which either merges with another corporation or acquires all of another corporation's stock assumes the environmental liabilities of the acquired company.[8] Further, with respect to acquisitions of particular assets, EPA has indicated that it considers the acquiring company to be a corporate successor, i.e., to have assumed the CERCLA liabilities of the selling corporation, if 1) the buyer expressly or implicitly agreed to assume all such obligations; 2) the transaction constituted a *de facto* consolidation or merger; 3) the purchaser is merely a continuation of the selling corporation; 4) the transaction was fraudulently entered into for the purpose of escaping liability; or 5) the purchasing corporation continues substantially the same business operations as the selling corporation.[9] Consistent with EPA's interpretation of the broad net of CERCLA liability, some courts have followed EPA's broad interpretation

---

[7] See, e.g., *Smith Land & Improvement Corp. v. Celotex Corp.*, 851 F.2d 86, 90-91 (3d Cir. 1988), cert. denied, 109 S. Ct. 837 (1989); *United States v. Crown Roll Leaf, Inc.*, 29 Env't. Rep. Cas. (BNA) 2018, 2024 (D. N.J. 1988).

[8] Memorandum on Liability of Corporate Shareholders and Successor Corporations for Abandoned Sites Under the Comprehensive Environmental Response, Compensation, and Liability Act (CERCLA), from Courtney M. Price, EPA Assistant Administrator for Enforcement and Compliance Monitoring, to the Assistant Administrator for Solid Wastes and Emergency Response, Associate Enforcement Counsel for Waste, Regional Administrators, and Regional Counsels, June 13, 1984.

[9] Id. Generally speaking, EPA's policy of holding corporate parties liable under the fifth option, i.e., the mere continuation of the same business operations, is viewed as a broad expansion of traditional notions of corporate law which hold corporate successors liable for the acts of their predecessors.

of corporate successor liability under CERCLA and held asset acquirors liable when they fell into one of the above categories.[10]

Because of CERCLA and corresponding state mini-CERCLA laws, there are now several ways in which a purchaser of real estate may become responsible for cleaning up contaminated properties. Even more disturbing, these parties could even become liable for remediating these sites without in any way having contributed to the environmental problem in the first place. For example, according to recent case law developments, an acquiror of real estate is certainly liable under CERCLA if it is the "present owner" of contaminated property, even if the contamination was caused by the prior owner.[11]

In addition, potential purchasers have to beware of CERCLA liability arising in several other ways. First, a corporate acquiror may have to assume liability as a generator of hazardous substances which "arranged for the disposal" of hazardous substances at a property owned by another party in the event that the seller previously disposed of its hazardous wastes at any offsite locations which are now contaminated and subject to CERCLA actions.

Moreover, as noted above, a corporate successor may conceivably become liable for any environmental problems associated with properties formerly owned or leased by its predecessor (since CERCLA liability extends to any owner or operator of a facility at the time hazardous substances were being disposed of). Thus, it is possible that the acquiror may be held liable for contamination on properties it has never even owned or used. This factual pattern actually occurred in a case decided by the U.S. Court of Ap-

---

[10] See, e.g., *Kelly v. Thomas Solvent Co.,* 29 Env't. Rep. Cas. (BNA) 1119 (W.D. Mich. 1988); In re Acushment River and New Bedford Harbor Proceedings re Alleged PCB Pollution, 712 F.Supp. 1010 (Mass. 1989).

[11] See, e.g., Shore Realty, 759 F.2d at 1043-45; Monsanto, 858 F.2d at 168-69.

peals for the Third Circuit, *Smith Land & Improvement Corp. v. Celotex Corp.* ("*Smith Land*"),[12] where a defendant successor corporation was held liable for the contamination of a property by one of its predecessors, even though the predecessor had sold the property several years prior to the predecessor company's acquisition by the defendant. In reaching its decision, the court in this case relied on both established doctrines of successor liability, and on its reading of the CERCLA statute, to conclude that CERCLA liability should be extended to corporate successors when one corporation either acquires or merges with another.

In light of the prospect of corporate successor liability, a company which is planning to acquire another company through a stock acquisition or merger should obviously identify and investigate the environmental condition not only of properties currently owned by the company to be acquired, but also of all properties formerly owned, leased or otherwise used by the company. The acquiror also should identify and verify the environmental status of all hazardous waste disposal sites presently or formerly used by the company.

Corporate Parent, Officer and Shareholder Liability Under CERCLA

Potential acquirors also should be aware that many courts, in addition to extending liability to purchasers of real property, have sometimes disregarded traditional corporate law principles regarding piercing the corporate veil in holding corporate parents, affiliates, officers and majority shareholders liable under CERCLA for the acts of their subsidiaries, or their affiliates, who may be involved solely in managing real estate properties. These courts have often decided, for example, that they can impose environmental cleanup liability directly on these corporate parents and related entities under CERCLA, and that it is no

---

[12] 851 F.2d 86 (3d Cir. 1988).

longer necessary to follow established corporate law common law principles when deciding whether these parties are responsible for cleanup of contaminated properties. In *U.S. v. Nicolet, Inc.*,[13] a court held that a parent corporation which was the sole shareholder of a subsidiary could be held liable for the subsidiary's CERCLA liabilities since the parent corporation had actively participated in the management of the subsidiary's affairs. In a subsequent federal appellate decision, the court in *U.S. v. Kayser-Roth Corp.*[14] held that a parent corporation could be held directly liable under CERCLA as an operator of a site, based solely upon its exercise of pervasive control over a subsidiary's business activities. Similarly, *Kelley v. ARCO Indus. Corp. (ARCO Industries)*[15] held that the controlling stockholder of a corporation, who was also the chairman of the company's board of directors and allegedly had overall responsibility for a facility, could be held liable under CERCLA as the owner or operator of a facility if he had the requisite knowledge, involvement, responsibility and control over the facility and its hazardous waste disposal practices and processes. *Arco Industries* also held that a president of a company, who had allegedly exercised day-to-day management of the facility, could be liable as an operator of a facility under CERCLA if these same criteria could be satisfied.[16]

While these recent key court decisions are indicative of the recent trends in environmental cases, they are by no means the absolute rule in all cases involving questions of CERCLA liability. For example, in a completely contrary opinion the United States Court of Appeals for the Fifth Circuit refused to extend CERCLA liability to a corporate parent and held in *Joslyn Corp.*

---

[13] 712 F.Supp. 1193, 1202-03 (E.D. Pa. 1989).
[14] 910 F.2d 24 (1st Cir. 1990), cert. denied, 111 S. Ct. 957 (1990).
[15] 721 F.Supp. 873 (W.D. Mich. 1989).
[16] Id.

v. T.L. James & Co., Inc.[17] that traditional notions of corporate law should still be applied when determining whether a corporate parent can be held liable under CERCLA for the actions of its subsidiary. The *Joslyn* court based its holding on the ground that nothing in either the statutory language itself, or its legislative history, indicated that Congress intended for CERCLA to modify well-established and traditional principles of corporate law in deciding whether to expand the net of CERCLA liability to potential secondarily liable parties. This court ruling renders uncertain just how far CERCLA liability will be extended in the future.

Because of the recent, widely divergent CERCLA case law rulings, many are now looking at Congress as the final arbiter of this wide-ranging debate. Unfortunately, Congress does not recent plan to address reauthorization of CERCLA until 1993 at the earliest, and if the last Superfund reauthorization debate is any indication, it may take as long as four years to pass another Superfund reauthorization law.

Common Law Liability

Purchasers of real estate should be aware that CERCLA and other federal and state statutes are not the only basis upon which an acquiror of real estate may be held responsible for the costs of an environmental cleanup. Perhaps even more importantly, many courts have begun to hold owners of property liable for environmental problems based on expanding theories of common law. In the recent landmark case of *T & E Industries, Inc. v. Safety Light Corp.*,[18] a court held a prior owner of property strictly liable to the current owner for the cleanup of contaminated property, finding that the previous owner's radium-processing activities at the site had constituted an "abnormally dangerous activity." Relying on the common law doctrine of *strict*

---

[17] 696 F.Supp. 222 (W.D. La. 1988), aff'd, 893 F.2d 80 (5th Cir. 1990), reh'g denied, 1990 U.S. App. LEXIS 6383 (5th Cir. 1990), cert. denied, 111 S. Ct. 1017 (1990).

[18] 587 A.2d 1249 (N.J. 1991).

liability, the court reasoned that companies which engage in abnormally dangerous activities such as radium-processing and disposal should fully realize the potential for harm arising from their manufacturing operations, and should therefore be held fully accountable for the costs attributable to their activities. This case illustrates both the growing trend toward holding property owners liable for environmental damages under traditional common law theories, and the expanding net of strict liability claims in environmental cases.

State Property Transfer Laws

Another area of potential significance in managing environmental liabilities arising out of real estate transactions is the potential impact of newly enacted state property transfer laws. These state laws typically require a seller to either disclose or actually clean up the environmental hazards on its property as a condition of the sale or transfer of the property. Various states, such as New Jersey, Illinois, Indiana and Connecticut, have imposed some form of environmental cleanup or notice requirements upon sellers who wish to transfer or sell real estate. In addition, a number of other states require transferors of property to file various notices or deed restrictions when they sell property which has been used for the disposal of hazardous substances or wastes.

The New Jersey Environmental Cleanup and Responsibility Act (ECRA)

The New Jersey Environmental Cleanup and Responsibility Act (ECRA)[19] is certainly the best known and most comprehensive of the current state property transfer laws. Under ECRA, a party which either sells or closes an "industrial establishment" (defined to include any facility which generates, manufactures, refines, disposes of, or otherwise handles hazardous substances,

---

[19] N.J. Rev. Stat. §§ 13:1K-6 et seq.

and whose operations fall within one of several Standard Industrial Classification codes established by the U.S. Office of Management and Budget) must complete a complex process of notifying the purchaser and the New Jersey Department of Environmental Protection and Energy (NJDEPE) of any environmental risks associated with the property and remediate all of the environmental hazards of this property in accordance with ECRA cleanup standards. Among the transfers which may trigger ECRA are stock transfers, mergers and various other corporate transactions, as well as outright sales of property.

The ECRA notice requirements basically contain two separate parts. First, the owner or operator of the covered establishment must file a completed General Information Submission (GIS) with the NJDEPE within five days of signing the agreement of sale or announcing the decision to close or terminate operations. The GIS is a statement outlining general information about the location, type and nature of the facility which is to be transferred or closed, along with the projected date for the transfer or closing.

Within 45 days of filing the GIS, the owner or operator of the industrial establishment to be sold or transferred must then, under ECRA, again file with the NJDEPE a second, much more comprehensive submission, known as the Site Evaluation Submission (SES). The SES must contain a detailed description of how the seller plans to clean up the facility and either a proposed sampling plan or a fully documented justification of why such a plan is unnecessary. After reviewing the SES, the NJDEPE will either approve the sampling plan or require the seller to make revisions and resubmit its plan. NJDEPE also will send an inspector to the facility to conduct a preliminary site inspection—possibly several months after submission of the original GIS. Following this inspection, the owner or operator may submit either a proposed cleanup plan or a proposed "negative declaration," stating that there has been no discharge of hazardous substances upon the property or that all such discharges have been cleaned up to the satisfaction of NJDEPE. If a cleanup plan is necessary, the owner/operator must also provide financial assurance to guarantee the cleanup. NJDEPE will then not approve a negative declaration until it is satisfied that the cleanup is complete.

Ordinarily, the transfer of a business establishment may not proceed until the NJDEPE has approved either the cleanup plan or the negative declaration. However, in order to help speed up real estate transactions and not unnecessarily delay critical financial activities, the NJDEPE may issue under various circumstances an Administrative Consent Order allowing a transaction to take place prior to completion of the ECRA process, provided one or more of the parties to the transaction provides adequate financial assurance to the NJDEPE that the cleanup will eventually occur. Alternatively, NJDEPE has the authority to defer the implementation of any cleanup plan for the site until after the closing of an establishment in those cases where the purchaser plans to use a facility in approximately the same manner as the prior owner.

Failure of the seller to comply with ECRA can lead in many cases to harsh results. ECRA violations may be grounds for allowing either the purchaser or NJDEPE to void the transfer and holding the transferor strictly liable for any damages to the purchaser resulting from the voiding of the sale.

Many businesses and others have argued that ECRA injects considerable costs, delays and major bureaucratic obstacles into routine commercial real estate transactions, and ultimately has had the net effect of discouraging industrial investment in New Jersey. These criticisms may have a genuine basis in fact: the complete ECRA process from the time of the initial filing until the approval of a negative declaration frequently extends more than a year, and can last even longer in certain complex cleanup cases.

The Illinois Responsible Property Transfer Act

In contrast to ECRA, the Illinois Responsible Property Transfer Act (IRPTA)[20] is an example of a statute which imposes comparatively mild but still significant burdens on parties involved in real estate transfers. IRPTA is triggered by transfers of real property upon which is located either 1) one or more facilities which are subject to the reporting requirements of section 312 of the federal Emergency Planning and Community Right-to-Know Act[21] (which applies to facilities which contain certain designated hazardous chemicals in quantities above threshold amounts) or 2) underground storage tanks which require registration with the State Fire Marshall.

Under IRPTA, a transferor (seller) of covered real property must provide a completed environmental disclosure document to the transferee (buyer) within 30 days following the execution of a contract, but no later than 30 days prior to closing (parties to the transfer may waive these time guidelines, provided the transferee receives the disclosure document prior to closing). This document requires the transferor to provide various information about its present and past use of the property. Within 30 days following the closing, the disclosure document must be recorded with the appropriate county recorder and filed with the Illinois Environmental Protection Agency.

IRPTA imposes several sanctions for violations of its notice requirements. For example, if the disclosure form reveals environmental problems previously unknown to the transferee, or if the transferor fails to deliver the form within the specified time frame, then any other party to the agreement (including prospective lenders) has the right to void the agreement or cancel a commitment to provide financing. The applicable county's or state's attorney also may initiate an action to assess civil

---

[20] Ill. Rev. Stat. Ch. 30 para. 901 et seq.
[21] 42 U.S.C. § 11022.

penalties against any transferor which fails to comply with the IRPTA disclosure requirements, and any private citizen who suffers losses through a violation of the act may file a private lawsuit against the alleged violator to recover damages.

Despite these enforcement and recording provisions, IRPTA is generally viewed as far less burdensome to private industry than the New Jersey ECRA. Among the major differences between IRPTA and ECRA are that: 1) IRPTA is primarily an environmental disclosure statute, while ECRA imposes both disclosure and cleanup requirements, and 2) ECRA requires governmental involvement and approvals at several stages of the ECRA process, while the role of the government under IRPTA is essentially limited to enforcing violations.

Similar to IRPTA, most other state notice and cleanup requirements tend to be less rigorous than ECRA. Since several states now have at least minimal disclosure requirements, it is prudent for any potential seller of real estate to find out, in advance of a proposed sale, whether there are any state or local laws that impose environmental notice or cleanup requirements in connection with property transfers and to adequately assess the effects of such requirements upon the proposed transfer.

Reducing the Risk of Environmental Liability

Contractual Allocation of Environmental Liability

Contractual Protections From the Purchaser's Perspective: As part of any real estate transaction which might involve environmental risks, it is advisable for the participating parties to specify in the purchase agreement how environmental liabilities are to be allocated. This is usually done in the written agreement of sale. Obviously, a buyer of real estate can effectively manage its potential exposure to environmental liabilities in purchasing contaminated property through a wide variety of useful contractual devices. Each of these devices offers one form or another of contractual protection of which parties can take advantage depending upon their bargaining power in a particular transaction.

One way for a prospective purchaser to protect itself from potential environmental liability in acquiring real estate is through a contractual indemnification provision expressly stating that the seller will indemnify the purchaser for all environmental liabilities that eventually arise in connection with the property. From the buyer's perspective, an ideal indemnification clause will allow that party to obtain indemnification from the seller for all environmental liabilities relating to any pre-closing operations of the facility or company to be acquired, regardless of when these liabilities arise or become apparent, and regardless of whether these liabilities arise as the result of government-initiated or private actions. In order to be most effective, the indemnification should cover liabilities from private toxic tort actions, as well as liabilities arising under all federal, state and local environmental laws and standards. It is important to indicate that an indemnification for pre-acquisition activities applies regardless of when these liabilities arise, since there is always a strong possibility in environmental cases that a pre-existing liability will not be discovered until several years following the sale of a piece of property when a governmental agency or private party discovers either a groundwater problem or soil contamination at the site.

For mergers, stock acquisitions and other transactions where a buyer may be liable as a successor corporation, a buyer should also seek indemnification and adequate representations relating to properties previously owned or operated by the seller. Such a provision will protect a buyer from the *Smith Land* problem, where, as noted previously, a buyer of a company was held liable for the activities of a previous corporate owner on property that the buyer never even owned.

In addition to contractual indemnification provisions, a purchaser of real estate can achieve an additional form of contractual protection by asking that the seller expressly warrant or represent in the purchase agreement that it is in compliance with all applicable environmental, health and safety laws and other governmental regulatory requirements. This representation should apply to both current and past operations. In addition, the sale contract should expressly provide that the seller will indemnify the buyer for any losses arising from any breach of this provision. In the event that the seller's operations turn out not to have been in compliance with environmental requirements, the buyer will then be able to assert claims against the seller for both indemnification and breach of contract. If the seller knows that it has violated one or more environmental or other related requirements and therefore is not in a position to make such a representation, the buyer should require the seller to make a list of each known violation in a separate appendix or exhibit to the contract, with the contract clearly specifying that the seller is in compliance with all applicable environmental, health and safety laws and requirements other than those violations explicitly listed in the attached appendix or exhibit.

In addition to obtaining the necessary warranties and representations, a purchaser should seek to include a provision in the purchase agreement specifying that the seller's permits and any other regulatory approvals necessary for the operation of the facility/business in question are transferable to the buyer, and that the seller will use its best efforts to facilitate this transfer. Finally, the contract should provide that the deal is voidable by the purchaser or provide alternative protections to the purchaser in the event that the purchaser is unable to obtain any permit or approval which is necessary to operate the facility/business.

Depending on the particular type of real estate transaction involved, other types of creative and innovative provisions can be drafted into a contract protecting purchasers of real estate from unknown environmental liabilities associated with the purchase of property. These provisions can range from more detailed warranties and representations made by the buyer to dedicated environmental cleanup escrow fund arrangements to cover potential cleanup costs. For example, if a situation arises where a private indemnification is likely to provide insufficient assurance to a purchaser against environmental liabilities, the buyer may wish to insulate itself from any possible type of environmental liability whatsoever by requiring the seller to clean up any environmental problems at its facility(ies) prior to closing. In asset purchases, a viable tactic might be for the buyer to simply "carve out" any environmentally problematic sites from the deal, so that the deal proceeds as planned minus the problem site(s).

Another potential alternative available to the buyer is to require the seller to set up an escrow account (possibly involving a portion of the purchase price) in a specified amount or for a specified number of years. This escrow account could be used to remediate environmental problems that arise in future years after the property is sold.

Of course, a final alternative in any transaction where the purchaser learns of potential environmental problems is to simply walk away from the deal.

As additional protection from possible environmental liabilities, a purchaser of real estate may wish to set up a subsidiary corporation and then acquire title to the real estate in the name of the subsidiary. By acquiring the property through a subsidiary, the purchaser can seek to shield the assets of the parent corporation from any future environmental liability in accordance with traditional concepts of corporate law. However, as noted earlier, such arrangements may not always be effective in protecting a parent corporation in the environmental area, since several courts have recently disregarded traditional corporate law principles and held parent corporations, corporate officers and even individual shareholders liable under CERCLA in specific cases where the court has found that these parties were actively involved in the operation of its subsidiaries' affairs.

After acquiring the property, a purchaser can take a number of other steps to help ensure that it will not be held liable for the acts of the prior owner of the property. For example, a purchaser should explore the possibility of using different sites to dispose of its hazardous/solid wastes than those used by the seller. By immediately discontinuing use of the seller's old hazardous waste disposal sites, a purchaser can eliminate any doubt that any hazardous/solid waste shipments from the acquired business/ facility to these sites were made by the seller and not the purchaser. Since many indemnification agreements protect the purchaser against liabilities arising from the seller's pre-acquisition activities, this practice of switching disposal sites immediately upon taking over a property/business can help to clearly confirm the purchaser's claims that it should be indemnified if it is named as a defendant in CERCLA cost recovery actions involving the company's prior disposal activities: should the disposal sites used by the seller ever become the subject of an environmental enforcement action or litigation, there will be no doubt that any hazardous waste shipments by the company/facility to these sites must have been made by the seller prior to the acquisition.

Contractual Protections From the Seller's Perspective

Examining the transaction from the seller's perspective, a seller will obviously want to limit its environmental exposure as much as its bargaining powers will allow. From the seller's perspective, an ideal contractual provision would specify that a buyer has had an opportunity to inspect the property, and agrees to buy the property "as is," with the buyer expressly assuming CERCLA and any other environmental, health and safety liabilities which arise following the date of sale, regardless of when the environmental conditions which led to these liabilities arose, and fully indemnifying the seller against all environmental liabilities. As noted in the earlier discussion on the *Southland* case, if the purchaser is going to assume environmental liabilities, it is imperative that the contract spell this out clearly.

If a seller of real estate cannot obtain this full contractual protection, there are many potential contractual alternatives that it may want to employ when it negotiates an agreement of sale with the purchaser. For example, if the purchaser insists on receiving some form of indemnification from a seller, a seller may seek to negotiate a limit on its potential liabilities by setting a maximum dollar amount or cap on its potential indemnification obligations following the sale, and/or bargaining for a limit on the length of time for which the indemnification provisions would apply. In addition, a seller should try to specify that any of its representations in the purchase agreement with respect to environmental matters are made based solely on its knowledge and belief. The seller also should seek to specify in any warranty or representation made to a potential buyer that its facilities are in *material* compliance, as opposed to *full compliance*, with any or all environmental regulatory requirements that apply to the facility's operations. By representing only that its facilities are in material compliance with environmental requirements, a seller leaves itself some room for minor or inconsequential violations of applicable federal or state environmental rules and regulations without being held in technical breach of the contract. This additional flexibility is significant, since an inspection can usually show that even the best-run facilities have some technical or minor violations of various environmental, health and safety governmental regulatory requirements.

No matter how far-reaching an indemnity clause may be, it is important to stress that private indemnification or hold harmless agreements would not affect either a buyer's or seller's potential CERCLA liability to governmental agencies which bring actions to force cleanup of the acquired site. CERCLA, as was noted above, expressly provides that neither private indemnification agreements nor other similar arrangements are effective to transfer liability from one party to another when claims are made by either the EPA or a state governmental agency.[22] The value of private indemnification agreements, therefore, is not that they fully transfer all responsibility for government-ordered cleanups to other parties, but rather that they allow one party to gain reimbursement from another in the event that it is subsequently held liable to a third party for the costs of environmental cleanups. Consequently, there may be times when the party offering the indemnification lacks the financial resources to provide adequate reimbursement in the event of a major environmental liability. Under these circumstances, an indemnity may prove to be of vastly limited value.

Recent Judicial Decisions

Most courts have shown a willingness to enforce privately negotiated arrangements for allocating CERCLA liability. CERCLA section 107(e)(1)[23] provides that:

> No indemnification, hold harmless, or similar agreement or conveyance shall be effective to transfer from the owner or operator of any vessel or facility or from any person who may be liable for a release or threat of release under this section, to any other person the liability imposed under this section. Nothing in the subsection shall bar any agreement for any liability under this section.

A majority of courts have interpreted CERCLA section 107(e) as stating that while no party may escape CERCLA liability to EPA or a state government, buyers and sellers are still free to allocate and/or transfer environmental liabilities in real estate transaction agreements, and to negotiate indemnification, reimbursement, or other contractual rights allowing one party to

---

[22] 42 U.S.C. § 9607(e)(1).
[23] Id.

recover from another in the event it is held liable under CERCLA to EPA or a state for the cleanup of contaminated property.[24]

However, because of recent case law, it is absolutely imperative for a real estate purchaser seeking to protect itself through contractual indemnification provisions to clearly specify that the indemnification covers CERCLA-type liabilities. As noted by recent courts, purchasers can still be held liable for the costs of cleaning up properties even if they had included a contractual indemnification provision in the written agreement of sale, unless that indemnity was clearly intended to cover environmental cleanup requirements. In *Southland Corp. v. Ashland Oil, Inc.*,[25] a court held that a contract which contained an "as is" provision in a sales agreement was not sufficient to transfer CERCLA liability from a seller to a buyer of contaminated property. The plaintiffs in *Southland* had filed an action for both private cost recovery under CERCLA section 107(a) and contribution under CERCLA section 113(f)(1). In reaching its decision, the court stated that the "as is" clause in a sales

---

[24] See, e.g., *Versatile Metals, Inc. v. Union Corp.*, 693 F.Supp. 1563, 1573 (E.D. Pa. 1988); *Chemical Waste Management v. Armstrong World Indus.*, 669 F.Supp. 1285, 1294-95 (E.D. Pa. 1987) ("Armstrong"). However, at least two courts have interpreted CERCLA section 107(e)(1) differently, holding that it not only prevents parties from contracting away their cleanup liabilities to EPA or a state, but also prevents potentially liable parties from contractually allocating their liability among one another. See *AM Intern. v. International Forging Equipment*, 743 F.Supp. 525 (N.D. Ohio 1990); *CPC International v. Aerojet-General Corp.*, 759 F.Supp. 1269 (W.D. Mich. 1991). These two cases have held that CERCLA section 107(e)(1) only allows contractual allocations of liability between a potentially liable party and other parties which could not otherwise be held liable to EPA or the state, such as insurers or guarantors, to cover the cost of Superfund cleanups, but does not allow private allocations of liability among jointly liable parties under CERCLA. 743 F.Supp. at 527-530; 759 F.Supp. at 1281-83. While purchasers of real estate should generally seek to obtain the most protective contractual indemnification arrangements possible, these two decisions should put purchasers on notice that some courts might not give effect to such agreements with respect to CERCLA liability.

[25] 696 F.Supp. 994 (D. N.J. 1988) ("Southland").

agreement was only a warranty disclaimer and only acted to preclude contractual claims, not those based on a statute like CERCLA.[26] Since neither of these claims was based on a breach of warranty, the court therefore found that they were not barred by the "as is" provision. The *Southland* court also stated that in order to transfer CERCLA liabilities, "there must be [some form of] an express provision which allocates these risks to one of the parties."[27] For contracts executed prior to CERCLA's enactment, the court indicated that a transfer of liability would require "some clear transfer or release of future 'CERCLA-like' liabilities."[28] In addition to *Southland*, several other courts which have addressed the question of contractual allocation of environmental liabilities have held that a transfer of environmental liabilities requires some sort of explicit contractual language.[29]

Even though many courts have followed the *Southland* rationale, judicial rulings in this controversial area of environmental law are not unanimous, and it remains to be seen how the courts will rule in cases as the stakes grow enormously in the environmental cleanup debate. For example, in *FMC Corp. v. Northern Pump Co.*,[30] a court held that a contractual release, signed in 1967, prevented the buyer from suing the seller for "all claims and causes of action which [it] had, has or may have [against defendant]." This broad release was interpreted to even cover CERCLA liabilities, and thus, the seller could not be held liable in any CERCLA contribution action or private cost recovery action for cleanup of contaminated property that it had previously sold. The court said that even though the release did not specifically mention environmental claims, the fact that the language of the

---

[26] Id. at 1001.

[27] Id. at 1002.

[28] Id.

[29] See Armstrong 669 F. Supp. at 1294-95; *Allied Corp. v. Frola*, 730 F. Supp. 626, 629-630 (D. N.J. 1990).

[30] 668 F.Supp. 1285, 1291-92 (D. Minn. 1987).

release included "all" claims was sufficient to bar claims against the seller for CERCLA liability.

Environmental Audits

Another way for a buyer to reduce its potential environmental risks in purchasing real estate is to conduct a pre-acquisition environmental audit of the facility and/or company to be acquired. EPA has defined an environmental audit as basically a "systematic, documented, periodic and objective review by regulated entities of facility operations and practices relating to meeting environmental requirements."[31]

Many companies have come to view environmental auditing as an effective tool to ensure environmental compliance with federal, state and local rules and regulations. Environmental audits, including both Phase I or Phase II audits, are now commonplace in most real estate transactions as a means to ensure that there are no hidden risks associated with buying a particular property and to avoid being caught in the expanding web of Superfund liability.

Conducting a pre-acquisition environmental audit can alert a prospective buyer of real property to potentially serious environmental liabilities in the seller's facility or company which might make the acquisition inadvisable. In less serious situations, an audit can inform the buyer of possible environmental problems with a site, so that the buyer is in a position to require the seller to clean up the property, reduce the sale price to cover expected environmental losses, or include various types of contractual protections in the written agreement of sale such as a broad form of indemnity obligation.

The seller also may benefit by conducting an environmental audit, particularly when the audit is performed by an indepen-

---

[31] EPA Environmental Auditing Policy Statement, 51 Fed. Reg. 606 (July 9, 1986).

dent consulting firm acceptable to potential buyers. In the event the audit does not identify environmental problems, the marketability of the seller's property is likely to increase. Also, an audit can help confirm the precise environmental condition of the seller's property at the time of sale, thereby providing the seller with a baseline upon which he may rely if he is subsequently named as a responsible party for cleanup of the site.

The following analysis focuses on some of the legal issues surrounding environmental audits, including the CERCLA "innocent landowner" defense, confidentiality concerns, and disclosure requirements. This discussion also reviews the EPA and Department of Justice policy on environmental audits. An appendix is included which contains a sample environmental audit protocol which might be followed in a general type of pre-acquisition audit.

The Innocent Landowner Defense

One of the benefits to purchasers of conducting a pre-acquisition environmental audit is that this action may assist them in asserting a defense to subsequent CERCLA liability known as the "innocent landowner" defense. Congress created the innocent landowner defense to CERCLA liability in the 1986 amendments to CERCLA.[32] This defense was added to the Superfund statute in response to claims that the statute had unfairly held innocent landowners liable for environmental contamination that really had been caused by their predecessors or other third parties over whom the landowners had no control.

As noted earlier, CERCLA had provided some very limited statutory defenses to liability prior to the enactment of SARA, one of which specified that a party would not be held liable for releases or threatened releases of hazardous substances resulting

---

[32] Superfund Amendments and Reauthorization Act of 1986 ("SARA") Pub.L. 99-499..

solely from the acts or omissions of a third party which was not in a *contractual relationship* with a defendant. This statutory defense to CERCLA liability could be asserted only when the party was able to demonstrate that it had exercised due care and took appropriate precautions against the foreseeable acts of third parties.[33] However, prior to 1986, EPA had interpreted the CERCLA definition of "contractual relationship" broadly to include even purchase agreements between buyers and sellers of real property. Because of this broad definition, CERCLA had been interpreted to effectively render the third party defense unavailable to innocent purchasers of contaminated property.

During the SARA debate in 1986, Congress created the "innocent landowner" defense in order to allow truly innocent landowners to avoid CERCLA liability in very limited cases. To achieve this goal, SARA amended the definition of "contractual relationship" to provide that a buyer of real estate is not considered to be in a contractual relationship with a seller if the buyer:

1) acquired title to a facility after the disposal or placement of hazardous substances at the property had occurred; and

2) can establish by a preponderance of the evidence that, at the time it acquired a facility, it did not know and had no reason to know that any hazardous substance which was the subject of the release or threatened release was disposed of on, in, or at the facility.[34]

This modification in the definition of "contractual relationship" under CERCLA was intended to allow innocent landowners to take advantage of the third party statutory defense. However, in order to assert the "innocent landowner" defense, SARA specifies that a purchaser also must have:

---

[33] 42 U.S.C. § 9607(b)(3).
[34] 42 U.S.C. § 9601(35)(A).

undertaken, at the time of acquisition, all appropriate inquiry into the previous ownership and uses of the property consistent with good commercial or customary practice in an effort to minimize liability.[35]

If a landowner can satisfy this requirement and also demonstrate that it exercised due care and took appropriate precautions against the foreseeable acts of third parties, then that party is not considered to be in a contractual relationship with its seller for purposes of CERCLA and therefore cannot be liable under CERCLA for pre-acquisition environmental liabilities.

Unfortunately, CERCLA provides relatively little guidance on how to satisfy some of the specific requirements of the "innocent landowner" defense. One of the most confusing problems has been the determination of what constitutes the "all appropriate inquiry" as required in order to assert this defense. In addressing this issue, CERCLA only specifies that a court should consider a number of the following factors:

> any specialized knowledge or experience on the part of the defendant, the relationship of the purchase price to the value of the property if uncontaminated, commonly known or reasonably ascertainable information about the property, the obviousness of the presence or likely presence of contamination at the property, and the ability to detect such contamination by appropriate inspection.[36]

However, CERCLA provides no further guidance on how to satisfy these general requirements for asserting the defense.

Moreover, EPA has provided relatively little additional guidance in interpreting the "innocent landowner" defense.[37]

---

[35] 42 U.S.C. § 9601(35)(B).

[36] Id.

[37] See Guidance on Landowner Liability under Section 107(a)(1) of CERCLA, De Minimis Settlements under Section 122(g)(1)(B) of CERCLA, and Settlements with Prospective Purchasers of Contaminated Property, from Edward E. Reich, EPA Acting Assistant Administrator for Enforcement and Compliance Monitoring, and Jonathan Z. Cannon, EPA

There have been, however, numerous legal commentaries written on how the "innocent landowner" defense should be interpreted. One of these articles suggests that purchasers must, at a minimum, 1) conduct a thorough review of a site history; 2) review federal, state and local records concerning the site; and 3) conduct an environmental study of the site, if completion of the first two steps suggests such a step would be necessary.[38] Notwithstanding such commentaries, the absence of any more substantive regulatory guidance from EPA still leaves a prospective acquiror of real property with little basis for determining if its pre-acquisition audit will sufficiently meet the requirements of the "all appropriate inquiry" criterion so that it will avoid the potential possibility of CERCLA liability.

Even without any additional guidance from EPA, it appears clear that the "innocent landowner" defense will still have somewhat limited utility for several reasons. First, because CERCLA itself limits the use of the innocent landowner defense to situations where parties had no reason to know of an environmental problem at the time of the acquisition of the property, the defense does not apply in cases where a pre-acquisition environmental audit does identify the presence of hazardous substances on a property, no matter how responsibly the purchaser acted to alleviate any environmental problems that were identified by the audit itself. Moreover, the innocent landowner defense also would not protect a purchaser which disposed of even a de minimis amount of hazardous substances at a facility, since the defense only applies when the disposal of hazardous substances occurs prior to the acquisition of property.

Acting Assistant Administrator for Solid Waste and Emergency Response, to Regional Administrators, Regions I-X, Regional Counsels, Regions I-X, and Waste Management Division Directors, Regions I-X, June 6, 1989.

[38] Edward E. Reich and Steven L. Leifer, "The Effect of CERCLA on Property Transfers," reported in Ronald D. Miller & Mark J. Bennett, "Due Diligence Techniques for the Innocent Landowner/Purchaser", 3 *TXLR* 434 (1988).

Further, although there have been relatively few cases interpreting the scope of the innocent landowner defense, those courts which have examined this defense have interpreted it very narrowly. Several cases have held, for example, that the defense does not protect a landlord whose lessee contaminates a property.[39] Another case has held that the defense did not protect a purchaser that knew at the time of purchase that a particular property contained certain heavy metal-containing slag, but mistakenly believed that the slag was harmless and inert.[40] In still another case, *BCW Associates Ltd. v Occidental Chemical Corp.*,[41] the court held that a defendant could be liable under CERCLA even though it had commissioned an environmental audit prior to purchasing a contaminated property and would therefore presumably be eligible for the innocent landowner defense. This case may, though, be distinguishable from the facts in other innocent landowner cases because there was clear evidence in this case that the defendant's own activities had inadvertently caused hazardous dust particles to become airborne inside a building.

At least one court, however, has shown signs that it might interpret the "appropriate inquiry" standard more leniently. In *U.S. v. Serafini*,[42] the court denied the government's motion for summary judgement against a landowner who in 1969 had purchased a site at which 55-gallon drums were visibly strewn across the property itself. The landowner had not actually visited the site prior to the purchase nor known that the drums were clearly visible upon inspection. In spite of these facts, the court rejected the plaintiff's motion for summary judgement because it found that there was an unresolved question of material fact as to

---

[39] See, e.g., Monsanto, 858 F.2d 160; *State of Washington v. Time Oil Co.*, 687 F.Supp. 529 (D. Colo. 1988).

[40] *Wickland Oil Terminals v. Asarco Inc.*, 19 Envtl. L. Rep. 20,855 (N.D. Cal. 1988).

[41] No. 86-5947 (E.D. Pa. September 30, 1988).

[42] 706 F.Supp. 346 (M.D. Pa. 1988).

whether the "all appropriate inquiry" standard for a purchaser in the defendant's position in 1969 would have included a site visit. This decision suggests that a court might determine whether the defendant had met the "all appropriate inquiry" requirement based on standards at the time and place where the deal actually occurred rather than at the time of a lawsuit or enforcement action.

In conclusion, the 1986 SARA amendments created a new defense for those "innocent" parties which conduct a proper commercial inquiry prior to acquiring a parcel of property. The enactment of this defense has created a new incentive for buyers to conduct pre-acquisition environmental audits. Obviously, by doing so these buyers will be in a much better position to protect themselves against the specter of CERCLA liability. However, because of the limited guidance available on how to effectively assert the innocent landowner defense under CERCLA, purchasers of real estate should not assume that the mere fact that they have conducted an environmental audit prior to acquiring a property will necessarily shield them from CERCLA liability. Purchasers also should remember that the innocent landowner defense only applies to CERCLA liability and does not affect a party's liability under other federal or state environmental law or in private toxic tort actions.

Confidentiality Concerns

One risk in conducting an environmental audit prior to the transfer of real estate is that the audit may uncover serious environmental problems or highly sensitive information which, if disclosed, could result in loss of valuable business trade secrets, embarrassment or even liability. This should be a particular concern for prospective sellers of real property which may face liability, enforcement action, or business losses as the result of such disclosures. Purchasers, of course, are less likely to face direct liability or other losses as the result of pre-acquisition audits, since they do not yet own or operate the property in question and can always walk away from the deal if the audit turns up negative information. However, the disclosure of adverse information can significantly affect the value of the targeted property and may even result in the imposition of environmental and cleanup or remediation obligations upon the purchaser should it elect to proceed with the transaction. Consequently, purchasers of real estate, like sellers, have an interest in preserving the confidentiality of environmental audits to the maximum extent allowed by law.

At the same time, there may be a legal obligation to disclose certain kinds of information discovered by the environmental audit, regardless of its sensitive nature. However, it may be possible to preserve the confidentiality of a significant amount of sensitive and/or trade secret information through the appropriate use of two well-established confidentiality rules, known as the "attorney-client privilege" and the "attorney work-product rule." Although it is impossible to absolutely guarantee the confidentiality of any portion of an audit, the early involvement of an attorney in the audit planning process can help to maximize the protection offered by these two rules of law.

The Attorney-Client Privilege

The purpose of the attorney-client privilege is to allow a client to discuss its situation with an attorney freely and fully without fear that the substance of the discussion will one day be disclosed. This privilege can be effectively used in various real estate transactions to protect certain confidential information related to the environmental conditions of the property, if the proper foundation for this privilege is laid.

There are essentially four key requirements which must be satisfied in order to claim the attorney-client privilege. First, the attorney must be providing legal advice to a party. Business or other non-legal advice provided by the attorney is not privileged. For that reason, any retainer agreement with an outside counsel involved in an environmental audit of a targeted parcel of property should specify that the attorney is being hired to provide legal advice with respect to the audit. If a potential buyer plans to use its own in-house counsel for the audit, the company should carefully distinguish between those situations where the attorney is acting to provide legal advice (which is protected by the privilege) and those situations where the attorney is acting in a general management role (where the privilege will not apply). Regardless of whether a company is using its outside or in-house counsel, all documents relating to the audit, including the initial letter retaining the attorney, should indicate that the purpose of the audit is to obtain legal advice related to the real estate transaction.

Second, the information for which the privilege is asserted must relate to communications between a lawyer (and his or her agents) and a client. However, it is important to note that the privilege does not protect the confidentiality of the underlying facts which are the subject of those communications. For example, a company which experienced an accidental spill of a toxic chemical could not use the attorney-client privilege to avoid a requirement to disclose the spill, even if it discussed the spill with an attorney. While the fact that a spill had occurred would not be privileged information, an attorney's specific legal advice to its client as to how to minimize the likelihood of lawsuits or civil penalties resulting from the spill would be covered by the privilege.

The U.S. Supreme Court has indicated that the attorney-client privilege may protect attorney communications with a wide range of its corporate client employees. In *Upjohn Co. v. United States*,[43] the Court held that attorney communications with even lower and middle level employees were protected under the attorney-client privilege if these communications were made at

---

[43] 449 U.S. 383 (1981).

the request of management for the purpose of providing legal advice to the corporation. Consistent with the *Upjohn* decision, it appears that a company can increase its chances of preserving the confidentiality of an audit by initiating planning for the audit by means of a written request from senior management to counsel. This written request should specify that counsel, acting in its legal capacity, is to undertake an environmental audit for the purpose of providing legal advice to the corporation and that this audit will consist of a number of interviews with a broad range of parties. This initial request should also specify that all material obtained as a result of the audit should remain confidential.

The attorney-client privilege, in addition to protecting communications between an attorney and a client, can also be used to protect certain communications between clients and non-lawyers where the non-lawyer is assisting an attorney in providing legal advice on the acquisition of a parcel of property. This principle is particularly significant in the context of environmental audits, which often make extensive use of technical consultants when investigating the environmental conditions of a property targeted for purchase, since it extends the attorney-client privilege to communications made by these consultants for the purpose of assisting an attorney in providing legal advice on the merits of buying the property. In many cases, it is advisable to have the attorney, rather than the client, retain the consultant, in order to substantiate a claim that consultant communications are made for the specific purpose of assisting the attorney in providing legal advice on the real estate transaction. For the same reason, consultants should also send their environmental audit reports and correspondence directly to the attorney, rather than to the client.

The third condition for properly asserting the attorney-client privilege is that all privileged information must be kept confidential. To meet this requirement, the company should stamp all material for which the privilege will be claimed as "privileged and confidential," and limit access to these materials within the company to those persons who have a need to know about the transaction in question. The company also should alert all those persons involved in the environmental audit to the need to maintain the confidentiality of specified documents. Moreover, an attorney should participate in the early planning of the audit to insure that a mechanism is in place for clearly identifying confidential materials and restricting their dissemination.

Finally, the last condition imposed on the use of the attorney-client privilege is that the party must not have waived its privilege by disclosing the information to outside parties. Intentional disclosure of otherwise privileged documents is generally considered to amount to a waiver of a party's right to assert the attorney-client privilege. For example, voluntary disclosure of privileged material to a government agency has been held to constitute a waiver of a party's right to assert a privilege of confidentiality, even though the party had agreed with that governmental agency that the material was not to be distributed outside the agency.[44] The fact that the material was distributed to one outside party was held to destroy the attorney-client privilege for that material with respect to all outside parties.[45] In addition, some courts have even ruled that inadvertent disclosure may result in a waiver of the attorney-client privilege.[46]

Several steps can be taken to help protect against violating this condition for asserting the attorney-client privilege. First, the stamping of privileged documents as "privileged and confidential" can both reduce the chance of inadvertent disclosure and provide a basis for arguing that any disclosure that occurred was unintended. Clearly documenting that information pertaining to an audit is to be kept confidential will provide written proof that

---

[44] *Permian Corp. v. United States*, 665 F.2d 1214 (D.C. Cir. 1981).
[45] Id.
[46] See, e.g., *Hartford Fire Ins. Co. v. Garvey*, 109 F.R.D. 323 (N.D. Cal. 1985).

the party intended this information to be covered by the attorney-client privilege. In addition, early involvement of counsel in the audit process can assist in establishing procedures for the prevention of inadvertent disclosure.

Attorney Work-Product Rule

In addition to the attorney-client privilege, the attorney work-product rule may be used to protect the confidentiality of environmental audits conducted prior to a real estate transaction under certain circumstances. The work-product rule provides qualified protection for information or materials collected in anticipation of litigation. This rule, which was first established by the U.S. Supreme Court in the 1947 case of *Hickman v. Taylor*,[47] is now codified in Rule 26(b)(3) of the Federal Rules of Civil Procedure.

The attorney work-product rule is generally much more limited than the attorney-client privilege in the types of materials it may protect. In contrast to the attorney-client privilege, the work-product rule applies only to documents and "tangible things," but not to "information" or "facts" generally. The rule also is limited to materials collected in anticipation of litigation. Although the litigation need not actually be ongoing, the anticipation of litigation must be realistic, as opposed to purely theoretical. Further, the material must have been prepared by or for a party to the anticipated litigation by or for that party's representative (including an attorney or consultant).

The work-product rule provides very strong protection for materials which reflect the mental impressions, conclusions, opinions or legal theories of the attorney. However, other materials may become discoverable if an adversary can show that it has a substantial need for the materials and that it is unable to obtain

---

[47] 329 U.S. 495 (1947).

the same information from other sources without undue hardship.

Because the applicability of the work-product rule is limited to materials prepared in anticipation of litigation, counsel should clearly document the reasons for believing that litigation may occur when seeking to take advantage of this rule. Companies should bear in mind the possibility that an adversary may not be able to obtain some or all of the material contained in the audit from other sources, and may therefore be able to meet the threshold for demonstrating substantial need or undue hardship. Also, as in the case of attorney-client privilege, companies should be mindful of the fact that disclosure to third parties may constitute a waiver of the work-product rule.

Self-Evaluation Privilege

Some courts and state legislatures have recently begun to recognize a new confidentiality privilege for materials generated during a company's self-evaluation process. The reason for this emerging self-evaluation privilege is to encourage companies to undertake critical self-evaluation to improve their environmental, safety and other standards without fear of public disclosure. The leading case in this area is *Bredice v. Doctors Hospital Inc.*,[48] which upheld a defendant hospital's refusal to turn over minutes and reports from medical staff reviews of patient treatment protocols in a malpractice case. In this case the court stated that preserving the confidentiality of such materials was essential to encouraging institutions to undertake critical self-evaluation, and that encouraging such self-criticism was in the public interest.

It is possible that this new self-evaluation privilege may be applied to protect the confidentiality of materials obtained in pre-acquisition environmental audits, particularly for sellers.

---

[48] 50 F.R.D. 249 (D.C. 1970), aff'd, 479 F.2d 920 (D.C. Cir. 1973).

As in the *Bredice* case, there are strong public policy interests in encouraging companies to undertake investigations to identify potential environmental violations and other problems. However, it is not clear whether this privilege could be interpreted to apply to prospective purchasers that conduct pre-acquisition environmental audits. Since a prospective purchaser is not yet the owner of the business/property that is the subject of the audit, it is not clear whether such an audit would be considered to be part of a *self-evaluation* procedure covered by the rule.

Although several states have enacted self-evaluation privilege legislation, the legal status of this privilege still remains uncertain in many jurisdictions. Consequently, attorneys should determine the status, if any, of this privilege in the applicable jurisdiction prior to initiating the audit. Regardless of the jurisdiction or whether a party is a purchaser or a seller, it is still not wise to rely solely on the "self-evaluation privilege" as a basis for preserving confidentiality.

Disclosure Obligations and Liability

Statutory Disclosure Obligations

Whenever a company considers performing an environmental audit of its real property or business, there is always the possibility that the audit may uncover information on violations or other environmental problems with the site which must be reported to various federal, state or local governmental agencies. This information could conceivably result in subsequent enforcement actions brought by governmental agencies, or even citizen suits to require a property owner to clean up its property.

If faced with this problem, many companies might initially think about whether it is really prudent to conduct an environmental audit in the first place, and what types of potentially damaging information will be obtained. The failure to report information required by government regulations can result in the imposition of severe civil and criminal penalties upon a corporation. Civil/criminal liability can even extend to company directors, managers or other "operators or "persons in charge" if they are held responsible for failing to submit any information required to be reported under federal/state environmental laws. Courts have held that criminal liability for a failure to report required information may extend to lower level employees, such as crew foremen, if they are deemed to be "operators" of a facility.[49]

Many of the key federal environmental statutes contain significant criminal sanctions for the failure to report required information or the knowing submission of false information. Some examples are as follows:

- CERCLA section 103(a)[50] requires that spills or releases of a "reportable quantity" of a hazardous substance be reported to the federal National Response Center. Persons who fail to meet this requirement are subject to civil penalties, criminal fines, and/or possible imprisonment for up to three years for a first offense.[51]

- The federal Emergency Planning and Community Right-to-Know Act of 1986[52] requires the reporting of spills or releases of a reportable quantity of extremely hazardous chemicals to state and local emergency planning authorities. As under CERCLA, knowing and willful failure to comply with this requirement may result in civil or criminal fines, and/or imprisonment for up to two years for a first offense.[53]

---

[49] U.S. v. Carr, 880 F.2d 1550 (2d Cir. 1989).
[50] 42 U.S.C. § 9603(a).
[51] 42 U.S.C. §§ 9603(b), 9609.
[52] 42 U.S.C. §§ 11001 et seq.
[53] 42 U.S.C. § 11045.

- The federal Resource Conservation and Recovery Act[54] subjects any party who knowingly omits or provides false information on any permit application or other record or report used for compliance with the statute to a criminal fine of up to $50,000 per day of violation, and/or imprisonment for up to two years.[55]

- Several other federal and state environmental laws, including the federal Toxic Substances Control Act, the Clean Water Act, and state spill reporting laws contain criminal penalties for knowing violations of reporting obligations. The above statutes also contain provisions for severe civil penalties for violations.

Various other agencies, in addition to EPA and state environmental agencies, also require the disclosure of information relating to potential environmental liabilities. For example, the federal Securities and Exchange Commission (SEC) regulations require a party which is filing a registration statement or a quarterly or annual report with the SEC to disclose the material effects which compliance with federal, state and local environmental laws may have upon the business, as well as estimates of material capital expenditures on environmental control facilities for at least the remainder of the current fiscal year and the following fiscal year.[56] The filing also must disclose the existence of any judicial or administrative proceedings arising under any federal, state, or local environmental law if the proceeding: 1) is material to the business or financial condition of the registrant; 2) involves potential damages in excess of 10 percent of the registrant's assets; or 3) involves a governmental authority as a party and the proceedings involve potential monetary damages,

---

[54] 42 U.S.C. §§ 6901 et seq.

[55] 42 U.S.C. § 6928.

[56] 17 C.F.R. § 229.101(c)(xii).

unless the registrant reasonably believes that the total damages will be less than $100,000.[57]

Outside counsel and consultants who perform environmental audits are not required to disclose the results of environmental audits in most cases. In fact, the applicable Professional Codes of Ethics in many jurisdictions may preclude outside counsel from revealing such confidences, unless the client intends to commit a crime[58] (in some jurisdictions, this restriction applies unless the client intends to commit a crime which is likely to result in imminent death or bodily harm[59]). By contrast, an in-house attorney or consultant may have an obligation to report a violation if he or she is a corporate official or manager or "person in charge" of a facility.[60]

EPA and Justice Department Policy

Both the U.S. Department of Justice and EPA have taken strong policy positions in an attempt to encourage voluntary environmental auditing by corporations. As part of that effort, several top EPA enforcement officials have recently stated publicly the agency's support for voluntary audits. Further, in its 1986 policy statement, EPA attempted to calm industry fears that the agency would automatically request the results of any completed environmental audits by noting that:

> EPA believes routine Agency requests for audit reports could inhibit auditing in the long run, decreasing both the quantity and quality of audits conducted. Therefore, as a matter of policy, EPA will not routinely request environmental audit reports.[61]

---

[57] 17 C.F.R. § 229.103.

[58] See Model Code of Professional Responsibility, DR 4-101(C)(3).

[59] See Model Rules of Professional Conduct Rule 1.6(b)(1).

[60] See, e.g., 42 U.S.C. § 9603(a).

[61] 51 Fed. Reg. 25,007 (July 9, 1986).

EPA's auditing policy statement went on to indicate that the agency would request such reports or portions of a report only when the needed information was not available by other means.[62] The agency further stated that it expected such requests to be limited and generally restricted to specific pieces of information.[63]

The Justice Department, meanwhile, indicated in a July 1, 1991 policy statement that it would view a company's policy of self-auditing, self-policing, and voluntary disclosure of environmental violations as a mitigating factor in potential enforcement actions.[64] Under this policy, a company which regularly audits its facilities and voluntarily discloses and corrects any violations would stand a strong possibility of receiving prosecutorial leniency, possibly avoiding prosecution altogether. By contrast, a company which makes little effort to identify or disclose violations, or which does so only when threatened with imminent prosecution, is unlikely to receive leniency.

Notwithstanding these governmental agency attempts to encourage voluntary environmental auditing, a number of commenters have criticized the EPA and Justice Department policy statements for failing to provide adequate safeguards to private companies to ensure that information obtained in voluntary audits will not one day be used against them in either civil or criminal prosecutions. They cite the fact that both EPA and Justice have retained the discretion to seek information obtained in audits and to prosecute private corporations and individuals on the basis of that information whenever they deem it necessary. The commenters also fear that criminal prosecutors are

---

[62] Id.

[63] Id.

[64] "Factors in Decisions on Criminal Prosecutions for Environmental Violations in the Context of Significant Voluntary Compliance or Disclosure Efforts by the Violator," U.S. Department of Justice Release, July 1, 1991.

likely to seek all information available to them in obtaining criminal convictions, regardless of the headquarters policies of EPA and Justice, and may well seize upon environmental audits as both a road map to a corporation's violations and as evidence that particular individuals had knowledge of these violations.[65]

No-Disclosure Agreements

Because disclosure of environmentally related information can lead to both civil and criminal liability in governmental and private action, buyers and sellers of real estate should consider appropriate actions to limit each other's rights to disclose information obtained during the course of a pre-acquisition environmental audit. Prior to initiating any pre-acquisition environmental investigation, it is often prudent for the parties to execute a formal agreement not to disclose any information obtained during the course of the pending environmental investigation to third parties (except, of course, when there is a legal requirement to disclose that information).

This non-disclosure agreement should extend to attorneys and technical consultants used by each party and should preclude disclosure of non-environmental information as well as information related to environmental compliance. In addition, any buyer or seller of real estate which retains a technical consultant to assist in a pre-acquisition audit should require that consultant to sign a similar non-disclosure agreement.

Conclusion

The net of environmental liability is expanding under CERCLA and other environmental statutes, as well as under common law doctrines. Unwary purchasers of real estate can

---

[65] See Edmund B. Frost, "Voluntary Environmental Compliance Audits: A DOJ Policy Failure," 5 *TXLR* 499, 501 (1991); James R. Moore, David Dabroski, John Daniel Ballbach, "Why Risk Criminal Charges by Performing Environmental Audits?" 5 *TXLR* 503 (1991).

readily find themselves being held liable for multimillion dollar cleanups of environmental contamination for which they are in no way responsible. Recent court decisions have held acquirors liable for environmental problems caused solely by previous property owners, and have extended this liability in certain cases to corporate parents, officers and directors, and individual shareholders. Consequently, a company contemplating a real estate acquisition should conduct a careful assessment of all significant environmental risks associated with the properties to be acquired, and should take advantage of those tools available for reducing environmental liabilities.

From the seller's perspective, it is often quite prudent to consider the impact on potential real estate transactions of any applicable state or local environmental property transfer laws. These statutes may require a seller to disclose information on and/or clean up environmental hazards on the property. In a few states, such as New Jersey, property transfer laws may add considerable delays and expenses to private transactions.

One important tool for minimizing environmental risks associated with the acquisition of real estate is private allocation of liability in the sale contract. One means of allocating liability is a contractual indemnification provision, in which one party (usually the seller) agrees to indemnify, or reimburse, the other party for certain specified environmental liabilities. Most courts have shown a willingness to honor such agreements. Unfortunately, private indemnification agreements usually do not affect a party's liabilities to government agencies or other third parties. However, they can allow a party to gain reimbursement from its indemnitor in the event such liabilities arise.

In cases where a seller lacks the financial resources to offer a reliable indemnification, a purchaser may wish to explore other options for reducing its potential liability. These options may include: 1) reducing the purchase price to account for anticipated environmental liabilities and cleanup costs, 2) withholding a portion of the purchase price until the seller cleans up any problem sites, 3) establishing escrow accounts to cover environmental liabilities, and 4) simply excluding the potential problem areas from the purchase. A corporation also may increase its protection against potential environmental liabilities by acquiring the property or company through a subsidiary, although the extent of this added protection is uncertain because several courts have refused to follow traditional corporate law principles and have held corporate parents accountable for their subsidiary's activities.

A second important tool for reducing the risks associated with a real estate transaction is to conduct a pre-acquisition environmental audit. An audit is essentially a systematic, documented review of a company's or facility's environmental practices and regulatory compliance. Environmental audits can alert a prospective purchaser to potentially serious environmental liabilities which might make the acquisition inadvisable.

Conducting a pre-acquisition environmental audit may allow a company to assert a defense to CERCLA liability known as the innocent landowner defense. However, the scope of this defense still appears limited: for example, it appears that the defense would not apply where the audit revealed a potential environmental problem, even though the purchaser did nothing to cause the problem and even where the purchaser did everything possible to minimize the problem. Further, most of the judicial opinions on the innocent landowner defense have interpreted this defense as a narrow exemption to CERCLA liability.

While a pre-acquisition audit may provide major benefits to prospective purchasers by allowing them to assess potential environmental risks prior to acquisition, there is a risk that an audit will identify evidence of violations or other damaging information. Because of this problem, an environmental audit must be carefully structured to meet the specific needs of the parties.

Moreover, conducting an audit raises a number of complex legal issues involving the preservation of confidentiality and potential disclosure obligations in the event that the audit detects violations. The involvement of either in-house or outside counsel in the earliest stages of the audit planning process can help to maximize confidentiality protections and avoid violations of environmental reporting obligations.

Appendix A
Conducting an Environmental Audit:
A Sample Protocol

The following is a list of some of the necessary materials and information that should be obtained in conducting a pre-acquisition environmental audit or due diligence review. This list is not intended to be exhaustive or complete. Rather, it is intended to provide a general overview of some of the more critical points to cover during an audit or due diligence review. Parties conducting an actual audit or other pre-acquisition environmental review should seek the advice of counsel for each specific situation, and should not rely solely on this list as their basis of information.

Compliance

- Examine copies of all (past or present) environmental permits, authorizations, or other approvals possessed by the facility (or company, in stock transactions). If permits are not available, find out why.

- Obtain copies of all notices of violations, notices of investigation, demand letters, administrative orders, and other correspondence relating to alleged noncompliance by the facility/company with any environmental laws or requirements (and documentation or other information on their resolution or current status).

- Obtain a copy of the facility/company's environmental, health and safety management organization chart and budget expenditures for recent years.

- Contact applicable federal, state, and local environmental agencies to determine if there are any current or past compliance or other environmental problems at the facility, or (particularly with respect to hazardous waste contamination) at nearby facilities.

- Review all hazardous waste manifests, water discharge monitoring reports, and emissions monitoring reports. If reports are missing or poorly organized, find out why.

- Review filings or reports made to any governmental agency relating to the presence or release of any hazardous chemical at the facility(ies).

- Identify all air emissions sources and water discharge points. Verify that each emission source or discharge point has all necessary permits.

- Locate onsite storage sites for hazardous wastes; verify that each such site is adequately bermed or has other secondary containment in the event of a spill.

Litigation

- Find out if there are any pending or threatened lawsuits against the facility/company relating to environmental matters, and request any documentation relating to these lawsuits (including "best estimates" of outcomes and "worst-case scenarios").

Identification of Potentially Significant Environmental Problems

- Speak with present (and former, if available and appropriate) facility employees to determine past hazardous waste disposal practices.

- Review facility(ies) site history (giving particular attention to past uses which may have involved the use or handling of chemicals). Include aerial photographs, if available.

- Identify known or suspected asbestos and PCB-containing materials.

- Identify all present and former underground and above-ground storage tank sites at the property, including date of installation and material(s) contained (older underground storage tanks containing hazardous chemicals present a high risk of leakage and potentially expensive cleanup (costs).

Miscellaneous

- Review any filings made to the Securities and Exchange Commission (which may list environmental liabilities, and/or may provide a basis for future legal actions if they fail to list known or reasonably anticipated material environmental liabilities).

- Visit local land title agencies to determine if there are any environmental (or other) liens on the property.

Stock Transactions

For a stock transaction, merger, or other transactions in which the purchaser may be liable as a corporate successor, the purchaser should do all of the above as well as the following:

- Obtain a list of all properties currently or formerly owned, leased, or operated, by the company to be acquired, and verify their environmental status.

- Obtain a list of all off-site hazardous waste disposal sites formerly or presently used by the company, and find out if there are any environmental problems at these facilities.

- Review key transaction documents relating to prior acquisitions and divestitures (giving special attention given to allocations of environmental liabilities and indemnification agreements, if any).

Chapter 5

Financial Implications of Environmental Compliance

David R. Chittick
AT&T

Introduction

Environmental problems can be traced in the headlines of today's newspapers: Superfund toxic waste dumps, toxic emissions, huge cleanup liabilities; new rules on air pollution; chemical spills; leaking underground tanks; hazardous materials. Superfund remediation costs are staggering: approximately 35 million dollars per site. Total liability is unknowable for corporations and for industries.

Increasingly, federal, state, and local governments push to solve complex environmental problems with ever more complex regulations: some 80,000 since 1981, most of them punitive. Permit requirements proliferate. So do environmentally based taxes and criminal liabilities for polluters.

A company can avoid such costs and liabilities by "doing the right thing" environmentally. However, if the "right thing" is defined as meaning only reactive, abatement-type compliance—the "end-of-the-smokestack" approach—only avoidance of fines and/or criminal prosecution will result. Pollution sources will remain unaffected.

The cost of this approach is high, because abatement devices are extremely expensive. Abatement involves high maintenance costs; involves administrative costs to deal with permits, etc.; and requires costly periodic monitoring, such as water and air-sampling, to ensure that the discharges are in compliance with regulations. Disposing of the byproducts of abatement is also costly.

Abatement also creates additional environmental problems: For example, when an activated carbon scrubbing device that adsorbs toxic chemicals passing up the smokestack is saturated, the contaminated carbon must be transported and disposed of, either landfilled or incinerated. It's impossible to escape the truism that any time you clean one thing, you dirty something else. It is far better to avoid these expenses by designing pollution out of the product and the manufacturing processes at the beginning.

So, if by the "right thing," we mean pro-active compliance—such as redesigning manufacturing processes to eliminate waste—then we can save money and gain other financial advantages as well.

AT&T is choosing this second approach—working to prevent pollution at the outset. While the company's efforts are meeting with considerable success, much remains to be done. Reaching our environmental goals is proving to be a complex, fascinating challenge, as reflected by the experiences of our Microelectronics Business Unit described later in the chapter. Nevertheless, the financial implications of pro-active compliance make this approach clearly desirable.

This chapter examines the financial implications of pro-active compliance from the perspective of AT&T.

Financial Implications

A pro-active stance can save a corporation millions of dollars in direct and indirect costs avoided or minimized. Direct costs typically avoided include:

- Costs of disposal: Labeling waste, transporting it; land-filling or incinerating it;

- Costs involved seeking appropriate vendors for transporting and disposing of waste and monitoring their activity;

- Costs of abatement: capital expenditures, maintenance, administrative, monitoring, and disposal;

- Cost of taxes on toxic, hazardous, or virgin materials;

- Costs for ever-harder-to-obtain and increasingly expensive materials such as CFCs;

- Cost of penalties for non-compliance: fines; legal fees, criminal liabilities;

- Cost of future Superfund liabilities and remediation;

- Cost of handling hazardous materials onsite: administrative, insurance, protective equipment purchase and maintenance, benefits payments;

AT&T avoided some of these costs with its aggressive program to reduce use of CFCs, before CFC prices and the excise taxes on them doubled. The company has reduced CFC emissions from over 2.6 million pounds in 1986 to less than 630,000 pounds in 1991.

Until recent years, chlorofluorocarbons (CFCs) were considered essential to the electronics industry as solvents and cleaning agents. But because they are believed to be a major cause of damage to the stratospheric ozone layer, 39 nations signed the Montreal Protocol in 1987, agreeing to cut CFC production worldwide in half by the end of 1998. Later, the mandate was strengthened: Phase out CFCs completely by the year 2000.

Manufacturers of CFCs were committed to eliminating the production of these chemicals. They also discontinued large-volume discounts which had the immediate effect of doubling prices for some customers. Additional price increases and excise taxes have doubled the price again.

AT&T's efforts to phase out CFCs, where possible, avoided much of these costs, proving the financial value of being proactive in environmental areas.

Pro-active compliance also has financial implications with regard to the avoidance of indirect costs such as:

- Cost of negative publicity on stock prices and share-owner relations;

- Cost of negative publicity on the brand name;

- Cost of decreased employee morale or confidence;

- Cost of diminished community confidence, civil torts, etc.;

- Cost of environmentalist or consumer activity, on the local, state, or federal level.

Quality management principles and a pro-active environmental posture not only help companies avoid such negative financial implications, but also provide positive opportunities for the future:

- Use of non-hazardous materials;

- Minimum process waste and/or destructible waste;

- Product and shipping containers that can be reused/recycled;

- Better customer acceptance and an enhanced reputation.

Tools for Improving E&S Management

AT&T employs two principal management tools in support of pro-active compliance: Total Quality Management, and Design for the Environment.

Total Quality Management

Total Quality Management (TQM) is an important tool to raise environmental consciousness among employees and managers and to help institutionalize environmental actions within the business. TQM is the application of continuous improvement to business processes. Any environmental crisis—air, water, or land—is a clear manifestation of a non-quality approach.

Design for the Environment

Environmentalist Barry Commoner says of the environment, "Everything is connected to everything." In quality language we say, "All work is part of a process." Both statements mean that if a company is going to prevent pollution, it has to focus on the design/manufacturing process as a whole. A company can't just solve one specific problem at some stage of the continuum if the solution causes additional problems elsewhere.

AT&T business unit managers are strongly encouraged to "think environment" so that environmental considerations are part of every design activity. Disposal, handling, energy and resource requirements or recycling needs can be reviewed before a manufacturing process is created. The process is called "design for environment."

Before R&D people design a process, before managers implement that process, both are encouraged to ask: "How can we create an environmentally preferable product? How can we design waste out of the process from the beginning?"

For example, AT&T uses arsine gas in the manufacture of semiconductors. Arsine gas is extremely dangerous and requires extraordinary precautions.

R&D people asked, "Why not develop generators of arsine gas to supply the gas for 'just-in-time' uses?" They developed such generators, and now the company can generate arsine gas when it's needed, where it's needed. No more high-pressure cylinders, no special piping, etc. Reduction in risk.

Doing it right the first time may cost more at the outset, but doing so keeps a company out of Superfund sites and other liabilities tomorrow.

AT&T's Environmental Goals

As part of AT&T's quality standards, AT&T has set aggressive goals for its environmental and safety performance, as well as the means to measure progress. The company's environmental goals are:

• **Phase Out CFC Emissions From Our Manufacturing Operations**

—50 percent by year end 1991

—100 percent by year end 1994

- **Eliminate Total Toxic Air Emissions**

    —50 percent by year end 1991

    —95 percent by year end 1995

    —Striving for 100 percent by year end 2000

- **Decrease Total Manufacturing Process Waste Disposal**

    —25% by year end 1994

- **Recycle Paper**

    —60% by year end 1994

- **Reduce Paper Use**

    —15% by year end 1994

AT&T's environmental efforts are meeting with considerable success as a result of Total Quality Management and Design for the Environment. Here are two examples:

- Three of AT&T's newest factories—in Bangkok, Madrid, and Guadalajara—were designed with new engineering technology to be free of ozone-depleting CFC emissions at start up;

- Scientists at AT&T Bell Laboratories' Engineering Research Center partnered with AT&T's factories to develop the Low Solids Fluxer, which eliminates the need to use CFCs for cleaning certain soldered printed wiring boards during manufacture. In April, 1990, AT&T's cordless telephone factory in Singapore became the company's first factory to become completely free of CFC emissions by utilizing the Low Solids Fluxer and by redesigning one manufacturing process to eliminate the need to clean the electronics components at all.

In addition to being environmentally safe, the Low Solids Fluxer lowers operating costs by reducing steps in circuit board manufacturing and by producing a higher quality product.

Waste Disposal

The cost of disposal of materials not recycled continues to spiral upwards. That's why scientists and engineers at AT&T Bell Laboratories' Engineering Research Center are working to prevent pollution two years, five years, even 20 years down the road.

The researchers use our Richmond plant as a "living laboratory" because it has several chemical-intensive internal business units. They've had to develop a "systems," or "cradle-to-grave," view of waste—from the raw material bought into a factory to the products that go out the door, even to recovery of those products at the end of their life. The team is very close to a documented waste-minimization process for all AT&T plants. Next, they'll see if they can completely design waste out of the process.

It makes good economic sense to recycle: landfill and waste disposal costs are going up as the availability of landfills decreases. Costs avoided by not sending waste to a landfill translate into lower total costs of service for building operations, saving the business expense money.

AT&T's headquarters locations have been recycling high-grade office papers for over 25 years. When New Jersey passed the Mandatory Source Separation Act in April of 1987, AT&T was already recycling approximately 287 tons of papers each month.

In 1990, AT&T employees recycled 44 million pounds of used paper, magazines, newspapers, and corrugated boxes, etc. By doing so they saved 374,000 trees, saved 55,000 barrels of oil, and diverted 72,600 cubic yards of waste from landfills. To close the loop, the company is increasing its purchases of recycled paper in a variety of applications.

The mission of AT&T's Corporate Recycling Process Management team, led by the company's Contract Services Organization, is to ensure that AT&T meets its stretch goals for recycling and reducing paper use. Team members say recycling paper doesn't add to AT&T facilities' costs. In fact, they say, revenue generated offsets the costs of recycling.

The Role of AT&T's E&S Engineering Organization

Overall corporate responsibility for AT&T's environmental and safety management lies with the 170-person staff of the Environment and Safety Engineering Organization (E&S). The group's mission is to establish for all of AT&T's operations and OEM (original equipment manufacturers) suppliers the direction, standards, and engineering support necessary to protect AT&T employees, customers, shareowners, the public, and the environment.

Corporate E&S develops corporate-wide programs, but the implementation of those programs takes place at the company's local facilities.

As a decentralized company with 20 business units, E&S deals with over 40 major manufacturing locations worldwide and approximately 2,500 administration locations. Language and understanding barriers, logistics problems, etc., make it difficult to get data regarding compliance with the corporate goals. Cost pressures are key.

Corporate E&S helps by impressing on the rest of the company—especially the leaders of the Business Units—the importance of supporting those individuals "in the trenches" with the necessary financial and staffing support.

Spreading environmental awareness throughout the company is challenging. The company is building environmental commitment and awareness, and this helps process engineers and others get the funding they need to continue their environmental efforts.

By setting aggressive corporate goals, AT&T has made progress. The credit belongs to the commitment of individual plant managers, engineers, and process engineers who have expended much time and effort to arrive at.solutions despite limited capital expenditures, but with a lot of time and effort.

An example of this commitment can be found in the words of individuals from one plant—Reading Works—of one business unit—Microelectronics—who are who are working diligently on the company's goal of phasing out CFCs. Their story is typical of what's happening throughout AT&T and shows the principles of Total Quality Management and Design for the Environment at work. It also reveals the magnitude and the extraordinary complexity of an effort in which "everything is connected to everything."

Microelectronics: A Microcosm

There are some 20 business units within AT&T. The Microelectronics Business Unit is one of them and is itself made up of several Strategic Business Units:

- High Performance Integrated Circuits (HPIC)—Reading

- Lightwave Technology—Reading

- Interconnection Technologies—Richmond

- Metal Oxide Semiconductors—Allentown

- Power Systems—Dallas

Microelectronics products get incorporated into equipment for customers: other AT&T Business Units, original equipment manufacturers, the Bell Operating Companies, international telecommunications consortiums, the Pentagon, etc. Microelectronics must provide extraordinary reliability for these customers. So if an engineer responsible for a Microelectronics product line wants to substitute a cleaning process for a CFC process already being used, that engineer must prove beyond a shadow of a doubt that the end product will be as reliable, and perform as well as it would with CFC cleaning.

Ted D. Polakowski is manager of corporate issues management for Microelectronics. He reports to that business unit's strategic planning director.

> Since divestiture, AT&T has tried to drive responsibility to the lowest level. We have 20 different business units, with a CEO in charge of each one. This means the income statement for each unit is the responsibility of the individual charged with running that business.
>
> In the new competitive, global marketplace, we live only on our ability to succeed. Actions contemplated with the best intention of helping the business may not be environmentally wise. That's why corporate E&S has asked for plans to meet the Environmental Goals from each business unit. E&S wants to keep environmental concerns at the forefront of everyone's mind.
>
> In my group I spend half my time on environmental concerns, working to formulate our group's plan to meet corporate goals. We have people in each manufacturing location who spend half of their time on environmental issues. This translates into five people working a year to develop our plan.
>
> We want to change the total culture and design waste out of the process at the front end. Traditionally, our designers have been concerned about what's best for the product but not necessarily best for the environment. So we're working to get the design process changed.
>
> I see a lot more environmental awareness than in the past. The presence of people in each business unit committed to environmental concerns is making a difference because when you bring it down to the business level and then to the personal level, you tap into the individual commitment of the people at that level.

Robert Lepiane, EH&S manager at the Microelectronics' Reading, Pennsylvania, facility, works closely with process engineers within the plant's two strategic business units: Lightwave Technology and High Performance Integrated Circuits.

> At Reading, we have our environmental action team with engineers representing all product lines in ME [Microelectronics]. This is so because there are reliability and yield consequences to substitution or process changes, and we need the engineers who know the specifics of a process to work with us.
>
> These engineers have the responsibility to ship product and improve yields. And if they're told to use a new chemical as a substitute for a CFC-based chemistry, they can't do that without testing and, in some cases, without extensive requalifying necessary to meet customer specs.
>
> Moreover, we can't just graft on chemistries or solutions that work in other AT&T plants, because our product line is different, our processes are different, our specs are different, our customers are different. There is no one "magic bullet."
>
> Just because Little Rock successfully eliminated CFCs from its operations doesn't mean that CFCs can be as easily removed from the manufacture of lightwave or HPIC products. In fact, a CFC substitute that works in Lightwave Technology doesn't automatically work for HPIC. So the problem becomes: How to do what has to be done and what priority to give it.
>
> Our success so far in decreasing the use of CFCs has resulted from awareness of better housekeeping—such as keeping lids on vapor degreasers, better minimization processes, etc., but we have a long way to go, even with substitutes. We don't have any good substitutes yet—but we believe they are out there. Compound the CFC goals with the attempt to eliminate chlorinated solvents and SARA-313 acids and you see the magnitude of the problem. And where do you get substitutes?
>
> One chemical supplier provided us with a promising substitute. Our action team visited that company, bringing parts which they cleaned in the proposed substitute, and then brought back for evaluation. The results were good. Although some capital investment would be needed to use

this solvent, Reading was willing to make the investment. Unfortunately, the substitute's ozone-depleting factor turned out to be much higher than originally calculated and, in fact, offered no advantage over some other CFC solvents.

A second possible substitute proved to have a toxicology problem, and so it was not introduced to the market. The search goes on. Probably, it will require a combination of approaches to reach our corporate Environmental Goals: substitution, design changes in the process, good housekeeping, some scrubbing.

According to product engineers, the less cleaning, the better the yield and the reliability. We've had great success in discovering that we don't have to clean parts as often as was once thought. A lot of cleaning has turned out to be just "insurance."

In many cases, someone asks, "Why are we using cleaners here?" And the answer is, "We've always done it that way;" or the answer is, "Well, we're doing it just in case someone handles it."

I think we're going to be ahead of the Clean Air Act. But we don't want to jump into expensive abatement efforts without first taking a crack at substitute chemicals. The capital expenditure for abatement is enormous. Maintenance of these abatement technologies—scrubbers for example—is also very expensive. Every time you ask an engineer for an estimate on the cost of abatement (scrubbing), that estimate gets higher and higher.

Our people are committed personally. We're all interested in the environment. We believe in the corporate environmental goals even though we believe them to be ahead of the industry in some cases. While technology is beginning to catch up, budgeting and priorities are also issues.

Dan Eiser, senior industrial hygienist and Co-chairman of Reading's CFC Task Force, deals with another aspect of CFC phaseout: employee safety.

My responsibility is Industrial Hygiene. My principle charge is process review: How can they be improved to increase employee safety & health within a plant setting?

I need to be assured that any substitute we use to replace CFCs is safe. The use of these materials requires us to carefully gather data on toxicity, etc.

CFCs were originally chosen in the industry as a safer alternative to chlorinated solvent cleaning. Chlorinated cleaning was a safer alternative than the method it replaced, that is, cleaning with flammable, toxic cleaners. In the race to achieve accelerated corporate goals minimizing use of freon materials, we have to be careful to avoid choosing substitutes that prove dangerous to employees or to the environment.

In the early stages of Reading's CFC reduction efforts, we were able to achieve the greatest reductions fairly easily. We eliminated redundant or unnecessary cleaning as we uncovered it. So we reduced solvent usage against the base year of 1986 by some 58 percent. The remaining task will be much harder as the easiest reductions have been made. In addition, since production had gone up, so has our solvent usage. Demand is based on society's desire for cellular telephones, VCRs, CD players, intercontinental phone service, faster computer systems, lap top computers, laser disks, etc.

In many industries, particularly the electronics industry, vapor degreasing is a standard method of cleaning parts. A CFC solvent, either pure or a blend, is put into a boiling sump where it vaporizes. Above the sump are coils filled with a refrigerant or with chilled water. These coils cause condensation of the vapor and help prevent loss of the solvent.

Parts to be cleaned are lowered into the steaming hot vapor. The vapor condenses on the parts because they are cooler than the vapor. Liquid now, the condensed solvent runs off, carrying impurities off the part and back into the liquid. Despite the condensing coils, there's always some evaporation of the vaporized solvent into the atmosphere.

So, in the long term, the use of vapor degreasers will have to be eliminated or redesigned for "zero emissions." But in the short term, we don't have an adequate substitute. Our task force is charged with finding substitutes for CFCs. The task force meets every two months to get updates, coordinate field trials, and get the members actively involved in the search for alternatives.

Unfortunately, there are built-in barriers to reaching the CFC Phase Out goals:

First, there's the culture within the federal government: Some government military specs still mandate the use of CFC cleaners. 100 percent reliability of parts is crucial to the military. Years of very expensive qualification and testing went into the development of these specifications. So to change any process, in many cases, demands requalification.

Second, there's the culture within the electronics industry: CFC cleaners have been the standard for the industry. They are known entities. So there is reluctance on the part of engineers to change what already works.

Third, there's the lack of data on safety performance of substitutes: There's much less data on the new substitutes for CFCs, which had such a well-documented record with regard to employee safety.

Finally, there's the matter of trading off pollution: We don't want to trade off air pollution problems for an alternative that creates water pollution.

There's no free lunch. There's no one answer—no magic bullet—that will solve the problem even if everyone were willing to pay the price for it. The answer, no doubt, lies in multiple solutions, especially in our business. But it's very difficult to get changes made.

As a process engineer who has worked in both Lightwave Technology and High Performance integrated circuits, Bruce J. Rhoades is charged with improving yield, shipping product—and phasing CFCs out of the processes he oversees.

We're making lasers for an AT&T customer to go in the ocean as part of the underseas connection to the rest of the world. Because these lasers must last 25 years on the ocean bottom without being replaced, only one device in a million is permitted to fail. So people are very reluctant to change the process of manufacture which has yielded this impressive reliability. It costs two to four million dollars to conduct qualification testing of these lasers.

Another barrier to change involves product life cycle. If we're in a three-year manufacturing cycle, and we're halfway through that cycle, we know that it will take at least six months to make changes. So we might say, "Let's continue to use a CFC cleaner, because the life cycle for the product will be nearly over before we can implement changes."

I have to maintain a shop—to make things. I can't stop to experiment. I don't normally have time or equipment to experiment. I have to prepare documentation, and quality audits, and communicate with management and with operators. However, I have managed to get some "skunk works" experimentation done. Sometimes it pays off.

For example, we have a process of polishing substrates to remove the wax from them. In the course of my readings, I stumbled across the fact that carbon dioxide can be used in such circumstances. In my spare time, under my departmental expense, I invested two or three thousand dollars, and bought a few tanks of carbon dioxide, a spray nozzle and tried the process. I warmed substrates and found that the carbon dioxide seemed to work well. But, before I could complete my experiments, I was transferred into another area. The process I had wanted to change continues to use CFCs.

However, I'm friends with another engineer, Paul Chen, who had been using CFCs to clean particles from the facet-coating of the lasers. I told him about my work with carbon dioxide and he saw how he could apply it to his needs. He used the carbon dioxide particles to knock off particles from the facets. He experimented and gathered data, a process that took about six months. He's now presenting his data to a Qualification Review Board, a committee of Bell Labs supervisors, a customer representative, and representatives of quality organizations.

So in this case, the skunk works approach paid off.

We process engineers have to be smarter at getting dollars for improving our processes. I didn't understand this financial process when I started and I'd see things I wanted to improve, but I didn't know how to get the funding.

People are asked to do so many more things so much more quickly. You don't have time to think about the process—about what's good for the product and for the environment. However, I see more grass roots concern for the environment. I see change. I see more thinking being done about the processes.

It will be difficult to meet the corporate Environmental Goals, nevertheless, I'm guardedly optimistic. What we're attempting to do takes time, and I'm a very impatient person.

Summary

Ever-burgeoning environmental regulations at the federal, state, and even local levels require increasingly complex and expensive compliance efforts by corporations in America. A similar pattern is occurring in the European Community and in the other countries of the world. Governments are realizing that pollution is a global problem and are passing restrictive laws to control toxic materials.

A pro-active approach to compliance has positive financial and other implications, as is proved by AT&T's experience in the areas of waste minimization, particularly recycling and phaseout of CFCs. Reaching a corporation's environmental stretch goals is a difficult, complex challenge. The management tools of Total Quality Management and Design for the Environment, coupled with individual commitment by plant mangers, engineers, researchers, and others makes it possible to meet that challenge.

Pro-active management that goes beyond mandate or regulation is clearly the right thing to do. It's also good business. Accidents, chemical spills, and toxic waste are defects in the process and thus quality failures. Pollution prevention reduces costs. And pollution prevention can help to reach that vision we all share: a clean and healthy planet—for ourselves and for our children.

Chapter 6

Economics of Waste Reduction, Resource Recovery, and Recycling

Joel S. Hirschhorn
Hirschhorn & Associates, Inc.

Overview and Introduction

In the environmental arena, there is little economic benefit and increasingly high costs for pursuing only regulatory compliance. Even the best of compliance goals get undermined by constantly changing and sometimes retroactive regulations and liabilities, unpredictable and often inconsistent enforcement and penalties, and the inevitable potential for people, out of malice, ignorance, or carelessness, to cause major corporate liabilities. Compliance itself is also a costly strategy to implement because so much time for technical, legal, and upper management staff is necessary. No matter what you do, including extensive company audits and comprehensive management data systems, future liabilities can not be eliminated as long as wastes and pollutants are produced.

The key question for corporate executives is: Would you like to take environmental accounts payable and turn them into accounts receivables?

The surest way to eliminate environmental costs and liabilities is to eliminate the circumstances that cause those costs and liabilities. Even if total elimination is not immediately achievable, then actively seeking zero wastes and pollutants is still the best path to economic success. This kind of zero-waste vision is key to the economic conversion of costs into profits.

Waste reduction, resource recovery, and recycling offer a better way for industry to satisfy the public's environmental and resource conservation demands. The alternative and smart environmental strategy, for the 1990s and the longer term, aims at converting public environmental demands into greater production efficiencies, materials substitutions and innovations, and new products. While adoption of these techniques may be the result of environmental concerns, the benefits they offer are more than environmental—they are economic.

Although a multitude of terms are used, waste reduction, waste minimization, source reduction, and pollution prevention generally cover the spectrum of reducing waste and pollutant generation and beneficially recovering, reusing, or recycling what might otherwise become waste. The main purpose of this discussion is to describe the strategic and management paths to obtaining maximum economic benefits from a new, opportunistic view of environmental issues and demands.

The Economic Dimension

Although environmentalists embrace all pollution prevention kinds of actions because of improvements in protecting public health and the environment and conserving natural resources, industry can and must justify the same actions because of a host of economic benefits. It is a classic win-win opportunity.

Unless economic benefits become the prime driving force for industry, the maximum amount of waste reduction and environmental benefits will not be obtained. Enlightened economic self-interest is nothing to be ashamed of if it also serves the public good. Moreover, there is no better time for American industry to seek and obtain the economic benefits achievable in the environmental area through a pollution prevention strategy. Various analyses have shown that industrial competitiveness at the company and national level is linked to minimizing waste generation (see "Prosperity Without Pollution"). Conversely, high amounts of waste generation are just another indicator of industrial inefficiency, which may reflect insufficient modernization, capital investment, and R&D. More attention will be given to "best industrial practice" as shown through waste and pollutant generation variations. Because environmental issues are global in nature, they will be increasingly potent sources of global competitiveness.

The tough challenge for people in industry and business is learning how to accurately and comprehensively understand—not only quantitatively, but also qualitatively—the whole range of direct and indirect, short and long-term economic benefits from waste reduction. While many people embrace the notion of turning environmental issues into profits, doing so over the long-term is terribly difficult because waste reduction becomes increasingly more technically difficult, risky, and capital intensive. Only a relatively small number of companies have demonstrated their ability to obtain substantial economic benefits from comprehensive and sustained waste reduction. While hundreds of positive examples are important to demonstrate the economic potential, they do not demonstrate the ability of all companies and managers to achieve truly substantial results over the entire spectrum of wastes, pollutants, and industrial processes. Just as people speak of sustainable economic development, it is appropriate to speak of sustainable pollution prevention or waste reduction. This implies the need to build the necessary company infrastructure, analytical methods, and incentives to sustain a long-term program with continuous improvement. But sustained pollution prevention offers continuous net economic benefits.

The complexity is that the economic benefits of pollution prevention may be much broader than what can be seen within the boundaries of a specific engineering project. Value is added to the company and its products when pollution prevention is accomplished, measured, and communicated. For example, a waste minimization program may offer significant economic benefits because of:

- an improved view of the company by financial analysts and stockholders, which increases stock prices;

- an improved view of the company's products, which increases market share;

- an improved view of the company's social responsibility, which makes recruitment of the very best professionals easier;

- free advertising through positive newspaper, magazine, and television coverage;

- the identification of new business opportunities (e.g. a company that manufactures a material goes into the business) of recycling that material;

- a significantly reduced probability of future civil and criminal prosecutions and reduced levels of fines and crimes;

- a more positive view of the company by government regulatory personnel, which reduces compliance costs and penalties;

- a reduction in worker health and safety problems and costs beyond what would otherwise be achieved;

- an improved view of the company, which facilitates acquisitions, mergers, and foreign activities;

- a more productive R&D program, which generates more significant innovations, such as totally new processes for making existing products and new products.

In fact, all of the above have been experienced, to varying degrees, by companies with impressive pollution prevention programs, even though they themselves may not have developed methods to explicitly account for such economic benefits. The trick is to reduce various economic benefits to concrete terms for specific projects. If economic benefits are to serve as an effective incentive for waste reduction actions, then those benefits must be explicitly understood and accounted for in any cost-benefit, project justification, financial, or capital investment analyses. If not, waste reduction will lose out to competing needs for capital and people's time.

At first, a lack of accounting for the full array of economic benefits may not be critical because early projects may have enormous direct benefits. However, over time the degree of direct, easily calculated economic benefit decreases relative to cost, and the omission of more indirect, long-term benefits becomes crucial. When the latter are systematically omitted, decisions systematically tilt against investments of money and people's time in waste reduction kinds of projects. That is, as the apparent marginal net economic benefit decreases, the need increases to refine and expand formal economic evaluations to include more benefits.

Evolution of Industrial Strategies

To understand the enormous range of potential economic benefits of waste reduction, it is useful to trace the historical development of industrial responses to environmental issues. At first, most companies implicitly or explicitly used a "defensive" strategy of regulatory compliance and use of end-of-pipe technology in their reaction to public demands and government requirements. The defensive strategy tacitly accepted the role of "bad guy" and fed the largely held belief that industry is not only the major cause of environmental problems, but also is guilty until proven innocent.

More recently, some companies have led the way in the use of an "enlightened" environmental strategy. Such companies have adopted waste reduction goals and tactics. From 3M's Pollution Prevention Pays, Chevron's Save Money and Reduce Toxics, and Dow Chemical's Waste Reduction Always Pays, the message has come that companies can, practically, improve their methods, operations, procedures, and technologies to cut costs. These and other companies in virtually every industry have presented many specific examples of their success, including net savings, profits, or returns on investments.

Moreover, this new enlightened strategy has helped astute companies build a positive environmental image as progressive, innovative, and responsible environmental problem solvers. Although it has taken some years, more attention is going to good environmental news and that news is about waste minimization, which is portrayed as a win-win strategy that benefits the public environmentally and industry economically. Scores of specific case examples from industry demonstrate significant and often substantial economic savings, often from actions taking relatively short periods of time and relatively little capital investment. In other words, returns on investment and other measures of financial success have been very good; the references at the end of this chapter are good sources of many specific industrial examples.

Another dimension of the new enlightened strategy is that a number of companies have discovered green consumerism, green products, and green marketing. A whole new world of lifecycle analysis, green product labeling, laws on environmental claims, and seeking market share and enhanced profits through redesigned, reformulated, and repackaged older products and the invention of entirely new products has emerged. Green product marketing is the ultimate market force that capitalizes on people's environmental values and translates them into business opportunities. Recycling, for example, becomes more than re-source recovery; it becomes an environmental product claim and, for many companies, even a business opportunity, that is to get into the recycling business.

But the enlightened strategy is really just a step in the right direction toward the ultimate economically smart strategy, which might be called Total Environmental Opportunities (TEO). The problem with the enlightened strategy is that there remain major disconnections between environmental issues and oppor-tunities, and the whole range of routine business activities and goals. Even more to the point, the enlightened strategy does not fully exploit new business opportunities that are in one way or another shaped by environmental issues and trends. The ulti-mate strategy is actually an environmentally driven business strategy because it is completely integrated into the entire business and is profit motivated. The enlightened strategy, in contrast, remains an environmental strategy and is seen as such by senior company executives.

TEO, the Environmentally Driven Business Strategy

With the TEO environmentally driven business strategy corporate culture is permanently changed to include environmental values. It is critically necessary to have every person passionately interested in advancing environmental progress and improvement, for the sake of their individual values and high-priority corporate values. The more genuine the environmental commitment, the more likely it is that people will find positive ways to cleverly exploit environmental opportunities and turn them into business success. Doing what is right environmentally can become a strong corporate bond because it advances company financial interests.

Moreover, with TEO there is just as much focus on the product itself, making it environmentally sound, responsible, and preferred, as there is on the manufacturing process. Product manufacture and marketing mutually reinforce total environmental performance, which in turn means more economic benefits. Clearly, environmental actions and benefits that go far beyond regulatory compliance and commonplace industry commitments drive the TEO strategy. or a sustainable program, absolutely every person in a company must think environmentally to achieve company objectives, especially marketers and researchers. Managers must finally recognize that every part of the company and every worker, has an environmental role to play, not only an environmental department and environmental experts, and not only people with technical functions. And every environmental role, if performed successfully, offers a competitive advantage and an economic payoff for the company. Technologically, it is pollution prevention, in all its forms, that translates the environmentally driven business strategy into successful practice. And it is an improved corporate culture with core environmental values that maximizes pollution prevention performance.

Ironically, the best regulatory compliance comes not from better management of wastes and control of pollutants at the end of the pipe (effects), but rather from reexamining what the company makes and how it makes and markets its products (causes) so that environmental regulations do not apply. Practicing pollution prevention, waste reduction, toxics use reduction, and green product marketing become the best way to reach ultimate regulatory compliance. More importantly, as discussed above, there are additional economic benefits from a TEO strategy: reduced direct and indirect costs, improved global competitiveness, increased sales and market share, and increased, sustainable profits. The environmental issues and trends that drive the strategy and its implementation also act as catalysts to trigger technological innovations, creative acquisitions and diversifications, new products, and aggressive marketing. That is, another goal of a TEO strategy is to rejuvenate and revitalize a company that is sagging because of lack of growth, diminished profits, and heightened competition.

Once they understand that the majority of people and customers, and not just government agencies, want improved environmental performance and quality, companies can make gains in marketing, manufacturing, and worker performance by being responsive to universal environmental concerns. The TEO environmentally driven business strategy rises above both social responsibility and regulatory compliance because it is profit driven in the best of capitalistic traditions. It is more than a response to public and legal demands, it is the way to exceed them and define new levels of excellence.

Managers must identify and seize market opportunities for new or improved industrial and consumer products in anticipation of emerging environmental concerns and not simply in reaction to past issues. An effective TEO strategy must be proactive and anticipatory. For example, many managers should now assume that it will become necessary to: take back any waste created by a product's use (a law in Germany); to eliminate the use of nearly all toxic heavy metals such as lead and mercury, to stop using chemicals based on chlorine, to not think that recycling is the ultimate answer; and to curb carbon dioxide emissions.

It is not a question of what is environmentally right or wrong, or scientifically proven or unproven. It is necessary to correctly diagnose the underlying environmental trends and their impacts on people (customers) and public policy (social consensus). This means that sharing the values, concerns, and fears of the most ardent environmentalists can be used to gain economic and competitive advantage. That frame of mind can motivate the kind of creativity which maximizes pollution prevention and gives a technologically competitive edge. In contrast, the traditional regulatory compliance perspective tries to combat, resist, and discredit environmental demands because they are sources of cost, not profits.

With a TEO strategy, efficiency in manufacturing operations is increased, and costs are reduced through a myriad of near- and long-term technical improvements that may extend beyond historical techniques. The necessary thinking is to conceive of new ways to keep existing customers and markets, even if it means using radically different raw materials, process technologies, and final products which make more sense environmentally. A petroleum based plastics manufacturer must seriously examine, for example, using agricultural raw materials to make products that are functionally equivalent to their existing products (e.g., Warner-Lambert is now commercializing its Novon materials made from corn or potato starch, and DuPont and ConAgra have formed a joint venture to make materials from food wastes); a chemical pesticide manufacturer must consider biological and genetically engineered products.

And if corporate culture is changed to include deeply ingrained environmental values and thinking, then there will be a steady stream of innovations by workers, including a host of unanticipated, non-environmental benefits within the framework of total quality management and customer satisfaction. Indeed, the TEO approach is just another path to quality and customer satisfaction. The critical need is to see innovative environmental advantages—achieved through continuous process and product improvement—as integral to both quality and customer satisfaction. This is the essence of the environmentally driven business strategy.

Key Management Actions for Maximum Economic Benefits

The key management actions for obtaining the maximum economic benefits of the TEO environmental business strategy are:

- create a bold environmental vision that even the most passionate environmentalists can embrace, and that is consistent with global sustainable economic development and total quality management

- develop a specific TEO environmental business strategy based on quantitative analyses of all the basic elements of the business (production, products, and markets), and the ways to capitalize on environmental issues, trends, and opportunities

- design a comprehensive program for workers, marketing, and technology for continuous environmental improvement through benchmarking and identification world standards of excellence in specific activities

- measure results of comprehensive, multimedia pollution prevention to improve internal management

- communicate positive environmental results to workforce, customers, government, environmentalists, and the news media

First Priority: Focus on People and Corporate Culture

Goal: Develop and Deepen Core Corporate Environmental Value

Key Steps:

- CEO communicates bold corporate zero–waste/zero–pollutant/zero–accident vision of environmental excellence and the policies and goals it entails to workforce; communicate that environmental commitment and continuous environmental improvement complement total quality management

- establish CEO level environmental management group with representatives from manufacturing, environment, marketing, R&D, financial, personnel

- survey and assess attitudes of managers and workers to identify problems, such as negative views or guilt about company's practices or products

- redesign job descriptions and responsibilities to incorporate environmental responsibilities for ALL employees

- design and implement training programs to improve environmental literacy and knowledge of personnel

- measure impacts on attitudes and information

- establish personnel evaluation criteria for environmental performance

- institute clear-cut rewards and incentives for personal and group environmental excellence and penalties for unsatisfactory environmental performance

Second Priority: Focus on Technology, Manufacturing Facilities, and Products

Goal: Improve Environmental Performance

Key Steps:

- express environmental vision and policies in technical terms and worker functions

- establish ambitious, specific goals beyond regulatory compliance consistent with the idealistic goal of zero waste and pollution

- build a waste reduction teams infrastructure

- design an internal information and technology transfer program

- conduct comprehensive waste reduction audits

- develop methods and routine procedures for measuring waste reduction progress appropriate for company's processes and products

- establish procedures for evaluating waste reduction capital projects

- formulate near- and long-term waste/toxics use reduction plans

- implement prevention/reduction programs in manufacturing, and product/packaging redesign

- review and redesign R&D programs

- measure progress of pollution prevention/waste and toxics use reduction, as related to production outputs

- communicate results to workforce, government, and outside groups

Third Priority: Focus on Products and Customers

Goal: Effective Green Marketing

Key Steps:

- define company's general environmental performance to position company environmentally

- identify environmental advantages and opportunities for products through lifecycle analyses

- examine changes in manufacturing and products to improve net environmental benefits (link to total quality management)

- assess potential for increasing market share of products through focused market research

- identify applicable state and federal laws and regulations for environmental claims and establish company guidelines for compliance

- use central authority for auditing and approving environmental claims, with major input from environmental experts

- define new green consumer, product stewardship programs (link to customer satisfaction program)

- design and implement comprehensive environmental communications (advertising, labeling, public and government relations)

- frequently reassess green marketing efforts relative to both success in marketplace and environmental performance

Conclusions

Most senior industry executives have become acutely aware of environmental issues and many have even chosen them as areas of personal concern. Waste minimization and pollution prevention programs focused on manufacturing have had remarkable success, at least in those companies with intensive efforts, and some green marketing efforts have begun to appeal to environmentally concerned customers. Nevertheless, there is little indication that companies, many of which are having serious problems that threaten their performance and survival, have genuinely grasped the full historic potential of using environmental issues and trends to reshape, restructure, and revitalize their entire business.

The concept behind the Total Environmental Opportunities business strategy presented is that companies in virtually every industry and business can make a profound change in their culture, thinking, and way of doing business. They should do so primarily for the economic benefits to be obtained for themselves. However, to be successful, it is necessary for senior managers to accept the fact that environmental concerns are here to stay; that is, we are witnessing the early phase of a major structural change in the global industrial economy. Indeed, we may be at the early stage of an industrial revolution driven by environmental concerns where whole new technologies and materials are created to replace existing ones.

The TEO strategy builds on current progressive efforts in many companies and takes them a major step forward not only to respond to current environmental concerns, but also to actively participate at the leading edge of change. Today, even the best of current environmental efforts are at the edges of company activities. What is needed is a bold new quantitative analysis of all of a company's activities, products, and markets to completely assess the potential economic benefits of the TEO strategy.

Quantitative analysis is crucial to moving from concept and broad strategy to precise implementation. TEO can add a strong new dimension to total quality management and customer satisfaction by bringing companies to the highest levels of global competitiveness necessary for survival in the 1990s. The technological steam engine for TEO is broad spectrum pollution prevention applied to raw materials, manufacturing, and products. The vision is a zero waste, zero pollution world of sustainable and profitable economic growth. Those who commit to that environmental vision will obtain its economic benefits.

Bibliography

Joel S. Hirschhorn and Kirsten U. Oldenburg, *Prosperity Without Pollution—The Prevention Strategy for Industry and Consumers*, New York: Van Nostrand Reinhold, 1991.

David J. Sarokin, et al, "Cutting Chemical Wastes," *Inform*, 1985.

Serious Reduction of Hazardous Waste—For Pollution Prevention and Industrial Efficiency, Office of Technology Assessment, 1986.

Waste Minimization, Air & Waste Management Association, 1990.

Chapter 7

Corporate Public Relations in the Green Era

Roger Strelow
Bechtel Environmental, Inc.

Introduction

According to U.S. Environmental Protection Agency (EPA) estimates, U.S. environmental regulations now cost the American economy some $100 billion per year, and this figure is likely to reach $200 billion by the end of the decade. In addition, environmental regulation is escalating rapidly abroad, especially in Europe and the Pacific Basin. U.S. multinationals must, of course, meet host country standards. But they are facing growing commercial and political incentives to go beyond foreign regulations in some instances, in order to ensure that their overseas operations meet the same basic criteria as their domestic facilities.

Leading U.S. multinationals are increasingly implementing, or at least considering, relatively uniform worldwide corporate environmental standards, analogous to the common policy of uniform worldwide product quality standards. Motivations include the desire to avoid criticism for operating abroad in a manner that is perceived as "less careful" than in the U.S. (an accusation made against Union Carbide in relation to the Bhopal incident) and the hope that exhibiting environmental leadership will help to make other nations more willing to welcome U.S. corporate activities, including acquisitions, within their jurisdictions.

Thus, the purely financial implications for U.S. corporations of living up to environmental expectations worldwide clearly meet the criterion so well described by former U.S. Senate minority leader, Everett Dirksen as "serious money." Because the financial impacts are so great, and because environmental demands can have such far-reaching implications, it is not surprising that these demands affect virtually every aspect of corporate activities. This chapter focuses on three such important aspects—strategic planning, public relations, and advertising. How environmental issues affect these three corporate activities may vary considerably according to the type and size of company, the nature of its business[es], and other factors, but some useful generalizations can be made.

Strategic Planning

Any successful corporate enterprise must constantly analyze its markets, its customers, its competitors, and its own strengths and capabilities in order to methodically determine what its direction and objectives should be and to develop an action plan for getting there. Such planning takes various forms and occurs in varying cycles within different companies, but it is inevitably addressed, at least indirectly, in the annual budgeting process. Such planning takes into account growth in current markets, development of new ones, business and facility acquisitions and divestitures, and technology opportunities.

Environmental demands impose constraints on corporate strategic planning, but they also afford certain opportunities. Until recently, both the constraints and opportunities were often only dimly recognized, at best, in strategic planning. This is one key reason why so many companies found environmental issues to be so frustrating during the first 10-20 years of the modern environmental awareness era (starting roughly in 1970). Now that corporate managers, in general, are increasingly sensitive to environmental demands, and environmental managers are increasingly involved in strategic planning, companies are better able to factor environmental considerations into overall business decisionmaking.

Environmental Constraints

Both the costs and the operational limitations imposed by environmental regulations on certain types of production activities (e.g., those involving the use and release of chemicals identified as carcinogens) must be taken into account realistically by strategic planners in assessing the potential attractiveness of both current and potential businesses. Public acceptance of certain technologies must be scrutinized objectively. For example, an electric utility considering construction of a new, coal-fired power plant—in an era of acute concerns about acid rain, visibility impairment and "greenhouse" gases that may induce global warming—will at least conclude that it must employ highly efficient emission control systems, and it may well decide that growth in demand can better be met by investments in energy efficiency. Development or expansion of a business or product line dependent on the use of chlorofluorocarbons (CFCs) probably does not make sense in the face of the multinational commitment to phase out the use of these chemicals which are implicated in the destruction of the earth's protective stratospheric ozone layer.

Not only can the viability of *products* be affected heavily by environmental factors, but also the viability of the *facilities* in which they are made. In the case of facilities, one must consider the potentially enormous environmental regulatory costs involved in buying or selling chemically contaminated property. A transfer of property may trigger a demand for costly cleanup that would have been deferred for a considerable period of time otherwise, especially in a state such as New Jersey, which requires a commitment to prompt cleanup as a condition of the transfer of industrial properties.

In anticipation of emerging trends, a strategic planner must take into account likely changes in the nature and scope of certain businesses because of environmental concerns. For example, there is a political movement in the direction of making producers and sellers of products "stewards" of their ultimate disposition. No longer will this responsibility rest solely with the consumer. Auto and refrigerator manufacturers, for example, will most likely soon be required to design their products, and perhaps to reclaim them, in order to maximize recycling of key materials and to prevent releases of potentially harmful substances at disposal sites.

Opportunities

Just as importantly, environmental demands are opening up profitable business opportunities that strategic planners need to identify and exploit. For example, the same manufacturer of refrigerators, referred to above, that may be constrained by the use of CFCs as a refrigerant or in foam insulation, can perhaps capture a larger share of his market by being the first to develop and employ an environmentally more benign product configuration.

There are major opportunities available, not only for redesigning a product to overcome environmental problems, but for providing environmental services. A corporation may have a technology or experience that has considerable potential market value if it is applied to solving the environmental problems of current or potential customers. Both computer and aerospace companies, for example, have been openly exploring or developing environmental services market niches. Some engineering and construction firms are increasingly applying their basic skills to the design and implementation of environmental cleanups.

Not only are manufacturers of consumer products (those sold at retail to the general public) faced with environmental opportunities. Manufacturers for industrial and commercial markets as well increasingly find that their customers also have a strong preference for environmentally reliable corporate suppliers. Environmentally sound products enable these customers to ensure the reliability of their deliveries (against the contingency of an environmentally caused interruption of production) and it can help them avoid adverse reactions from their customers and shareholders to the use of a "dirty" supplier.

The issue of "green products" and advertising will be addressed below.

The process of strategic planning illustrates very well how important it is that the management of environmental issues be fully integrated with overall corporate management policy. During most of this modern environmental era (1970 to the present), and in most companies, management of environmental issues has been perceived and treated as an extraneous nuisance, a necessary evil. Environmental regulation was seen as conceptually unexceptionable but often excessive in practice—and, in any event, an inevitable drag on the "bottom line." More recently, corporate managers have seen that smart planning can often make an environmentally driven expenditure a productive and cost-beneficial one. Several leading petroleum and chemical companies now openly proclaim that, in essence, smart pollution reduction practices are good business.

Public Relations

Public relations ("PR") is the management of a company's relations with the general public, often through the media. Certain important segments of the public are usually handled separately from an organizational standpoint—e.g., employees and shareholders. An important subset of PR is community relations—the interaction with a defineable group of plant-site neighbors and other nearby residents with a particularly direct interest in how that facility is operated, especially from an environmental and safety standpoint. Not surprisingly, an increasing share of corporate PR attention has been focused in recent years on environmental issues.

Some major companies now have designated or de facto environmental specialists in their PR groups. At the same time, enlightened environmental managers have increasingly hired or trained key environmental employees to be adept in PR themselves. Often it is the PR specialist who can best plan and orchestrate environmental PR efforts, while it is the PR-trained environmental specialist who can best perform many of the "out front" roles—e.g., chairman of a community meeting, interviewee on a local TV talk show. This is because the environmental specialist can often best answer, or at least address, concerns about toxicity, technology or other key issues in an environmental controversy.

Controversies

In the past, the vast majority of corporate environmental PR activity was in the form of response to events generating controversy—an EPA fine for non-compliance, discovery of hazardous chemicals from a plant site in the groundwater serving nearby residential wells, an application for an EPA permit to operate a hazardous waste incinerator at the plant site. Not surprisingly, much of such PR was defensive and reactive—and not very successful.

In recent years, a number of companies have significantly improved their ability to deal with such controversies. They have learned a number of lessons and put them into practice. These include:

- Keep communications with the community and media as open and continuous as possible.

- Ensure that communications are truly two-way, so that community concerns and media interests can be identified and addressed in their early stages, not after some crisis has erupted.

- Furnish objective, unvarnished information early and often. Develop a reputation for reliability rather than advocacy (e.g., in the case of discovery of offsite groundwater contamination, don't focus on arguing that the contamination is not harmful, but rather on laying out clearly what you're going to do about it).

- Learn how and when to say "we're sorry" when that is appropriate, by putting yourself in the relevant audience's position.

- Open your doors. Many public fears are partly based on lack of knowledge about a "mysterious" plant. Invite reporters and neighbors in, show them around, explain what goes on and why.

Reporting

An increasing share of corporate environmental PR is reporting rather than reacting. Several major companies have issued "environmental" annual reports in addition to their normal annual reports. Others have issued special reports. The Securities and Exchange Commission (SEC) has pushed public companies to be more forthcoming about the details of environmental liabilities in routine reports such as the 10-K.

Under prodding from some public interest organizations, many companies are now exploring how some type of objective audit of environmental compliance might be routinely shared with the public, much as auditors reports are included in annual reports. There are substantial challenges and sensitivities involved here. Not the least of them is that, despite (or, sometimes, because of!) the detail and complexity of environmental regulations, it is not always clear whether a particular activity or condition is, in fact, in or out of compliance.

However, companies will come to see regular, objective environmental reports as a means to ensure both that the right things are done internally on a timely basis, and that the public is given the reassurance on this score that they increasingly want.

Advertising

The first and foremost lesson that can be derived from the past several years' experience with advertising of "green" products is probably BE CAREFUL. On several occasions, companies anxious to portray their product as environmentally benign or desirable, or as better than some alternative type of product (e.g., disposable paper diapers vs. reusable cloth diapers), have been publicly taken to task by those who dispute their assessment. If the environmental advantages of a product are not overwhelmingly clear and widely accepted, it may well be more prudent—and effective—to avoid making environmental claims for it.

Several initiatives are in place or under development to establish some standards and procedures for environmental advertising. They are largely focused on providing some sort of meaningful "Good Housekeeping seal of approval" which should both reassure consumers and give advertisers more insulation from possible attacks.

But there is also a risk associated with advertising or otherwise publicizing a company's environmental record or accomplishments. This is the "perceived hypocrisy" factor. One large chemical company that has been outspoken as an environmental leader recently was attacked by certain public interest groups alleging numerous regulatory violations. Quite apart from the merits of this or other such disputes, a company contemplating environmental advertising or publicity must carefully assess the likely net impact on the public and customers from environmental "crowing" that may provoke claims of hypocrisy.

Conclusion

Companies today are seizing new opportunities, and at the same time still facing tough challenges, in connection with the impacts of environmental demands on strategic planning, public relations and advertising. Despite difficulties and uncertainties that remain, efforts to bring environmental issues more into the mainstream of corporate management and activities, in an integrated fashion, are headed in the right direction. Such mainstreaming will best ensure that companies manage their environmental challenges and opportunities effectively.

Chapter 8

Allocating Corporate Resources for Environmental Compliance

Gabriele G. Crognale
Science Applications International Corporation

Overview

An article that appeared in *Engineering News Record*[1] began with the caption "EPA's RCRA Program Gets Tough" which poignantly portrays the ultimate driving force behind environmental compliance at this time. This "command-and-control" approach to compliance has been the norm that Congress set for EPA in its present enforcement program. To complement this and to put more bite into its enforcement penalty assessments, EPA issued its revised RCRA Civil Penalty Policy (RCPP) in October 1990 in a concerted effort to convince companies that penalties are not just a part of doing business as was previously perceived by many organizations.

---

[1] Hazel Bradford, " EPA's RCRA program gets tough," July 22, 1991, p.8.

Since then, different EPA regions have begun to impose hefty penalties on companies in violation of RCRA, such as $3.7 million[2] on a heavy machinery manufacturer for both RCRA and TSCA violations, and $3.0 million[3] on a large multi-disciplined manufacturing company; and in violation of CERCLA, over $60 million[4] in cleanup costs assessed to two specialty chemical companies, and four other parties in a Superfund settlement; and an estimated $60-80 million[5] for cleanup assessed to another heavy machinery manufacturer. Such penalties have undoubtedly caught the attention of many CEOs of companies that could face similar fines and cleanup costs.

These are not aberrations or isolated incidents; on the contrary, many companies seem to have taken EPA's actions seriously, and, as a result, have initiated programs to keep their companies not only in compliance, but striving to exceed compliance requirements. They do so in order to find themselves free from these exacting penalties, and more importantly, from the potential of having to face expensive cleanup costs or future corrective action under both the HSWA Amendments and Subpart S of RCRA.[6]

It is interesting to note that a recent survey[7] by a management consulting firm found that the environmental compliance

---

[2] *Hazardous Materials Intelligence Reporter*, Vol. XII, No. 31, 2 August 1991, p.4.

[3] *Chemical & Engineering News*, May 20, 1991, p.17.

[4] David Stipp, *Wall Street Journal*, "Firms to Settle A Superfund Case for $69.5 Million," July 9, 1991, p.A4.

[5] *Engineering News Record*, September 2, 1991, p.19.

[6] EPA issued the proposed rule on July 27, 1990. It specifies goals for corrective action of solid waste management units (SWMUs) at hazardous waste management facilities. The Hazardous and Solid Waste Amendments (HSWA) require corrective action for all permitted facilities and for those facilities seeking a permit.

[7] *Engineering News Record*, "Corporate Spending Rises," June 3, 1991 p.11. (Reference previously made in Chapter 3 on Environmental Liability).

programs of many U.S. corporations were costing as much as 65 percent of net income to stay in compliance. These programs are usually the main responsibility of the company's environmental manager, who also has to control staff management and resource allocations to pay for these programs.

The level of effort required by the manager to maintain compliance is staggering. It is a position that many a manager finds himself or herself in without much preparatory school curriculum training, although there is a growing trend in many universities to offer environmental management courses. The managers' backgrounds are somewhat varied, ranging from chemical engineering to biology. Most have bachelors and some have master's degrees.[8] As presently structured, the manager's position is one that is in a constant state of flux, requiring constant fine-tuning as each crisis is encountered and overcome.

Of course, those managers that have been in this position for some time, or are new to the position, with previous experience as a regulator or environmental consultant, or from another company, are much better equipped to handle their responsibilities than someone not as familiar with the regulations, regulators and processes. Add to this responsibility the tremendous workload and research required to stay current with the regulations, and you have the makings of a very stressful position. Those sentiments were echoed by the respondents of the NAEM survey referenced earlier.

The question one may ask about this is, why all the concern? Besides the obvious specter of the "Pollution Police" swooping down on these companies, which is not an appropriate portrayal of EPA or state regulators (they are dedicated to uphold the law), many companies are very much concerned about their corporate

---

[8] Survey of NAEM (National Association of Environmental Management) members released at Haz Mat 91 International, June 1991.

image. Emerging forces, such as shareholder concerns, public relation departments concerns, and a growing "green awareness" trend[9], are starting to take effect in many U.S. companies.

In addition, some companies are beginning to see these new compliance costs as the new cost of doing business, an "insurance policy" against future liability. The real cost of a RCRA enforcement corrective action is not the penalty assessed, but the costs associated with the RFA/RFI[10] that typically follow the Administrative Order and initiate the first phase of corrective action at a facility that has had a documented release of hazardous materials.[11] In this regard, RCRA is becoming more like CERCLA, and it is not uncommon to see such corrective action span three to five years. As an example, one particular EPA Administrative Order (a Section 3013 Order) cost a company approximately $100,000 in fines. The RFA portion, which is still going on after four years, has cost the company far in excess of that fine in consulting and soil-boring contractor fees alone. This is ultimately what many companies, whether generators or TSDs, are attempting to avoid, as best possible, in their compliance programs today.

The Common-Sense Approach to Environmental Compliance

As evidenced in many companies that have complex programs, the environmental manager has to wear many hats. In smaller companies, this may be compounded by the fact that

---

[9] The Environmental Marketing Claims Act of 1991 was introduced in the U.S. House by Rep. Sikorski that would establish a program to regulate environmental marketing claims.

[10] RCRA Facility Assessment/RCRA Facility Investigation.

[11] The corrective action track being discussed may either involve a facility that has submitted its Part B permit application, or a facility that must undergo corrective action as a result of an enforcement action. (See Footnotes 2, 3 & 4).

environmental managers are not only responsible for environmental and/or health and safety, but may also be responsible for quality control and product management, among others. In general, though, the environmental manager typically falls into either a corporate consultation or facility compliance role. To further define this term, it is important to distinguish the organizational functions that each role entails.

Briefly, the environmental managers in a "Corporate Consultation" role are typically in a corporate function that involves broad authority over the company's environmental programs. Their responsibilities typically include: establishing compliance policies; performing or monitoring environmental audits; participating in community relations; managing safety and health policies, and performing other allied functions. Whereas, the environmental managers in a "Facility Compliance" role are involved in a more focused position at the facility or plant. These managers are typically the "front line" that deal in a compliance-oriented mode with the regulators.[12] This chapter deals with both, not exclusively one or the other.

In the context of this discussion, the manager's role will focus on environmental, health and safety. Therefore, the manager must be thoroughly knowledgeable in the applicable regulations, most usually RCRA, TSCA, SARA, Air and Water, and be adroit in handling other duties, such as: staffing, budgeting, hiring of contractors, and filling out the required compliance forms. It is obvious then, that a structured game plan is very important if that manager is to stay on top of all of this and still be in compliance. From the environmental manager's standpoint, it is a very difficult task, especially when measures to correct noted deficiencies noted require sizable capital expenditures, and more importantly, corporate approval to obtain and spend the funds.

---

[12] *Environmental Management in the 90's: A Snapshot of The Profession*, NAEM report, July 1991. (See Footnote 8).

Where does one start to attempt to manage this task, and do it efficiently?

It is important at some juncture early on for the manager to begin to learn as much about the company as possible. A logical starting point would be to track a specific product from beginning to end (final waste stream). Following such a path, the manager is then able to not only learn about the company as he or she goes on, but also begin to pick up the process of how the product is made. A supplementary benefit of this "walk through" is that the manager could also be apprised (or informed) of potential areas for waste minimization, which is one of the major thrusts of EPA in the 1990s. The manager is also able to see where the end product goes out the door, and more importantly, from a compliance perspective, where and how the waste is being stored. This exercise, simple as it seems, is probably the most important cornerstone in compliance activities. A seasoned inspector will most likely ask to be walked through the waste stream generation process; if inspection logs are required (as in TSDFs[13]), it will be to the manager's benefit to know where to look to inspect effectively and to have these documents readily available for inspectors to review; and, if the facility plans to conduct an environmental audit, there is a good likelihood that some astute auditor will request the same. Environmental audits will be discussed in greater detail later in this chapter.

Of course, the manager is not expected to do all of this alone, and having the right mix of technical staff should make this task easier. The scope of the compliance program and the budget allocated for compliance may be a direct function of the size of the company, and its commitment to environmental compliance. Other factors may include: the number of facilities to be managed, and the availability of capital to maintain the staff. Presuming that a particular company is sufficiently solvent, another impor-

---

[13] Treatment, Storage and Disposal Facilities

tant tool for the manager is knowing the strengths and weaknesses of his or her staff and being able to fit them where their talents do the most good. For example, the manager might want to utilize a staff member proficient in filling out and tracking manifest forms to handle this task. That person might also be utilized as an in-house trainer if the need arises. Another individual could have a working knowledge of the regulations, and could be instrumental in troubleshooting the management of the facility's hazardous wastes, or maintaining the required records. This list is only limited by the knowledge that the manager has of the staff, the time that the manager has to train his or her staff, the manager's creativity in filling all the gaps, or a combination of any of these.

Another important task for the environmental manager to effectively direct is the management and updating of the facility's [14] compliance records, which include the required RCRA records, SARA Form Rs, NPDES discharge permits and records, and all other applicable federal and state air, solid and medical waste requirements.

By far, the most voluminous compliance records are typically those required by RCRA, which covers both the generators and the facilities. With the push for multi-media[15] inspections by EPA becoming more prevalent, other media program records may become just as voluminous, and equally cumbersome for the manager if not managed properly.

There is no real management guidance on how to maintain records, since it is a personal call as to how each manager wishes to maintain the facility's records. One tip worth noting is that the manager may wish to consider a "tickler" file, possibly patterned

---

[14] Discussion will concentrate on referring to companies as facilities, ie., treatment, storage or disposal, although most usually a facility refers to a storage facility. Generators will be referred to as generators.

[15] RCRA, TSCA, Air and Water Programs, to name a few.

after EPA's ERP,[16] in order to better track those items that require some priority in being addressed.

The bottom line is that the manager should use whatever filing system best fits in his or her particular situation. Creativity is highly recommended.

Another aspect of effective facility environmental management that should be evaluated by the manager early on and on a regular basis, is the assessment of the facility's environmental strengths and weaknesses, expanding on the strengths as a guide to help shore up the observed weaknesses.

Taking into account the previously identified pieces of information, the manager should now be in a position to appropriately evaluate the facility's strengths and weaknesses.

Specific items that should be considered include:

- Inspection records

- Manifests (up to three years prior required by EPA)

- Incidence reports

- Environmental audit reports

- Follow-up/corrective action (based on audit findings)

- EPA/State correspondence, including NOVs or AOs [17]

- Contractor work, such as consultant studies or reports, soil data and groundwater monitoring reports, to name a few.

---

[16] EPA's Enforcement Response Policy, a tracking tool that alerts RCRA support staff of high priority (HPV) or recalcitrant violators.

[17] Notices of Violation or Administrative Orders.

In addition, it would be advantageous for the manager to establish lines of communication with other managers of sister facilities, or even to establish an ad hoc managers group or roundtable group to brainstorm ideas and try to formalize solutions to problems encountered. The old axiom "two heads are better than one" is very appropriate in the management of environmental affairs. For this reason, there are various brainstorming groups in existence in various parts of the country. It would be prudent to have the manager inquire if such groups exist in his or her local area.

This discussion has focused on the collection of various bits of data on a facility, which the manager may now be able to apply to the compliance process. He or she may wish some form of corrective action strategy to address noted deficiencies in the facility's environmental management program, or plan actions that may be perceived as general improvements, or best management practices.

Of course, it would be ideal if environmental managers were able to convince senior or corporate management to make every correction noted in a timely manner. However, as is often the case, budgetary constraints may dictate that priorities be established to rank those corrective actions that need immediate attention, and those that can wait since they may require staff and resource allocations over a longer period of time. In other instances, the environmental manager may face some resistance from corporate management, which may not be completely convinced that all these corrective actions are necessary. This may be due, in part, to a lack of one of several factors including: resources, dialogue, communication and cooperation with both upper management and the rest of the organization.[18]

---

[18] See Footnote 8.

A growing argument that appears to be swaying more corporate officials is that the manager should put all the relevant factors regarding environmental compliance into perspective.

As previously shown, maintaining a proper compliance program for any facility, or several facilities, of a corporation is very costly.[19] It is costly because the corporation is paying for a dedicated environmental group to try to keep the corporation free from expensive enforcement penalties. This being a relatively new field where experienced people are not easy to find also adds to the cost of maintaining compliance, but, if all these are considered in the context of a "bigger picture" the environmental managers are worth it to the corporation.

In addition, those penalties have increased significantly with EPA's issuance of its RCPP in October 1990, as previously mentioned, mainly as a deterrent to non-compliant actions by generators or facilities of hazardous waste. Furthermore, the "do nothing" approach, especially if deficiencies were noted in an environmental audit, could put the facility and/or parent corporation into the "willful blindness" category that Justice could prosecute as criminal.[20]

Violations that fall under RCPP can incur civil penalties up to a maximum of $25,000/day per violation, while the criminal penalties can go as high as $50,000/day per violation. Clearly, it is not in the corporation's best financial interest to stay non-compliant.

In addition, the argument can be raised to corporate management that certain costs may be viewed as capital improvements, which would undoubtedly require corporate accounting to assess

---

[19] See Footnote 7.

[20] Presentation by Barry Hartman of the Department of Justice, AWMA Conference, June 1991. (Prior discussion on criminal actions presented in the chapter on environmental liability).

the validity of each claim. They could even consider these improvements at least as tax write-offs, something that penalties and order mandated corrective action would not be. There is even the possibility, depending on the particular circumstance, that certain improvements may become potential waste minimization/pollution prevention vehicles that could bode favorably for the company's corporate image.

Finally, there is a growing trend among many of the largest polluters to want to be viewed favorably by the public, the consumers of their products, and even their shareholders, who are starting to become more open about their concerns.

In this regard, EPA, in July 1991, initiated a new and different program, the Industrial Toxics Project, more commonly referred to as the "33-50 Program,"[21] which is aimed at allowing the largest industrial polluters to voluntarily reduce their pollution levels (primarily air).

For a further incentive, EPA is establishing an awards program to recognize the voluntary company commitments and the accomplishments that each company successfully attains. The Awards Program will recognize different aspects of exceptional company performance in successive program years. Although actual achievement in reducing releases is a central goal, EPA does explicitly state that the role that pollution prevention plays in achieving these reductions will be an important factor in the Awards Program. As a further incentive, these prestigious awards will be selective and competitive in keeping with the national level of the 33-50 Program.[22]

---

[21] EPA asked over 600 companies in July 1991 to voluntarily cut their 1992 emissions by 33 percent of their 1988 levels, and their 1995 emissions by 50 percent of 1988 levels. Hence the name 33-50.

[22] "What's Next" portion of the EPA document, *EPA's 33-50 Program A Progress Report*, July 1991.

Some companies, such as Chevron, 3M, DOW, Texaco and Polaroid, have either issued environmental reports or made videos that highlight their environmental programs in an effort to explain to the public their progress in achieving their individual commitment goals. More detail on both the 33-50 Program and each of these companies will be provided later in this chapter.

Other companies, sensing the public's desire for more environmentally acceptable products, have devoted tremendous energy and marketing and advertising dollars to promote their products as being "environmentally friendly." In a move aimed at protecting the consumer from potentially misleading advertisements, a task force of attorneys general issued a report which calls for establishing standards for marketing claims.[23] The Environmental Marketing Claims Act of 1991 (H.R. 1408) has been introduced in the U.S. Congress, and EPA is looking to set standards to ensure a product's environmental marketing claims.

All of these programs and trends together demonstrate an increase in environmental awareness and what it really costs at all levels to maintain.

Yardsticks to Measure Compliance

An environmental audit is defined by EPA[24] as a systematic, documented, periodic and objective review by regulated entities of their facility operations and those practices related to meeting environmental requirements.

It may be interpreted that the main purpose of the audit is to allow the audit team to fully apprise the environmental manager

---

[23] "The Green Report II" was issued in May 1991, and included the attorney general from NY, CA, MA, UT, WA, to name a few.

[24] Environmental Auditing Policy Statement, 51 Fed. Reg. 25004 (July 9, 1986).

and/or corporate officers of deficiencies or nonconformities of the facility's environmental management program. The audit is predominately a management tool and any findings contained in the audit report should be acted upon by the manager or corporate executives in a prudent fashion. Of course, as explained previously, the extent that the audit's findings can be acted upon in a timely manner by the manager are dependent upon key factors, such as: staff, budget, cooperation and commitment from upper management,[25] to name a few.

Depending upon the staff and time the manager has to devote to conducting self-audits of the facility, a corporate or third-party audit could give the manager a cross-sectional snapshot of his or her facility in a relatively short amount of time. During such audits, if the manager is part of the team, the information obtained can be a tremendous benefit to him. In addition, if the audit also concentrates on training records, it could uncover items of interest to the manager that might be used in future on-site environmental training.[26]

Apart from being required by law,[27] employee training, including Haz Mat training, is probably the first line of defense in any generator or facility's hazardous waste management program. As is typically discovered by EPA or state inspections, a facility's program is usually only as good as its least trained, least competent employee responsible for some aspect of hazardous waste management. Therefore, as noted time and again in numerous EPA inspection logs or enforcement actions,[28] many

---

[25] Steve Fradkoff, *Environmental Manager*, "Environmental Audits: Not for the Halfhearted," July 1990. Also see Footnote 8.

[26] See "Auditing Answers," *Environmental Protection Magazine*, p.45, July/August 1991.

[27] 40 CFR 265.16 or 264.16 (RCRA).

[28] EPA/State inspectors log their inspection findings as violations in the Compliance Monitoring Enforcement Log (CMEL), which

noted violations could have been avoided if the required training had been expanded (presuming that it had been conducted), or the trainer could have taken more time to ensure that the class had clearly understood the lecture. It appears as though the mindset of some line operators, possibly third shift, is still in a mode where training is just something his supervisor requires him to take. It could also be that the operator is not clear about what is required, or worse, may have a casual attitude about the whole compliance program. As an example, one may notice dark blotches or stains on property grounds or discolored vegetation which may indicate that something may have been dumped or spilled that was probably hazardous, and if so, is probably a RCRA violation. Observations like that may indicate to a seasoned inspector that something is amiss and he or she may want to investigate further. If so, this may become problematic for the facility if it results in an enforcement action.[29]

Therefore, it is important to stress that an effective employee training program is one that, at a minimum, gives the trainee a feeling that the training is something good for him or her, promotes responsible attitudes, could allow for advancement, and bodes well for the company and the environment.

If, at times, the audience finds itself lost or confused, the trainer should consider providing a format that places emphasis less on regulatory citations that seem like the regulations are being read out loud, than on actual case studies of what not to do (like throw oil-based paint and solvent down the toilet), or what can go wrong, like having an EPA or state inspector see the solvent stain on the ground. The key is to use as many graphic

---

subsequently enters the Hazardous Waste Data Management System (HWDMS), EPA's tracking compliance tool.

[29] In such an action, EPA issued complaints and assessed $495,900 in penalties for RCRA violations to a commercial TSDF for alleged spilled solvents onto the ground. (Ref: *Hazardous Materials Intelligence Reporter*, Vol. XII, No. 4, 25 January 1991, p.3).

examples as possible to bring the point home. Such an example could be an incident similar to the tragic death of two employees of a paint company in central Massachusetts that were killed when a drum they were using to mix solvents in exploded. The accident may have been caused by improper grounding of the drum.[30]

If those aren't effective training tools, perhaps some form of a monetary reward–punishment incentive could be introduced. Let's face it. If "Joe" neglects to slap a label on a 55-gallon drum, or leaves a drum of waste in an inappropriate or dangerous location as he runs off to break or lunch, and an inspector just happens to be on site, it could become very costly to the company. In such instances where fines could result from such negligence, it may be appropriate to inform the trainee that it may be reflected in his or her next pay raise, or worse, be grounds for dismissal. A generator in Rhode Island has incorporated such a program. The company keeps a log of employees' activities that are then factored into their pay scales.

Of course, these are just some suggestions that may be utilized by the trainer, depending upon the audience, their degree of knowledge, experience, etc., but the bottom line again, in training, as in the environmental program in general, is to use common sense to come to a workable solution.

Responsibilities of the Environmental Manager

As in any other discipline that requires a responsible, knowledgeable individual to control day-to-day operations, a hazardous waste operation requires the same degree of intensity and control.

---

[30] That occurred in March 1989 and the fatalities were investigated by EPA and referred to OSHA.

As previously noted, the environmental manager wears many hats ranging from firefighter to salesman. First, rushing to put out those pesky compliance "fires" and second, trying to sell the solution to supervisors and corporate executives.

This task is by no means an envious one, and possibly not a glamorous one, but for the manager who has made a concerted effort to maintain a tight compliance program, there may not be that many instances where "fires" need to be put out, and the position can be one that allows for noteworthy accomplishments.

There is a sense of satisfaction, for instance, in knowing that the employee training program has begun to pay off, especially after an inspector has walked through the facility and found no violations. In the same manner, the manager can convey a sense of accomplishment to the staff after a corporate or third party audit has not revealed any findings or made recommendations for "best management practices" during the audit.

In reviewing the responsibilities of the environmental manager, the following stand out:

- Ensuring knowledgeable staff are assigned to the proper tasks to accomplish the company's program goals.

- Constantly re-evaluating staff needs to ensure these goals are met or exceeded.

- Securing corporate resources to fund these goals.

- Maintaining open lines of communication with regulators before, during and after inspections, as well as being apprised of recent regulatory/legislative trends, and attending, when possible, regulatory-oriented (or EPA-sponsored) seminars.[31]

---

[31] There are companies that offer courses on topics such as "RCRA Regulations," "Environmental Audits," and "Waste Minimization." If interested, the reader should contact the author or publisher.

- Maintaining open lines of communication with sister facilities and other facilities, either within the local area, or through business contacts.

- Constantly reassessing priorities and following up on the previously discussed items.

Following these steps should put the facility much closer to total compliance with the regulations. They should not be perceived as being all that difficult or unobtainable. It will, however, require much hard work and patience on the part of the manager and his or her staff in order to make it happen.

If successful, this is something that can be shared with other companies through networking or roundtable discussions and managers meetings.[32] This could become a means to gauge compliance from one facility to another, where the manager could discuss the inspection or audit findings with a close colleague to assess the situation.

This would be similar to the way regulators brainstorm noted inspection violations as enforcement actions are contemplated. Guidance documents, directives, or policy memoranda that come down from EPA/HQ are also brainstormed in a similar fashion in regional offices, as well as state agencies.

The Role of Pollution Prevention and Waste Minimization

The previous sections of this chapter have dealt primarily with strategies for maintaining effective and manageable compliance programs in everyday dealings with hazardous sub-

---

[32] There is an Environmental Managers Group in the Greater Boston area whose members include high tech and other manufacturing companies' environmental managers who brainstorm such general interest items.

stances from manufacturing processes to waste generation and disposal.

The focus has been on getting the job done right and training and managing employees to ensure continued success in this endeavor. The common factor in each discussion has been the management of some form of pollution that comes out of the process, whether it be from the end of the pipe, treatment hopper, or top of the stack.

Beyond recognizing the problem, a subtle and fairly recent change in the regulatory mindset has shifted gears towards preventing pollution at the source. This has moved into the forefront with remarkable swiftness since 1987 and coincides with the beginning of Superfund's Toxic Release Inventory.[33]

Pollution prevention, or waste minimization, was one of the highlights of EPA's RCRA Implementation Study.[34] The study acknowledged that it would take a concerted effort by both the regulators and the regulated community to achieve maximum potential. Just before that document was released, EPA completed the "Pollution Prevention Research Plan: Report to Congress," which presented a comprehensive pollution prevention research program. Then, in November 1990, Congress passed the long-awaited Pollution Prevention Act of 1990.[35]

An excerpt from the Act reads as follows: "There are significant opportunities for industry to reduce or prevent pollution at the source through cost-effective changes in production, operations, and raw materials use. Such changes offer industry

---

[33] This may have been introduced as a result of incidents, such as Bhopal, India.

[34] EPA/OSWER study, "The Nation's Hazardous Waste Management Program at a Crossroads," (EPA/530-SW-90-069), p.1, July 1990; BNA's *Environment Reporter*, p.602, July 12, 1991.

[35] PL 101-508 Title 6, 104 Stat. 1388

substantial savings in reduced raw material, pollution control, and liability costs as well as help protect the environment and reduce risks to worker health and safety."[36]

EPA further defines pollution prevention as an umbrella term for a wide range of source reduction activities, which may include toxics use reduction, chemical substitution, process modification, product redesign, and better management practices.

Better management practices, the common sense approach, can conceivably become the cornerstone of waste minimization, especially in light of EPA's subsequent strategy for dealing with waste minimization/pollution prevention activities, part of which was the formulation of the Industrial Toxics Project.[37] This ambitious undertaking by EPA is striving to have companies voluntarily curb their emissions of 17 toxic chemicals, mostly chlorinated hydrocarbons or heavy metals, by 33 percent of 1988 levels by 1992, and up to 50 percent by 1995.

In addition, another important element of the Act is the requirement that companies begin to document and quantify their efforts to reduce waste through: source reduction, recycling and treatment. Under SARA, Title III,[38] companies are also required to fill out their Toxic Chemical Release Inventory Reporting–Form Rs on a yearly basis, which includes an estimate of releases of chemicals into all media (air, water and soil), as well as an inventory of all wastes shipped off-site.

It would seem that the combination of these requirements (or voluntary requests) are EPA's way of further persuading compa-

---

[36] EPA publication, *Pollution Prevention Training Opportunities in 1991*, p.1.

[37] See Footnote 22.

[38] Section 313 of the Emergency Planning and Community Right-To-Know Act (1986).

nies to undertake voluntary reduction actions.[39] This is a different approach for EPA, where the regulatory mindset has historically been geared towards "command-and-control" for compliance gauging instead of actively seeking voluntary compliance efforts from industry.

In promoting this endeavor, it may be that the Chemical Manufacturer's Association's own Responsible Care® Program has received its first big endorsement from the EPA by having the administrator, William Reilly, acknowledge Responsible Care as a significant voluntary effort already in progress.[40]

It will be interesting to see how effectively all these factors affect the reduction of pollution at the source, and if indeed, the generators, both large and small, are committed to this common goal.

Case Studies

If you scan typical compliance journals or publications, it appears as though the trend has been toward the highlighting of enforcement cases and penalties as a possible deterrent to other recalcitrant or would-be violators.

With the advent of pollution prevention opportunities, it appears that the environmental do-gooders will finally have a chance to bask in the limelight in a positive way.

That does not imply that, up until now, there have been hardly any companies that have exemplified positive compliance attitudes. Unfortunately, public attention has not been focused on

---

[39] Lois Ember, *Chemical & Engineering News*, "Strategies For Reducing Pollution At The Source Are Gaining Ground," July 8, 1991.

[40] *Chemical Week*, "Listening To-And Taking On The Skeptics," July 17, 1991, p.85.

these companies as quickly as on those found in violation of federal regulations.

In pollution prevention, the 3M Company merits recognition for having produced two videos, available through the Pollution Prevention Clearing House[41], that highlight the achievements and strategy of 3M's highly successful, corporate-wide pollution prevention program. The strategy is based on source reduction and the reclamation and reuse of process waste.

One of the videos is intended to encourage formulating chemists and other key players in 3M laboratories to eliminate or reduce waste in products.

In similar fashion, the Chevron Corporation merits recognition for its production of a video titled "Smart Moves," which describes Chevron's successful waste reduction program, called SMART (Save Money and Reduce Toxics), which was also highlighted in a report published by Chevron. It is titled, *1990 Report on the Environment: A Commitment to Excellence* and gives a detailed, well written account of where this oil company is headed in minimizing pollution. The report also notes the company's success with its environmental audit and SMART programs.

In addition, Dow Chemical merits recognition for its video production titled, "The WRAP (Waste Reduction Always Pays) Awards" which presents a brief overview of Dow's awards, which reward those company divisions that demonstrate innovative pollution prevention programs.

Texaco, Inc. stands out for its production of a report released in 1990 titled, *Environment, Health and Safety Review*. That report highlights its "Compliance-Plus" Program which strives to

---

[41] These are entitled " 3M's Pollution Prevention Pays Program" and "Challenge To Innovation," which are listed as training films in EPA's booklet, *Pollution Prevention Training Opportunities in 1991.*

maintain a dedicated corporate environmental awareness, and like Chevron, maintains a successful environmental audit program.

In waste reduction, Texaco launched a WOW (Wipe Out Waste) campaign aimed at reducing waste for a cleaner environment. WOW relies on research and technological effort to solve complex waste management problems. Topping that list is the appropriate disposal of hazardous materials that are generated from various petroleum refining and chemical manufacturing operations. For a short time, Texaco published a comic book featuring Captain WOW to get across the message that it was important to wipe out waste.

Another company that merits recognition for its commitment to its environmental responsibilities is the Polaroid Corporation for its Toxic Use & Waste Reduction (TUWR) Program. They subsequently published a report titled, *Making Commitment Work—Polaroid Report on the Environment April 1991*. This report stresses the company's efforts to minimize waste. The program actually began in 1987-1988, when Polaroid set its own goal of reducing waste by 10 percent per year over a five-year period ending in 1993.

Polaroid has openly acknowledged its pride in those employees who make TUWR work, and their commitment to the environment in their everyday routine.

As the report highlights, Polaroid has effectively reduced toxic use and waste by 20 percent since 1988; established a new Marketing Environmental Group Advisory Board and appointed someone to manage the newly created Marketing Environmental Program; extended the company's energy conservation efforts to include charter membership in EPA's Green Lights Program; and completed a grass-roots community survey to measure the familiarity of civic leaders and neighbors with the company's environmental objectives in Massachusetts, where Polaroid has production centers . The company has also solicited feedback in an effort to improve communications. The report also listed comments from employees on environmental concerns as indicated by references to: environmental representatives becoming facilitators; the adoption of new attitudes towards environmental issues; and waste reduction's dependence upon commitments. All of these seem to point towards an earnest attempt by the company's employees to maintain their commitment to the environment.[42]

Changing the Corporate Mindset

As shown in the preceding sections, each one of the actions illustrates a growing trend toward changes in corporate attitudes. Corporate decision makers are now leaning toward the integration of these program aspects: a sound environmental program; a skilled environmental manager to oversee this program; and a willingness of the corporation's public relations department to divulge more about the company's environmental program.

Corporations are realizing that it pays to be seen in a favorable light on environmental issues by the public, consumers, shareholders and the regulators, who are the ones set the tone. In addition, the message that EPA means business has been received loud and clear by the regulated community. This message is really for those recalcitrant companies that still look at the fines and penalties as just the cost of doing business today.

As evidenced by the details in this chapter, this attitude is quickly becoming the exception, since many corporate executives appropriately are very much concerned about their public image. As an item of interest, recently conducted polls and surveys have found that corporate executives feel they are doing a good job in managing their environmental problems and have changed their

---

[42] *Making Commitment Work-Polaroid Report on the Environment,* April 1991.

corporate attitudes while increasing awareness.[43] That could be viewed as a willingness of the corporate executives to devote more resources to accomplish these goals, and also provide information to satisfy shareholders, who are becoming more vocal about their desire to be informed about their corporation's environmental progress. In addition, there are many public interest groups that are constantly monitoring corporations and their efforts to actually implement their programs. These include Greenpeace, the Environmental Defense Fund, The Sierra Club, and The Coalition for Environmentally Responsible Economies (CERES), to name a few, that are committed to the preservation of the environment.

Green considerations are becoming more prominent as additional driving forces to change the corporate mindset, and with the passage of the Environmental Marketing Claims Act, the issuance of the Green Report, and the combined energies of the EPA, the U.S. Office of Consumer Affairs (OCA), and the Federal Trade Commission (FTC) to initiate a product labeling program[44], the message is coming in clear that green marketing is very much a regulatory concern. It will probably require being factored into any responsible company's corporate environmental structure at some future point.

The last topic that seems to be slowly gaining more prominence is that of global considerations of the U.S. multinational companies. Some of the situations that may be encountered as a result of heightened global awareness and concerns raised by foreign governments could be more stringent regulations and what impact these may have on the multinational companies abroad.

---

[43] Susan Ainsworth, *Chemical & Engineering News*, "Industrialists laud own environmental efforts," July 1, 1991, p.35.

[44] EPA Newsletter - *Reusable News*, Winter 1991

EPA's Office of International Activities established a detail in the American Embassy in Mexico to work on environmental issues specific to the region. In another area, Mexico's equivalent of EPA, the Secretary of Urban Development and Ecology (SEDUE) is concerned, along with the U.S., of possible air and water pollution, and hazardous waste contamination of the so-called "maquiladora" industries.[45] The term *maquiladora* refers to foreign companies that set up centers in Mexico to assemble products that require much manpower to produce. Since labor is cheaper in Mexico, the final products are assembled there, and then exported to market. If a free trade agreement is reached with Mexico, these companies may find their operations under the jurisdiction of both U.S. and Mexican environmental laws. Moving closer in this regard, EPA administrator William Reilly briefed Congress on the first steps toward a joint environmental planning effort between EPA and SEDUE.[46] In addition, both agencies have developed a strategy for combating pollution problems along both sides of the border.[47]

In the Pacific Rim countries, the Taiwan EPA, the Hong Kong SPEL[48], the Japanese, South Korean, Australian, and other governmental ministries or agencies, are beginning to take

---

[45] Mexico established a "maquiladora" program in 1985 that allows duty-free imports of manufacturing components to Mexico for processing or assembly.

This was a footnote in a GAO report on U.S. and Mexico trade (GAO/NSIAD- 91-227).

[46] Hazel Bradford, *Engineering News Record*, "Mexican trade pact gains support in Congress," May 20, 1991, p.7.

[47] *Environmental Protection News*, "Border Pollution Plan Presented," Vol. 6, No. 17, September 8, 1991, p.5.

[48] The Secretary for Planning, Environment and Lands, and their advisory body, The Environmental Pollution Advisory Committee. More information on Hong Kong's environmental progress is contained in the report, *Environment Hong Kong 1990 - A Review of 1989*, Environmental Protection Department of Hong Kong.

strong forward strides, and will become forces that multinationals will have to deal with in the foreseeable future.

In South America, rich with its natural resources, the environmental ministries of Columbia, Brazil and Venezuela are also moving forward with tougher environmental regulations. Coincidentally, world focus was on Brazil when that country played host to ECOBRASIL '92, in conjunction with the United Nations Conference on Environment and Development—UNCED '92. That event gathered delegations from over 160 nations, thousands of environment specialists and more than two thousand foreign journalists.[49]

Looking at a broader context, approximately 30 U.S. multinational companies have already committed to reducing their toxic pollutant levels of the 17 listed chemicals in the 33-50 Program as well as other chemicals used at their facilities outside the U.S. It is probably a prudent move on their part to look ahead and anticipate future regulatory changes throughout the world.

Furthermore, with the unification of the European Community (EC), there has emerged a growing interest by the EC member states in implementing regulations to allow the regulators and the public to better understand certain industrial activities within the member states. Thus the Commission of the European Community issued a proposal on March 5, 1992 for a council regulation to allow industrial companies within the member states to participate voluntarily in the EC's ECO-audit scheme. *ECO-audit* is the EC term for environmental audits as conducted in the U.S. The voluntary nature of the ECO-audit is intended to encourage affected companies to act more responsibly in their business areas, and to facilitate the dissemination of information to both the regulators and the public, much like the practice of the more responsive publicly held corporations in the U.S. In

---

[49] Program flyer for ECOBRASIL '92.

addition, the Basle (effective May 1992) and Lome IV Conventions have put into motion requirements for standardized international waste shipments, and with the Lome Convention, an outright ban on radioactive waste shipments.[50]

All these emerging trends point to a growing globalization of environmental concerns, and we may conceivably see standard global environmental regulations by the year 2000, but it will take tremendous cooperation, commitment and trust in our governments, industries and each other, if this is to become a reality.

Steve Fradkoff, formerly of EPA, and Tom Robinson of Nyacol Products, provided the technical review and some of the referenced material in this chapter.

---

[50] Jan McAlpine, "International Trade in Hazardous Wastes: Public Sector Management Responses in the United States and Abroad," Haz Mat 91 International, June 1991.

Chapter 9

Environmental Market Opportunities

Roger H. Bezdek & Robert M. Wendling
Management Information Services, Inc.

Introduction: The Pollution Abatement and Control

Industry as an Opportunity for American Business

To most businessmen, entrepreneurs, and corporate executives a clean and healthy environment, while good in the abstract, is nevertheless an expensive luxury. Sure, they argue, a high level of environmental quality is desirable. Pursuing this goal, however, damages the U.S. economy, so we must always be on guard lest we spend too much on "wasteful" environmental programs—wasteful because they destroy jobs, depress profits, decrease productivity, and produce a host of either real or imagined woes.

A recent manifestation of this phenomena was the heated debate over acid rain and the Clean Air Act Amendments of 1990.

By the late 1980s it was no longer credible to deny that the problem exists; rather, it was more fashionable for those opposed to the legislation to maintain that the costs of acid rain clean-up were too high. Once again the litany of lost jobs, impoverished communities, and devastated industries likely to be caused by acid rain control and prevention programs was brought out, dusted off, and given a new face.

However, rarely mentioned in this debate and largely unnoticed by the general public is the fact that since the late 1960s, protection of the environment and abatement and control of pollution have grown rapidly to become a major sales-generating, profit-making, job-creating industry. As illustrated in Figure I and Table 1, expenditures for pollution abatement and control (PABCO) have grown (in constant 1991 dollars) from $23 billion per year in 1970 to nearly $130 billion per year by 1991—increasing much faster than GNP over the same period.

Many companies, whether they realize it or not, owe their profits—and in some cases their existence—to PABCO spending. Many workers, whether they realize it or not, would be unemployed were it not for these expenditures. So much for the contention that protecting the environment destroys industries and costs jobs.

Further, while the rate of growth in PABCO expenditures is forecast to decline during the 1990s, these expenditures will continue to increase at about twice the rate of GNP. In the early years of the next decade PABCO expenditures will likely equal and then exceed the U.S. Department of Defense budget—both PABCO spending and the DOD budget will total $200 -$220 billion (1991 dollars) and will comprise about three percent of GNP.

The question may be asked, aren't investments in environmental protection "nonproductive?" Wouldn't spending lots of money on anything—for example, building pyramids in the desert—stimulate industry and create jobs?

Figure 1
Pollution Abatement and Control Spending in the United States, 1970 -2005

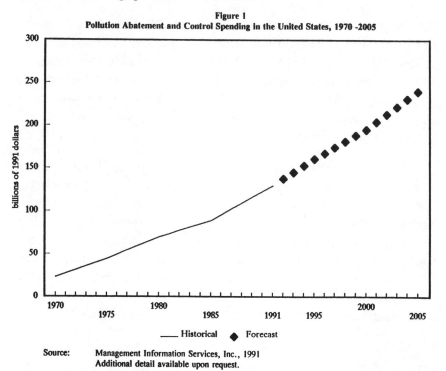

Source: Management Information Services, Inc., 1991
Additional detail available upon request.

Table 1
**Historical and Forecast Pollution Abatement and Control Spending
in the United States, 1970-2005**
(millions of 1991 dollars)

	1970	1975	1980	1985	1991	1995	2000	2005
Pollution Abatement and Control, Total	$22,803	$44,220	$69,562	$88,826	$129,064	$160,112	$194,900	$239,435
Air Pollution Control	6,680	13,122	21,162	27,935	34,806	44,990	55,259	72,780
Radiation Pollution Control	16	278	263	280	580	791	1,075	1,418
Water Pollution Control	7,884	18,151	29,694	39,769	53,695	64,252	76,960	90,473
Land Pollution Control	8,044	11,748	16,334	19,090	35,704	44,590	55,378	67,125
Chemical Pollution Control	83	217	1,067	928	2,262	2,967	3,470	4,463
Multi-Media Pollution Contr	96	704	1,042	824	2,394	2,522	2,758	3,176

Source: Management Information Services, Inc., Washington, D.C., 1991.
Additional detail available upon request.

These investments are not at all like building useless pyramids. Rather, they produce a healthier, safer, cleaner, and more livable environment. Environmental protection is an exemplary public good, and according to the Harris pollsters this issue has consistently enjoyed wider and stronger public support than virtually any other issue over the past quarter-century.[1] Investments in plant and equipment which produce this strongly desired public good are as productive as those that produce automobiles, television sets, golf balls, or defense systems that we are willing to pay for personally or through the government.

Don't environmental standards penalize certain states and regions at the expense of others? Sometimes, yes. This point has been so overused, however, that almost any state or region suffering economic hardship places some of the blame on unreasonable environmental laws.

According to our initial estimates, the acid rain abatement program contained in the Clean Air Act Amendments of 1990 will, annually, create 115,000 jobs and generate $1.5 billion in corporate profits.[2] It is significant that many of these benefits will flow directly to states such as Pennsylvania, Michigan, and Illinois who presently see only costs and disadvantages from acid rain legislation. American business must recognize that funds expended on pollution abatement and control programs are not wasted. Investments in environmental protection contribute as much to the well-being of the nation as money spent on other goods competing for scarce private and public funds.

Over the past quarter century protecting the environment has been a major U.S. priority. The legislation enacted has signifi-

---

1 This is one reason why spending on environmental protection programs will likely increase rapidly throughout the 1990s.

2 See Robert M. Wendling and Roger H. Bezdek, "Acid Rain Abatement Legislation--Costs and Benefits," International Journal of Management Science, Vol. 17, No. 3 (1989), pp. 251-261.

Table 2
Air Pollution Control Expenditures in the United States, 1975-1991
(millions of 1991 dollars)

	1975	1980	1985	1991
Air Pollution Control, Total	$13,122	$21,162	$27,935	$34,806
Federally Mandated	13,122	21,162	27,935	34,806
Stationary Sources	9,874	15,958	20,132	25,404
Federally Mandated	9,874	15,958	20,132	25,404
Federal (Non-EPA)	227	301	361	496
State & Local Govt.	502	812	974	1,210
Private	9,146	14,844	18,622	23,590
Mobile Sources	2,891	4,812	7,523	9,042
Federally Mandated	2,891	4,812	7,523	9,042
Private	2,891	4,812	7,523	9,042
Undesignated Source	343	392	280	361
Federally Mandated	343	392	280	361
EPA	343	392	280	361

Source: Management Information Services, Inc., Washington, D.C., 1991.
Additional detail available upon request.

Table 3
Radiation Pollution Control Expenditures in the United States, 1975-1991
(millions of 1991 dollars)

	1975	1980	1985	1991
Radiation Pollution Control, Total	$278	$263	$280	$580
Federally Mandated	278	263	280	527
EPA	22	18	19	32
Federal (Non-EPA)	256	245	261	493
Private	-	-	-	54

Source: Management Information Services, Inc., Washington, D.C., 1991.
Additional detail available upon request.

cantly improved the nation's environment and has set in motion ongoing programs that will have significant effects on the nation's environment and economy well into the next century. Importantly, protection of the environment and remediation of environmental problems will continue to be one of the most rapidly growing and profitable industries in the U.S. Astute businessmen and entrepreneurs must be cognizant of these exciting opportunities.

International Market Opportunities for U.S. Business

Pollution abatement and control programs represent an important opportunity for U.S. companies to increase their exports. Some of the largest and most lucrative opportunities for U.S. exports of environmental technology and services are with the rapidly industrializing Asian nations, such as Taiwan, South Korea, and Thailand, with which the U.S. presently has large trade deficits. These nations, and others, will be spending heavily over the next decade to clean up their environment.

American companies, using technologies and equipment developed over the past 25 years in U.S. pollution control and abatement efforts, can obtain a large share of this Asian business.[3] Indeed, for many of these companies the Asian market may represent a golden opportunity for further sales and profits. Success abroad will also narrow the nation's trade deficit as millions of dollars of equipment—from large electrostatic precipitators and hazardous waste incinerators to delicate and sensitive monitoring instruments—are sold abroad.

This is one area in which U.S. companies still maintain a strong competitive advantage, and American companies have an excellent chance to capture a substantial share of the emerging

---

3 For example, the U.S. leads, by far, the rest of the world in the number of flue gas desulfurization systems (scrubbers) in operation, with (according to MISI estimates) 160 installed and more than 50 on order.

Asian market. MISI estimates that the world-wide market for air pollution and control equipment alone will reach $25 billion annually by the late 1990s, with well over half being spent outside the U.S. and Europe.

Waste management will be another high-growth field, as small, densely populated countries such as Taiwan, South Korea, and Singapore are forced to cope with ever increasing amounts of

Table 4
Water Pollution Control Expenditures in the United States, 1975-1991
(millions of 1991 dollars)

	1975	1980	1985	1991
Water Pollution Control, Total	$18,151	$29,694	$39,769	$53,695
Federally Mandated	16,789	27,526	36,683	49,476
Water Quality	16,789	27,316	36,451	48,984
Federally Mandated	16,789	27,316	36,451	48,984
Point Source	16,087	26,539	35,528	47,978
Federally Mandated	16,087	26,539	35,528	47,978
EPA	1,387	4,134	5,621	7,036
Federal (Non-EPA)	424	613	794	1,367
State Govt.	1,284	1,564	1,794	2,176
Local Govt.	5,652	7,696	10,754	14,503
Private	7,337	12,533	16,566	22,123
Non-Point Source	703	740	923	1,006
Federally Mandated	703	740	923	1,006
Federal (Non-EPA)	110	143	186	209
State Govt.	250	224	259	251
Local Govt.	287	316	344	378
Private	56	94	133	168
Drinking Water	1,362	2,378	3,318	4,711
Federally Mandated	-	210	232	492
EPA	12	109	104	130
State Govt.	-	48	83	136
Local Govt.	919	1,814	2,557	3,632
Private	206	407	572	814

Source: Management Information Services, Inc., Washington, D.C., 1991.
Additional detail available upon request.

hazardous wastes. To cite only one example, the pressing need for environmental cleanup in Taiwan, coupled with the nation's low international debt and large dollar reserves, make it likely that the nation will lead the way among the rapidly industrializing nations in expenditures for pollution control and waste management.[4]

U.S. consultants and engineers can play an especially important role in breaking into new international markets. If they win contracts to identify and propose solutions for pollution problems, it is likely that their proposals will be designed around American made equipment, giving American manufacturing an edge in bidding against their Japanese and European competitors.

The Emergence of the PABCO Industry Over the Past Two Decades

Tables 1 through 7 and Figure 1 illustrate the growth of the pollution abatement and control industry over the past two decades. They show that PABCO has been one of the most rapidly and consistently growing "recession proof" industries in the economy for the past 20 years.

Real PABCO spending (1991 dollars) increased from $23 billion in 1970 to $129 billion in 1991. This represents a more than five-fold increase in expenditures in 20 years—a sustained real average annual rate of growth of nearly 11 percent per year over the period. This compares with an average annual rate of growth of GNP that averaged between two and three precent during the 1970s and 1980s. That is, since the late 1960s, spending for pollution abatement and control has been increasing at a rate four times as large as GNP.

As might be expected, this rate of growth has not been constant. In the early 1970s, PABCO expenditures were increasing

---

4 While Taiwan's environmental problems are acute, the nation has $75 billion in foreign exchange reserves and no net overseas debt.

Table 5
Land Pollution Control Expenditures in the United States, 1975-1991
(millions of 1991 dollars)

	1975	1980	1985	1991
Land Pollution Control, Total	$11,748	$16,334	$19,090	$35,704
Federally Mandated	751	1,091	2,800	25,098
RCRA [a]	11,748	16,334	18,715	33,155
Federally Mandated	751	1,091	2,425	13,505
Solid Waste	11,748	16,334	17,504	21,703
Federally Mandated	751	1,091	1,214	2,052
EPA	29	137	2	17
Federal (Non-EPA)	143	152	354	527
Local Govt.	4,717	5,603	6,853	8,677
Private	6,859	10,441	10,295	12,480
Hazardous Waste	-	-	1,211	6,992
Federally Mandated	-	-	1,211	6,992
EPA	-	-	186	287
Federal (Non-EPA)	-	-	13	713
Private	-	-	1,012	5,982
UST [b]	-	-	-	4,459
Federally Mandated	-	-	-	4,459
Superfund [c]	-	-	374	2,549
Federally Mandated	-	-	374	2,549
EPA	-	-	235	1,157
Federal (Non-EPA)	-	-	56	672
State Govt.	-	-	37	216
Private	-	-	47	504

[a] Resource Conservation and Recovery Act
[b] Undeground Storage Tanks
[c] Comprehensive Environmental Response, Compensation, and Liability Act

Source: Management Information Information Services, Inc., Washington, D.C., 1991.
Additional detail available upon request.

nearly 15 percent per year, whereas by the late 1980s they were increasing at about seven percent annually. This is to be anticipated as the industry grew and matured—but even recent growth rates of seven percent are more than twice the growth rate of GNP. In 1970 PABCO spending accounted for 0.8 percent of GNP, while by 1991 the U.S. was devoting 2.3 percent of GNP to pollution control and abatement.

More interesting, perhaps, is the "recession-proof" nature of this industry:

- In the late 1970s the U.S. economy was reeling from inflationary shocks, record interest rates, energy crises, and anemic economic growth, but between 1975 and 1980 PABCO expenditures grew 60 percent, from $44 billion to $70 billion.

- In the early 1980s the U.S. experienced the most severe economic recession in half a century, with many industries experiencing depression-level problems, but between 1980 and 1985 PABCO spending increased by $19 billion—27 percent.

While spending on pollution control grew substantially across all environmental media over the past two decades, the distribution of spending shifted significantly among media control programs:

- In 1970 spending for the control of water pollution accounted for 35 percent of the total; in 1991 it represented 42 percent of PABCO expenditures.

- In 1970 spending for the control of air pollution accounted for 29 percent of the total; in 1991 it represented 27 percent of PABCO expenditures.

- In 1970 spending for the control of land pollution accounted for 35 percent of the total; in 1991 it represented 28 percent of PABCO expenditures.

Table 6
Chemical Pollution Control Expenditures in the United States, 1975-1991
(millions of 1991 dollars)

	1975	1980	1985	1991
Chemical Pollution Control, Total	$217	$1,067	$928	$2,262
Federally Mandated	217	1,067	928	2,262
Toxic Substances	6	515	364	959
Federally Mandated	6	515	364	959
EPA	6	95	104	173
Federal (Non-EPA)	-	325	139	166
Local Govt.	-	-	-	436
Private	-	95	121	185
Pesticides	211	553	564	1,302
Federally Mandated	211	553	564	1,302
EPA	43	83	70	73
Federal (Non-EPA)	-	17	11	10
State Govt.	1	28	22	25
Private	168	426	461	1,194

Source: Management Information Services, Inc., Washington, D.C., 1991.
Additional detail available upon request.

Table 7
Multi-Media[a] Pollution Control Expenditures in the United States, 1975-1991
(millions of 1991 dollars)

	1975	1980	1985	1991
Multi-Media Pollution Control, Total	$704	$1,042	$824	$2,394
Management and Support (EPA)	152	257	325	454
Energy (EPA)	52	220	52	29
Interdisciplinary (EPA)	41	44	67	151
Undesignated (Federal, Non-EPA)	461	521	379	661
EPCRA [b]	-	-	-	1,099
Local Govt.	-	-	-	46
Private	-	-	-	1,054

[a] Includes costs that cannot be specifically allocated to a specific medium.
[b] Emergency Planning and Community Right to Know Act

Source: Management Information Services, Inc., Washington, D.C., 1991.
Additional detail available upon request.

- In 1970 spending for chemical and for multi-media pollution control were negligible; in 1991 they each represented about two percent of the total.

Even as spending on all media increased rapidly, there have been notable shifts within media as well, as illustrated in Table 2. These reflect shifting national priorities and indicate the dynamic nature of the business opportunities involved:

- In the control of air pollution, proportionately more money has been devoted to mobile sources, reflecting increasing concern with automobile pollution.

- In water pollution control, spending for drinking water programs has increased most rapidly, but still comprises only ten percent of the total water pollution control market.

- In controlling land pollution, there has been phenomenal growth in spending for the control of hazardous wastes and for the Superfund program. Expenditures for hazardous waste control programs increased from virtually nothing in 1980 to $7 billion in 1991—almost 20 percent of the total. Superfund spending increased from a negligible amount in 1985 to $2.4 billion in 1991— seven percent of the total.

- Spending for chemical pollution control has been increasing the most rapidly and consistently for two decades, from $200 million in 1975 to $2.3 billion in 1991.

Tables 2 through 7 also illustrate the importance of the different funding sources for the PABCO expenditures and the pervasive nature of federal mandates. The federal government usually enacts the legislation, sets the standards, and mandates the spending, but it is private industry and state and local governments that actually have to spend the money to achieve the desired environmental goals. This dichotomy between the source of the mandates and the source of the funding has important implications for public policy and, more importantly, for emerging business and marketing opportunities for private industry.

Thus, for example, all air pollution control spending is mandated by federal law, but almost none of it is directly financed by the federal government. In 1991, of the $35 billion expended to abate air pollution, private industry spent $10 billion and state and local governments funded most of the rest.

Table 8
1991 Employment Created by Pollution Abatement and Control Expenditures
(thousands of jobs)

Manufacturing, Total	1,337
Textile and Apparel	33
Chemical & Petroleum Products	208
Fabricated Metal Products	67
Machinery	182
Transportation Equipment	94
Other Manufacturing	748
Agriculture, Forestry & Fisheries	87
Mining	226
Construction	130
Transportation, Communications and Utilities	563
Wholesale and Retail Trade	261
Finance, Insurance, Real Estate	84
Services	396
Government (Federal, state, local)	385
TOTAL, ALL SECTORS	3,469

Source: Management Information Services, Inc., 1991. Additional detail available upon request.

For controlling water pollution in 1991, federal laws will mandate $49 billion out of the $54 billion total. Of the $54 billion, private industry will pay $22 billion and state and local governments will pay most of the rest.

On the other hand, for programs to control land pollution in 1991, federal legislation will mandate only about $25 billion of $36 billion. However, local governments will fund $9 billion in programs, and private industry will pay most of the remaining costs—the federal government and the state governments will pay little of these expenses.

Similarly, all of the $2.3 billion that MISI estimates will be paid to control chemical pollution in 1991 is federally mandated. However, the federal government will directly pay only $400 million of these costs, private industry will pay $1.4 billion, and local governments will pay $400 million.

The Current (1991) Size and Structure of the Industry

If "PABCO" were a corporation, in 1991 it would rank at the top of the Fortune 500:

- We estimate that in 1991 PABCO expenditures will total $129 billion.

- In 1990 General Motors, which was ranked by Fortune as the largest U.S. industrial corporation, had sales of $126 billion.

- In 1990 the number two U.S. industrial corporation, Exxon, had sales of $108 billion, while the third-ranked corporation, Ford Motor Co., had sales of $98 billion.[5]

Clearly, providing the goods and services required for environmental protection has become a major U.S. industry with

---

5 The source of the data on U.S. industrial corporations is *Fortune,* Vol. 123, No. 8 (April 22, 1991).

Table 9
Jobs and Sales Created in Each State in 1991
by Pollution Abatement and Control Expenditures

State	Jobs (thousands)	Sales (billions)	State	Jobs (thousands)	Sales (billions)
Alabama	62	$2.1	Montana	8	$0.3
Alaska	7	0.3	Nebraska	23	0.7
Arizona	44	1.6	Nevada	13	0.5
Arkansas	30	1.0	New Hampshire	16	0.6
California	424	15.7	New Jersey	122	4.8
Colorado	63	2.2	New Mexico	16	0.6
Connecticut	64	2.4	New York	270	10.5
Delaware	9	0.3	North Carolina	91	2.9
District of Columbia	9	0.3	North Dakota	9	0.3
Florida	145	5.2	Ohio	130	6.2
Georgia	83	2.8	Oklahoma	43	1.6
Hawaii	13	0.5	Oregon	42	1.4
Idaho	13	0.4	Pennsylvania	121	7.1
Illinois	123	5.7	Rhode Island	15	0.5
Indiana	79	2.9	South Carolina	43	1.3
Iowa	39	1.3	South Dakota	9	0.3
Kansas	28	1.1	Tennessee	72	2.4
Kentucky	40	1.4	Texas	239	8.1
Louisiana	50	1.9	Utah	23	0.7
Maine	15	0.5	Vermont	8	0.3
Maryland	64	1.8	Virginia	109	4.1
Massachusetts	109	3.8	Washington	67	2.5
Michigan	165	5.9	West Virgiania	38	1.2
Minnesota	70	2.3	Wisconsin	70	2.6
Mississippi	30	1.0	Wyoming	25	1.0
Missouri	67	2.3			
			Total	3,469	$129.0

Source: Management Information Services, Inc., 1991.
Additional detail available upon request.

significant effects on the economy and labor market. In 1991 we estimate that PABCO expenditures of $129 billion will generate:

- $270 billion in total industry sales

- $22 billion in corporate profits

- 3.5 million jobs

- $76 billion in federal, state, and local government tax revenues

Table 8 illustrates that in 1991 PABCO spending created about 3.5 million jobs, including 1.3 million jobs in manufacturing.

This represents about three percent of total 1991 employment, and more than five percent of total 1991 manufacturing employment.

Table 9 shows the geographic distribution among the states of the total sales and jobs created by 1991 PABCO spending. It is seen that these are spread widely among the states, significantly impacting every region of the nation.

Prospects for the Future

As indicated in Table 10, PABCO is forecast to continue to be a rapidly growing, "recession proof" industry well into the next century, offering unique entrepreneurial and profit opportunities throughout the economy for all types of businesses. MISI forecasts that real expenditures (1991 dollars) will increase from $129 billion in 1991 to:

- $160 billion in 1995

- $195 billion in 2000

- $239 billion in 2005

Throughout 2005 spending on PABCO will continue to increase substantially faster than the rate of growth of GNP, although the rate of growth will decline from seven percent in the late 1980s to about three-to-four percent annually by the early years of the next decade. Thus, PABCO expenditures as a percent of GNP will continue to gradually increase, reaching 2.6 percent of GNP in 1995 (2.8 percent in 2000, and 3.1 percent by 2005. The growing significance of the magnitude of PABCO expenditures is not fully appreciated:

- By the early years of the next century—within about ten years—PABCO expenditures will equal and then exceed the nation's spending on national defense.

In 1991 the Department of Defense budget was $292 billion and accounted for 4.9 percent of GNP. Under the Administration's

Table 10
Forecast Pollution Control Expenditures in the United States, 1991-2005
(millions of 1991 dollars)

	1991	1995	2000	2005
Pollution Abatement and Control, Total	$129,064	$160,112	$194,900	$239,435
Air Pollution Control	34,806	44,990	55,259	72,780
Stationary Sources	25,404	31,426	38,070	48,473
Mobile Sources	9,042	13,316	16,968	24,021
Undesgnated Sources	361	248	221	286
Radiation Pollution Control	580	791	1,075	1,418
Water Pollution Control	53,695	64,252	76,960	90,473
Water Quality	48,984	57,832	69,076	80,655
Drinking Water	4,711	6,420	7,885	9,818
Land Pollution Control	35,704	44,590	55,378	67,125
RCRA [a]	33,155	38,962	45,666	56,120
Solid Waste	21,703	24,406	26,762	32,976
Hazardous Waste	6,992	11,052	14,474	18,014
UST [b]	4,459	3,504	4,429	5,103
Superfund [c]	2,549	5,628	9,712	11,332
Chemical Pollution Control	1,885	2,967	3,470	4,463
Toxic Substances	799	1,343	1,481	2,145
Pesticides	1,085	1,624	1,990	2,318
Multi-Media Pollution Control [d]	2,394	2,522	2,758	3,176

[a] Resource Conservation and Recovery Act
[b] Underground Storage Tanks
[c] Comprehensive Environmental Response, Compensation, and Liability Act
[d] Includes costs that cannot be specifically allocated to a specific medium.

Source: Management Information Services, Inc., Washington, D.C., 1991.
Additional detail available upon request.

scenario, 1993 defense spending will be (in 1991 dollars) about $275 billion, or about 4.3 percent of GNP.[6] Given present trends—the end of cold war, continuing strategic and conventional arms limitations agreements, the disintegration of the Soviet Union,

---

6 These estimates were obtained from the Budget of the United States Government, Fiscal Year 1991, U.S. Government Printing Office, 1990.

reductions in the size of the armed forces, etc., for the foreseeable future Pentagon spending will continue to decline in real terms (1991 dollars) and as a percentage of GNP: to $255 billion in 1995, $210 billion in 2000 and about $190-$200 billion by 2005.[7] Thus, in about ten years PABCO expenditures will equal—and then exceed—national defense spending.

This is truly a momentous development deserving of some reflection. Over the past four decades intense interest has focused on the economic impacts of defense spending on the economy, the effect of this spending on business, the jobs created, and related issues. An entire economic sector was created and nurtured—as were many large and profitable companies and millions of jobs—for more than forty years. Within about a decade this "engine" of the economy will (for better or for worse) be eclipsed by the PABCO industry. The implications of this dramatic shift in national priorities and in the allocation of societal resources are profound and pervasive.

At least as important for future marketing and business prospects, PABCO represents a growing industry, in terms of absolute spending, real dollars, and percent of GNP, whereas defense spending is a "declining industry" and will remain so indefinitely. During the 1990s traditional defense-oriented corporations will be fighting over a shrinking pie as Pentagon

---

7 The U.S. Office of Technology Assessment expects defense spending to decline to 3.8 percent of GNP in 1996, and by the turn of the century we anticipate that it will decrease to about three percent of GNP. See U.S. Office of Technology Assessment, *Redesigning Defense: Planning the Transition to the Future U.S. Defense Industrial Base*, Washington, D.C., 1991. The Electronics Industries Association, whose periodic forecasts of defense spending are widely respected for their accuracy, predicts an even sharper decline to $200 billion (1991 dollars) in 2000. See Electronics Industries Association, *Defense Electronics Market Ten-Year Forecast: U.S. Department of Defense and National Aeronautics and Space Administration Budgets, FY 1991-FY 2000*, Washington, D.C., October 1990.

spending gradually declines, while at the same time spending to control and abate pollution will be growing about twice as fast as GNP. The implications of these trends are obvious for astute entrepreneurs and corporate executives.

The distribution of PABCO spending over the next two decades will shift:

- By 2005 spending for air pollution control will represent 30 percent of the total, compared to 27 percent in 1991, reflecting (in part) the implementation of the provisions of the Clean Air Act Amendments of 1990.

- In 2005 water pollution control expenditures will represent 38 percent of the total, as opposed to 42 percent in 1991.

- Spending for land pollution control will remain at 28 percent, chemical pollution control spending will remain at two percent, and expenditures for multi-media control programs will decrease to about one percent of total PABCO spending.

The PABCO spending priorities will also shift within the media categories:

- Among air pollution abatement programs, spending on mobile source (cars and trucks) control will increase the most rapidly, from $9 billion in 1991 (26 percent of total air pollution control spending in 1991) to $24 billion (33 percent of the total) in 2005.

- Spending to enhance the quality of drinking water will increase rapidly (reflecting SDWA legislation enacted during the late 1980s), from $4.7 billion annually in 1991 (nine percent of total water pollution control spending) to $9.8 billion (11 percent of the total) in 2005.

- Expenditures on the Superfund program (CERCLA) will increase dramatically, from $2.5 billion per year in 1991 (seven percent of land pollution control spending) to $11.3 billion in 2005 (20 percent of the total).

- Spending for the control of hazardous wastes will increase nearly three-fold, from $7 billion in 1991 (20 percent of total land pollution costs) to $18 billion per year by 2005 (27 percent of the total).

- Expenditures for chemical pollution abatement programs will more than double, from $1.9 billion in 1991 to $4.5 billion in 2005.

The business and profit opportunities represented by these and related trends illustrated in Table 5 are clear, and some of these are discussed in greater detail below.

Major Emerging Environmental Issues and Business Opportunities During the 1990s

The Clean Air Act of 1990

The Clean Air Act Amendments of 1990 represent the most significant recent environmental legislation and will drive environmental policy for the next two decades.[8] MISI estimates that this legislation alone will result in additional environmental expenditures of at least $15-$20 billion annually through 2010. The major sections of the Amendments pertain to: the attainment and maintenance of ambient air quality standards, mobile sources, air toxics, acid deposition control, permits, and enforcement and reauthorization.

The act will have a major economic impact on private industry throughout the 1990s and well into the 21st century. The

---

8 Clean Air Act P.L. 88-206, December 17, 1963; last amended November 15, 1990.

estimated costs vary widely, between $15 billion and $30 billion per year for the next two decades. The figure which the White House is using (which MISI feels is accurate) is approximately $20 billion per year. However, industry sources have developed much higher estimates of annual compliance costs. For example, the Clean Air Working Group claims that by the late 1990s the act could be costing the economy between $60 and $65 billion per year.[9] There is general agreement that the major cost of the legislation will arise from the sections covering mobile sources, air toxics, and acid deposition.

The mobile source provisions will add additional layers of regulations and requirements to all aspects of the motor vehicle industry, and by the mid-1990s will result in additional spending of between $2 and $4 billion per year. Consider just the alternative fuels section: vehicles using alternative fuels will cost about $500 to $1,000 more per unit, the costs to modify existing petroleum refining facilities for methanol and reformulated gasoline could exceed $2 billion by 1995, and the cost to each service station to convert to a methanol capability will be $50,000 to $100,000 per station. Note that the alternative fuels Section is only one of two dozen in the mobile sources section of the bill.

The air toxics portion of the bill covers about 200 chemicals released by many industries, and its effect will be ubiquitous throughout the economy, significantly influencing everything from the corner dry cleaners and service stations to the largest steel mills and factories. Estimates of the cost of this range as high as $10 billion during the 1990s. However, this estimate could easily be low by a factor of five or more, since the regulations for

---

9 Clean Air Act Legislation: House/Senate Side-By-Side Comparison, report prepared for the Clean Air Working Group by Denny Technical Services, 1990.

most of these chemicals remain to be written and more toxic chemicals will undoubtedly be identified.

There is little doubt that the acid deposition section of the act will be very costly, for it will radically affect every fossil-fuel electric power plant and industrial/commercial boiler in the country. MISI has extensively analyzed the costs and benefits of the acid rain provisions and estimates that these will cost the economy between $6 billion and $9 billion per year for the next 20 years.[10] The industries affected the most include electric utilities, heavy industrial processes, chemicals, petroleum refining, coal mining, and iron and steel manufacturing.

The acid deposition section of the bill is notable for another reason: it will revolutionize the conduct of U.S. environmental policy, moving it from an engineering "command and control" approach to a free market approach. The emissions trading mechanism it establishes will result in more cost effective, efficient achievement of environmental goals. It will also result in the creation of a new $6 billion per year industry in marketable pollution allowances—see Section VI.H below.

Nuclear Waste Cleanup at DOD/DOE Facilities

The appropriate handling, transportation, storage, disposal, and cleanup of the nuclear wastes which have been generated over the past half-century by the nation's nuclear weapons program will be a major environmental issue during the 1990s and beyond. The estimated costs of this remediation continue to escalate, and MISI forecasts that the costs will be in the range of $200 billion for 10,000 contaminated sites over the next three decades, including:

---

10 See Wendling and Bezdek, Ibid., and James H. Easterly, "Acid Rain Legislation Could Drain U.S. Utilities," Modern Power Systems, November 1987, pp. 18-25.

- $70 billion to $130 billion for environmental restoration at inactive sites.

- $60-$70 billion to dispose of radioactive wastes.

- $30-$40 billion to decontaminate and decommission unused facilities.

- $10-$20 billion to bring facilities up to compliance with existing environmental laws.

Several billion dollars to begin this work has already been approved by Congress, and the projected expenditures rapidly escalate in the out-years.

Hazardous Wastes

The handling and disposal of hazardous wastes will remain a major environmental issue during the 1990s. RCRA mandates have historically concerned "cradle to grave" monitoring, but legislative efforts in the future will focus primarily on solid waste and stress mandatory recycling as the way to deal with this growing problem. At present there are about 4,700 land disposal, incinerator, and treatment storage facilities that fall within RCRA authority.

Estimating costs to industry of hazardous waste disposal is very difficult. The costs of one proposed EPA rule change alone is up to $50 billion over the next ten years, while another would impose a $7.50 per ton fee on the use of virgin materials in a variety of products, including plastics, paper, batteries, and packaging material. The revenues generated by this fee would be placed in a trust fund to assist states in hazardous and solid waste management.

The direction of future legislation is clear: mandate the recycling and treatment of wastes before they get to dumpsites. Remediation and recovery is already a $7 billion per year industry and will likely grow rapidly as it is emphasized more.

MISI estimates that control of hazardous wastes will be a $11 billion a year industry by 1995 and a $14 billion a year industry at the turn of the century.

Another important area related to RCRA—not Superfund—is that of underground storage tanks for petroleum products. There are two million such tanks at 750,000 sites regulated under RCRA by EPA rules. Owners have until 1998 to bring these into compliance, including adequate tank corrosion protection. The estimated costs to do so range from $10 billion to $40 billion; MISI estimates that annual expenditures for this purpose will total $3.5 billion in 1995 and $4.4 billion by 2000.

Effective monitoring and testing of all wastes and sites is crucial for the successful operation of any RCRA program, as those who wish to operate these sites will need this information. It should be noted that the costs of corrective actions at a RCRA site will often equal or exceed those required at a Superfund site.

Superfund

Between 1980 and 1990 $10.1 billion was spent under the original 1980 Superfund legislation and SARA.[11] This figure will be greatly exceeded in the coming decade: The 1991 Superfund-related costs total $2.5 billion, by the mid-1990s they will total nearly $6 billion annually, and by 2000 MISI estimates that Superfund cleanup expenditures will likely approach $10 billion per year.

There are currently more than 1,200 toxic waste sites on the National Priorities List, and an additional 9,000 have been identified which may be added during the 1990s. The total cleanup

---

11 Comprehensive Environmental Response, Compensation and Liability Act--Superfund (P.L. 96-510); Superfund Amendments and Reauthorization Act (P.L. 99-499).

costs for all of these sites could total $500 billion over the next three decades.

One of the most difficult problems with the Superfund program is determining what constitutes permanent and effective cleanup. The technologies involved are changing rapidly, and more sites are constantly being discovered and identified. Three major cleanup technologies exist: Mobil/incineration ($100-$2,000 per ton), bio-remediation ($50-$250 per ton), and separation technology and chemical fixations.

Public Water Systems

There are 200,000 water systems in the U.S., including 60,000 systems for year-around residents. The Water Quality Act Safe Drinking Water Act Amendments of 1986 greatly strengthened requirements for establishing and enforcing new regulations.[12] The net effect of the 1986 Amendments is that the nation's water supply system will have to spend an additional $2-$4 billion per year, every year between 1991 and 2000, in capital outlays for water treatment. At present, total capital outlays for water treatment are only $1.5 billion annually. Annual outlays may thus have to triple over the next decade and will likely exceed the total spent during the previous half-century.

MISI estimates that annual expenditures for safe drinking water programs will increase from $4.7 billion in 1991 to nearly $10 billion by 2000.

Asbestos Remediation

Asbestos containment and removal is mandated by both OSHA and EPA regulations. MISI has analyzed this issue and determined that by 1991 asbestos remediation has become a large and rapidly growing industry with annual revenues of exceeding two billion dollars. There are between 600,000 and 800,000 non-

---

12 Safe Drinking Water Act (P.L. 93-523).

residential buildings in the U.S. constructed prior to 1980 that have an asbestos problem. It is becoming increasingly difficult for these buildings to be sold or leased without the problem being solved, while federal and state laws mandate the removal in schools and other public buildings.

The total costs to remedy this problem (estimated on the basis of laws already on the books) is likely to be $100 billion to $125 billion over the next two decades. MISI estimates that by the mid-1990s the annual revenues of the "asbestos remediation" industry will total $4-$6 billion.

Municipal Solid Waste Management

The management and disposal of the nation's 175 million tons of annual municipal solid waste (MSW) is already a $16 billion per year industry which has been growing inexorably. Landfilling is the most common disposal method, but EPA estimates that 80 percent of all landfills currently in operation will be closed within 20 years. This is not as serious a problem as it might seem, since the average life of a MSW landfill is only between ten and 15 years. Nevertheless, many areas of the country are experiencing shortfalls of permitted landfill capacity and rapidly rising landfill costs and tipping fees.

The real problem is that new landfills are not being developed at anywhere near the required rates, and landfill capacity is declining because:

- Older landfills are reaching the end of their expected lives.

- Environmental restrictions are being tightened by state and local governments.

- Siting new landfills is increasingly difficult due to public opposition.

The alternatives are not promising. Waste-to-energy facilities—seen as a panacea a decade ago—have not generally proven to be economically viable and suffer from technical problems. Incineration—also once thought to be the main alternative to landfilling—is being increasingly restricted by air pollution control legislation at all levels of government. Ocean dumping is also being increasingly restricted.

The alternatives for the 1990s include the development of new technological processes, but will primarily rely on recycling and on better management and control of MSW. The monitoring of existing and new landfills will become increasingly important, to better utilize the facilities, to establish efficient materials management, and to develop secondary markets for the separated and recycled products.

MISI forecasts that the MSW management and disposal industry will continue to grow throughout the 1990s, reaching $24 billion annually by 1995 and totalling $27 billion per year by 2000.

Emissions Brokering

One of the most significant features of the Clean Air Act Amendments of 1990 is the establishment of an emissions trading system to control acid rain more efficiently and less expensively. MISI estimates that this free market approach will be 25 percent to 30 percent less expensive in achieving the same acid rain abatement and control as the traditional, inefficient engineering/regulatory approach followed for the past three decades.

Thus, in a major departure from "command and control" approaches, the CAA establishes a system of marketable allowances that will give utilities great flexibility to comply with SO_2 emissions reductions. EPA will allocate the allowances to utility plants that burn fossil fuels according to formulas specified in the legislation, and is directed to develop a list of allowances to be allocated by December 31, 1992. The act establishes an allowance tracking system that will include a continuous emission monitoring system to sample, analyze, measure, and provide on a continuous basis a permanent record of emissions and flow.

Each emission allowance (EA) is a federal permit to emit one ton of SO_2 per year. If a utility's emissions exceed the allowances available, it will be in violation and subject to a penalty of $2,000 per ton of excess emissions. The utility must offset the excess emissions the following year.

No utility will be subject to any penalty for exceeding its allowances for a given calendar year until that year has ended, when all transfers of allowances applicable for that year have been completed. Allowances are annual, and thus temporary increases or decreases in emissions within utility systems or power pools do not require allowance transfers or recordation so long as the total tonnage emitted in any year matches allowances held for that year. Utilities, must, therefore, "true up" at year end to ensure that the allowances match emissions for each unit.[13]

Utilities that reduce their emissions below required levels can bank the excess allowances for future use, or sell them directly to other utilities. To ensure that the allowance market system works, that utilities do not "hoard" allowances, and to make allowances available to new units, the act contains both auction and direct sale provisions.

EPA will reserve 150,000 allowances (2.8 percent of the 5.3 million allowances available) during Phase I, and 250,00

---

13 See the analysis of emission trading in Management Infor-mation Services, Inc., and Management Analysis Co., *The Effect of the Clean Air Act Amendments on the Need for Reviving the Nuclear Energy Option*, prepared for the American Nuclear Energy Council, 1991.

allowances (2.8 percent of the 8.9 million available allowances) for each year of Phase II, and will be required to sell these reserved allowances to the highest bidder. For utilities wishing to sell their allowances directly, the bill establishes a direct sale price at $1,500 per ton.

In sum, the act creates a market in pollution futures. This market mechanism gives utilities incentives to invest not only in future generating capacity, but also in future pollution abatement capacity. This section of the act will create unique opportunities for private industry.

In Phase I of the act (1995-2000) the value of the EAs to be sold/traded will be $5 billion to $10 billion annually. Even for a modest sized start-up firm, annual revenues could quickly reach $20 million to $40 million, under the conservative assumptions that only 20 percent of the EAs are traded, commission rates are 20 percent, and a market share of 10 percent is achieved.

The market will grow rapidly. Since the volume of the EAs is fixed, they will gradually acquire a scarcity value, and their value will increase as U.S. metropolitan areas are forced to meet the standards of the CAA and as additional environmental legislation is enacted.

The small current market in pollutant brokering is growing more than 30 percent per year. At present, the competition is limited, but this will change in the near future as major companies like Kidder, Peabody and Company enter the market. In July 1991 the Chicago Board of Trade voted to create a private market in EAs, thus creating the world's first sophisticated market in pollution credit futures.

Chapter 10

Insurance Coverage for Environmental Risks

Ronald M. Oster & Grace A. Carter
Paul, Hastings, Janofsky & Walker

Introduction

As the scope of environmental liabilities expands, businesses are turning increasingly to insurance coverage as a potential means of limiting their ultimate exposure. Of course, preventive strategies, such as waste reduction and compliance monitoring, can limit a company's liability for known environmental hazards. But the burgeoning number of newly discovered hazards, as well as the growing liability for latent hazards, make it impossible to manage every environmental risk.

Insurance coverage is one means of shifting the risk of liability to an entity which received premiums in exchange for accepting just such risks. The average company faced with environmental claims or potential claims is pursuing coverage on two fronts: (1) negotiating for increased coverage in current policies, and (2) maximizing the coverage still available from policies issued years earlier.

In response, insurance companies have become more reluctant either to assume additional environmental risks in new policies or to accept liability for such risks in earlier policies. The actual and potential environmental liabilities for insurers dwarf any of their other large exposures in recent years, including the claims arising from toxic torts, pharmaceuticals and asbestos. Insurers contend that taking on the aggregate of the "bet your company" environmental liabilities faced by their individual corporate insureds could soon become a "bet your insurance industry" problem.

Yet, absent an unlikely governmental bailout, the insurance industry is probably the best positioned of all affected parties in the 1990s to spread the risk of the massive environmental liabilities. Given its traditional function as a "spreader of risk," and the breadth of the coverage provided in the last thirty years, the insurance industry should accept its responsibility for the environmental problem. The industry should pay for the environmental harm for which insureds are being held legally liable, and insurers should charge their insureds a premium commensurate with the true magnitude of the responsibility. Finally, the corporate insureds should pass on that premium charge, in the form of increased prices for their products and services, so as to spread the risk throughout society in the same way that companies have spread the cost of product liability judgments. While the environmental problem is larger than any other exposure faced by insurers or insureds in recent years, the problem is susceptible to many of the same solutions applied to similar exposures in the past.

The next section analyzes some of the trends affecting environmental coverage, both in American business generally, and in the insurance industry. It is followed by a review of the insured's strategies for maximizing coverage under both current and older policies, and the insurer's counter-strategies designed to limit liability. The final section presents a blueprint for the long-over-due "greening" of the insurance industry.

Trends Affecting Environmental Coverage

Trend No. 1: *The ever-expanding discovery of environmental harms due to advances in scientific research and increased public awareness means that preventive environmental programs alone will not protect a company from environmental liability.*

The last 10 years have seen an enormous growth in awareness as to the number and magnitude of potential environmental hazards. In the 1970s and early 1980s, a company which neither produced large amounts of hazardous wastes nor polluted the air with known contaminants could be relatively certain of limiting its environmental liabilities through a compliance and monitoring program. During the last several years, however, a number of "new" environmental hazards have come to the forefront, many of them arising out of activities previously believed to be innocuous.

The recent controversy over electromagnetic fields (EMF) is a case in point. Electric utilities, cogeneration facilities, and other producers of electricity are increasingly subject to claims by individuals and property owners concerning exposure to EMF. These claimants assert that their proximity to electrical lines or substations is responsible for causing a wide variety of ills, ranging from emotional distress to cancer, as well as reduction in property values. Similar controversies over exposures to radon, irradiated food, video display terminals and indoor pollution emphasize the newly found hazards seemingly inherent in everyday activities. As scientists and researchers are progressively able to pinpoint the causes of disease apparently attributable to commonly used substances, the companies which sell or generate those substances are finding themselves increasingly targeted as the parties responsible for the injuries (whether real or speculative) that allegedly result.

Even more widespread are the latent liabilities arising out of recently discovered contamination due to long-buried hazardous wastes. Thus, in addition to the obvious need to minimize air, water and surface pollution, companies are faced with the need to avoid causing unknown and perhaps unknowable hazards. Even the most careful and prudent environmental strategy, standing alone, cannot insulate a company from such liability—given the discovery of new harms from activities which were previously presumed "safe."

Trend No. 2: *The legal system responds to advances in scientific research and public awareness of hazards by expanding the scope of environmental liabilities and the number of potentially responsible actors (risk spreading).*

In the area of product liability, which is the closest analogue to the current environmental liability situation, the legal system over the past thirty years has greatly expanded the responsibility of even the most careful corporate actors. Under the laws in effect until the middle of the twentieth century, manufacturers of products were liable only for those defects and harms that were due to the manufacturer's negligence. This fault-based system worked relatively well in a less complex society, but became outdated when large quantities of mass-produced goods entered the marketplace.

A shift from fault-based liability to a system of "strict" liability was the result of this change. Under strict liability, the manufacturer can be held legally liable for harm caused by a product defect, without regard to any fault on the manufacturer's part. This system was intended, in large part, to place the risk of damages due to injuries on the party who was best able both to prevent the defect and to spread the cost of harm resulting from that defect. Because the companies producing manufactured goods were increasingly large and capable of passing the costs of any liability on to the mass consumers who purchased their products, courts viewed manufacturers as the entities best-suited to "spread the risk" of defective or harmful products. In fact, the existence of liability insurance for manufacturers has been a major factor cited by several courts in imposing strict liability on manufacturers (and ultimately their insurers) for product defects.

Environmental liability has followed the same evolutionary pattern of strict liability. Until the last twenty years, legal remedies applicable to pollution damage were rooted in traditional common law notions of negligence and causation. However, Congress passed a series of laws, including the original Superfund law in 1980 (the Comprehensive Environmental Response, Compensation, and Liability Act or CERCLA), which increasingly removed the element of "fault" from environmental liabilities. First, a company could be held liable for damage to natural resources even if the company had complied with then-existing federal and state laws, and even if every known preventive measure had been taken. Second, a company could be held liable even if its only involvement with the contaminated property was as an owner, and even if the actual contamination was caused by another party, such as a lessee or a previous owner.

This system of strict liability for environmental damage, without regard to fault, has led to a massive expansion in the enforcement activities of the Environmental Protection Agency (EPA) and similar state and local agencies. Freed from the need to show negligence in every case, the EPA has been able to bring massive Superfund actions against hundreds of companies and to extract millions of dollars in cleanup costs. The expansion of environmental liabilities has, in turn, led companies to turn to their insurers for assistance in paying for the enormous costs imposed by the government, as well as private parties.

Trend No. 3: *Although the insurance industry historically has responded to a growth in the size and number of claims by paying them and spreading the cost throughout society, more recently insurers have responded to mushrooming environmental claims by attempting to cut losses through narrow interpretations of existing coverage and by refusing to issue any new coverage for such claims.*

Traditionally, the insurance industry has responded to an increase in the number of large claims in a given area by following the time-honored rules of insurance underwriting: when losses go up, the insurer makes up those losses by raising premiums and using investment income generated by those premiums to keep the insurance company solvent until the losses diminish. When the losses are large, the insurer may raise premiums not just for the insured (or category of insureds) responsible for the losses, but for a broad spectrum of other insureds as well.

Because of the sizeable number of individuals and companies insured by a given insurer, the premium increase may be relatively minor for each insured. The system has a built-in mechanism to prevent excessive increases in premiums: If the premiums rise too far or too fast, insureds will turn to other insurers charging lower premiums, will self-insure either individually or through the formation of insurance mutuals, or, as a last resort, will go without insurance.

In the 1980s many of the usual rules changed. As the large drug and toxic tort claims—including those related to DES, Dalkon Shield, and, particularly, asbestos—staggered the insurance industry, the insurers responded not only by raising premiums, but also by issuing blanket exclusions or by refusing to insure certain risks at any price.

A similar pattern has emerged during the 1990s regarding insurance for environmental claims. The only difference is that the stakes are even larger. While asbestos claims and most drug claims affect only a segment of industry, the environmental problems affect virtually every company that either manufactures products, or that buys or sells real estate, or that acquires a company that has engaged in these activities. The EPA has estimated that by the year 2000, the combined environmental cleanup efforts of industry and government will cost over $200 billion per year. Given that there are thousands of companies being pursued by the EPA and other agencies for large and small contamination liabilities, and given that nearly every company was insured at one time or another under a general liability policy that potentially covers those claims, the insurance industry has, perhaps understandably, adopted a siege mentality.

But the insurance industry's response to the expansion of environmental claims may have become an overreaction. Many, if not most, insurers have insisted on inserting exclusions in their policies for pollution liabilities. According to the insurers, the latest versions of these provisions now expressly exclude any coverage for any contamination or pollution claims. Under traditional insurance underwriting practices, such "absolute" pollution exclusions would be difficult to justify. The reason is that if nearly every company has the potential for environmental liabilities, and if such companies are concerned about the potential for environmental claims, then many insureds would probably be willing to pay increased premiums (and in some cases, greatly increased premiums) for the security of knowing those claims were covered. Yet many insurers currently are not offering coverage for environmental risks.

Strategies for Maximizing Environmental Coverage

The most obvious solution for an insured facing increased liabilities—to buy more insurance—is generally not available in the environmental context due to the current insurance industry retrenchment. However, the insurance industry is cyclical; when the environmental risk can be better defined, limited and "rated," or in effect understood by the insurance industry, the insurers probably will return to the market and begin offering insurance more widely for these risks.

Meanwhile, until the market for new environmental coverage rebounds, an insured's primary source of coverage will be existing or older policies. The average business in the 1990s will still find it more profitable to pursue insurers for coverage under older policies than to expect coverage under policies being issued today or in the future.

Why do insurance policies written 15, 20 or even 30 years ago provide coverage for environmental claims brought against a company today? The answer lies buried in the wording of the typical comprehensive general liability (CGL) policy issued to most corporate insureds until approximately 1985. The standard form CGL policy provided insurance for an "occurrence" of bodily injury or property damage which takes place during the policy period. An "occurrence" has been interpreted to include anything from the initial deposit of waste, to the contamination of the natural resource, to discovery of the damage caused by the contamination.

Thus, the policy can be triggered by any of a number of events that may have taken place many years ago but have only recently led to a claim. Some courts have ruled that all of the policies from first deposit of waste through discovery of the damage are triggered. It is important, then, to assume that *every* policy from the first deposit of waste through discovery of the damage will potentially apply.

Another cardinal rule is to examine all potential types of coverage. The above discussion focuses on bodily injury and property damage coverage under the "occurrence" provision in the standard CGL policy, but other provisions may likewise provide coverage. For example, the "personal injury" provision in the CGL policy may provide coverage where the claimant alleges trespass, nuisance or other wrongful entry of hazardous substances onto the property.

In addition, some companies purchased Environmental Impairment Liability (EIL) policies designed specifically to cover environmental risks. Finally, environmental harm to the insured's own property (as opposed to harm caused by the insured's activities which spill over onto the property of others) may be covered under a first-party property policy which also typically covers fire, theft, and similar risks.

The insured must also examine potential sources of coverage purchased by other entities. Insurance policies issued to predecessor companies of the insured, to lessors or lessees of the property, or to other companies in a contractual relationship with the insured may provide an additional source of funds that can be drawn upon to cover the insured's environmental liabilities.

Implementing an Environmental Coverage Strategy

Several key steps must be taken at the earliest possible time to maximize the insured's chances of enforcing the coverage it purchased for environmental liabilities:

- Locate and maintain complete copies of current and older insurance policies, as well as other types of policy evidence (ledger entries, premium payment records, accounting records, claim correspondence with the insurer or broker, and so on). The insured will have the burden in any insurance coverage action of proving the existence and key terms of the policies, and must be able to demonstrate coverage through complete copies of the policies or, if policies are unavailable, through secondary evidence.

- Give notice to the insurers immediately of any environmental claim or potential claim by a governmental agency or private claimant. Even though no lawsuit has yet been filed, a letter from the EPA identifying the company as a Potentially Responsible Party ("PRP letter") may be sufficient to trigger the notice requirements in the insurance policy. In some states, courts have held that delayed notice of a few months or even weeks may cost the insured its right to receive any benefits under the policy. While other states require the insurer to show substantial prejudice from any delayed notice in order to deny coverage, the better practice is to give notice as promptly as possible of any claims.

- Obtain the insurer's commitment to defend the governmental or private party action against the company. Once a lawsuit or administrative proceeding is brought, the insured's first priority must be to enforce the insurer's obligation to defend the suit or pay defense costs on the insured's behalf. In most states, the duty to defend is broader than the duty to pay the claim after a settlement or judgment, and the insurer must defend even if the claimant has very little likelihood of actually recovering against the insured. Because defense costs can sometimes be as financially burdensome as the actual settlement or judgment, the insurer's defense obligation is often the most important benefit of a CGL or other liability policy.

- Consider early settlement negotiations or alternative dispute resolution methods to enforce the insurer's obligations. Despite the insurance industry's "hard line" position in insurance coverage disputes, a coordinated settlement strategy will sometimes persuade the insurer that resolution without the need for costly coverage litigation is in the interests of both the insurer and the insured. Enlisting the help of a mediator or other dispute resolution professional may narrow the issues and lead to an early settlement.

- When the only solution is the filing of a lawsuit to enforce insurance coverage, the insured can save litigation costs and obtain a more favorable result by structuring the coverage suit to maximize coverage. The insured will want to obtain promptly a court order requiring the insurer to defend the underlying environmental case, while reserving certain issues of coverage and potential exclusions until after the underlying case has been resolved. The prospect of an open-ended defense obligation, with little possibility of a quick decision on the coverage itself, will place some pressure on the insurer to come to the bargaining table and attempt to settle with the insured.

Insurer's Counter-Strategy in Environmental Coverage Actions

To understand the insurer's likely counter-strategy in an environmental coverage action, it is important to understand the insurer's perspective derived from the drug, toxic tort and asbestos battles of the late 1970s and early 1980s. When the onslaught of these types of claims began, many insurers were caught off guard and were slow to realize the full import of both the number of claims and the size of the overall problem. Insureds were able, by taking the offensive in coverage actions, to obtain favorable rulings which required the insurers to pay large sums of money under their policies to defend and indemnify their insureds. For example, in the asbestos context, insureds won a number of key cases adopting the "continuous trigger" rule—that is, that every policy from first exposure to asbestos through the manifestation of asbestos-related disease was triggered and every insurer over a period of many years was thus held liable.

In the environmental context, the picture is more complex. The large liability insurers learned their lessons in the asbestos insurance wars and have taken the offensive in the new environmental coverage battles. Examples of this new aggressive posture include the following:

- In many cases, an insurer will file its own environmental coverage action against the policyholder in an attempt to obtain a favorable outcome or to start the action in a state with more pro-insurer coverage rulings. In some cases, insurers have attempted to create favorable judicial precedents by filing actions against policyholders known to have limited financial and legal resources. In other cases, insurers have made settlements on the condition that a judicial decision favorable to policyholders be withdrawn by the court. These efforts to control the development of judicial precedents have been criticized by courts and commentators alike.

- Insurers increasingly seek to enforce exclusions and other restrictions on coverage contained in their policies. For example, the insurers argue that the "pollution exclusion" contained in the standard CGL policy before 1986 allows coverage only if the contamination occurs abruptly and without warning. Because most environmental claims involve gradual pollution damage, occurring over a period of many years without the insured's knowledge, the insurers have sought to reduce drastically the coverage available by giving the clause this narrow reading. The pollution exclusion controversy is only the tip of the proverbial iceberg: many insurers, in responding to an insured's coverage lawsuit, will allege 30 to 40 separate exclusions and other limitations on coverage, and will seek to enforce them all. While insureds have been successful in obtaining court rulings rejecting the insurers' narrow policy interpretations, resolution of the many coverage issues raised by the insurers takes time and money.

- Insurers often attack the policyholder as a deliberate polluter and seek to avoid coverage by claiming that the contamination and resulting damages were "expected or intended" by the policyholder. By portraying their own insureds as unprincipled polluters who lack any regard for the environment, some insurers apparently hope not only to win favor with judges and juries who have undergone their own "greening" transformation, but also to defeat coverage by bringing the insured's conduct within a restriction in the policy. While this tactic may be successful if the insured has deliberately dumped pollutants into a river for many years, it is destined to fail if the insured, like many companies, was disposing of wastes in a manner that was acceptable (and often government-sanctioned) at the time.

The Greening of the Insurance Industry

The recent history of insurance coverage litigation, especially in the asbestos and environmental contexts, demonstrates the ultimate futility of the current battle between insurers and insureds. By taking an increasingly hostile stance, by filing coverage actions in multiple forums on issues previously decided in other states, and by refusing either to admit the possibility of coverage or to settle environmental coverage actions without protracted court battles, the insurance industry has only exacerbated an already difficult situation. The net effect is that both sides—insurers and insureds alike—diminish their resources in a war of attrition in which no ultimate resolution is obtained.

The insurance industry should, instead, begin to recognize its share of responsibility for the environmental risk-spreading taking place in society at large. So long as society has determined to fasten environmental liability on manufacturers and other companies without fault, insurers will not be able to escape their own share of liability which derives from the policies they drafted and the premiums they received. While insurers may be able to exclude coverage for the most egregious conduct by willful polluters, their attempts to evade coverage for contamination arising from commonplace industrial activities should fail.

The greening of the insurance industry is long overdue and may require a major shift in attitudes among both insurers and their policyholders. The outlines of an environmental awareness program for the insurance industry include:

- An increased willingness to work with insureds to resolve both the underlying environmental actions and the coverage disputes that result. Today, most environmental claims give rise to two kinds of disputes on which legal fees and other resources are expended: the environmental claim itself and the insurance lawsuit to decide coverage for the claim. Much of the money spent by insurers to defend the environmental claim and to fight the coverage lawsuit could be profitably used for remediation, cleanup and other measures that would resolve the entire matter more quickly and more cheaply.

- A channeling of the insurance industry's resources into better loss prevention and risk management programs that would benefit both insurers and insureds. The insurance industry, including brokers, insurance companies and industry-wide underwriting groups, has an enormous capacity for gathering knowledge on effective environmental control strategies and for disseminating that knowledge to the bulk of American businesses, their insureds. By working in a partnership with insureds to implement effective compliance, monitoring, and control methods for environmental risks, the insurance industry could become "part of the solution" rather than simply a part of the problem.

• As an outgrowth of better environmental control strate-gies, the insurance industry could begin to return to its traditional function as the ultimate risk-spreading entity by re-entering the environmental insurance market. Rather than simply fleeing the environmental problem by issuing policies absolutely excluding pollu-tion-related claims, the industry could, for example, limit coverage to situations where (a) the insured has followed an acceptable environmental risk manage-ment program, subject to review and site assessment by the insurer; and (b) the insured has been sued or otherwise notified of a claim that does not involve an insured's deliberate or knowing contamination or dam-age to natural resources.

Already, some bright spots have appeared in the environmen-tal coverage picture. Insurers, both the established liability carriers and some new environmental insurers, have begun to issue particularized policies for certain "niche" markets: envi-ronmental consultants, lenders, contractors, and others. Some efforts to develop an insurer-insured protocol to resolve the environmental coverage problem have commenced, although their ultimate result remains to be seen. In any event, just as insureds must implement strategies to eliminate potential envi-ronmental liabilities in the future, the insurance industry should devote its considerable resources not to resisting coverage for environmental claims but to arriving at reasonable compromises with insureds.

Bibliography

Kenneth S. Abraham, *Environmental Liability Insurance Law* (Englewood Cliffs:, NJ: Prentice Hall, 1991).

Environmental Protection Agency, *Environmental Investments: The Cost of a Clean Environment* (Dec. 1, 1990).

Marianne Lavelle, "Industry, Insurers at Odds," *The National Law Journal* (March 30, 1992).

Robert A. Matthews and Peter L. Gray, *Superfund Claims and Litigation Manual* (Executive Enterprises, 1990).

Office of Technology Assessment, *Coming Clean: Superfund Problems Can Be Solved* (1989).

Roger Parloff, "Rigging the Common Law," in *The American Lawyer*, March 1992.

Report on "Environmental Risk Management" in *Business Insurance*, October 21, 1991.

Note: The authors of this chapter have also written a book which covers the environmental insurance topic more extensively. Contact Government Institutes for additional information regarding the Environmental Insurance Handbook.

Chapter 11

Tax Consequences of Environmental Cleanups

Thomas H. Yancey
Sidley & Austin

Introduction

Your business has just been notified that it has been designated as a "potentially responsible party" (PRP) by EPA in a court action for site remediation under the Comprehensive Environmental Response, Compensation and Liability Act (CERCLA). Almost before you know it, you are confronted with numerous tasks and deadlines arising from the cleanup process, including deciding how to participate in the negotiation of a consent decree and the management of the cleanup. As negotiations proceed on the consent decree, estimates are made of the overall cleanup cost and formulas are specified for apportioning liability among the PRPs. Eventually, you are faced with choosing among cash-out and work settlement options with EPA and among the other PRPs. Various premiums are attached to your potential choices,

241

different "reopeners" are specified triggering additional liability, and some options require immediate funding while others call for contributions only as the cleanup is performed.

Your ability to make intelligent decisions will depend to a large degree on the availability of information about the costs of the remedial action and the likelihood that it will be successful in addressing the release of hazardous substances from the site. But another area often overlooked in dealing with cleanup liability is income tax planning. Failure to understand the income tax ramifications of cleanups can cause management to miss opportunities to save taxes and significantly reduce the after-tax cost of government-ordered remediation. As the following discussion demonstrates, tax planning should be made an integral part of the cleanup process, starting with the negotiation of a consent decree and remediation agreements among the PRPs.

The major factors to consider are the deductibility of cleanup costs, the timing of the available deductions, and the tax treatment accorded to any fund or organization created by the PRPs to fund the cleanup. Each of these factors will be discussed in turn.

Deductibility of Cleanup Costs

Cleanup costs generally are imposed under CERCLA and similar state laws for compensatory or remedial purposes, making them deductible as ordinary and necessary business expenses under the Internal Revenue Code. Amounts paid as fines or penalties for violations of those laws, however, cannot be deducted. Thus, except to the extent that a PRP incurs costs under the penalty provisions of those laws, it will be able to secure deductions for its cleanup costs.

In order to take a deduction for any expenditure, however, the taxpayer must be able to show that the expense does not create a capital asset (i.e., a permanent improvement or betterment to property or other asset, having a useful life of more than one year). Capital costs can only be recovered through depreciation or amortization deductions, generally over the useful life of the asset created. An asset having no ascertainable useful life cannot be depreciated or amortized for tax purposes.

Generally, cleanup costs should not be treated as capital costs because they are imposed by law as an imminent liability that must be resolved and the taxpayer does not acquire any useful assets from incurring the costs. But if a PRPs cleanup costs result in the cleanup of its own property so that its original useful life is extended, it is suitable for a different use, or the need for the cleanup was foreseeable when the property was acquired, the costs may constitute nondeductible capital expenditures. Similarly, if cleanup costs are used to purchase facilities, equipment or machinery owned by the PRP, they will be treated as capital expenditures subject to depreciation and amortization.

If the PRPs form a corporation to perform a cleanup, payments to the organization may be treated as nondeductible capital contributions. That treatment is also a possibility if the IRS successfully re-characterizes a trust, escrow or other cleanup funding arrangement as a corporation or business association. Deductions for the loss of the contributed capital used to perform the cleanup can only be obtained upon the liquidation of the organization involved.

Timing Of Deductions And The Economic Performance Rules

Effect of Reopeners on the All Events Test

Subject to the capitalization rules, accrual method taxpayers (which include corporations having annual gross receipts of at least $5 million) can take deductions when all events have fixed the fact of a liability and its amount can be estimated with reasonable accuracy (the all events test) and economic performance has occurred. It is crucial for a PRP to understand how these rules apply in the context of an environmental cleanup in order to evaluate the tax effect of the various cleanup options available.

In the typical cleanup it is relatively easy for a PRP to satisfy the all events test. The entry of a consent decree or judgment under the environmental laws fixes the fact of liability and the PRPs cost can be estimated with reasonable accuracy using the cost studies and sharing arrangements used to organize the cleanup.

To the extent that a PRP's share of the cleanup costs may be changed under a "reopener" arrangement, then the all events test would not be met. If the reopener can only operate to increase the PRP's expenditures above a certain amount, however, that would not prevent the all events test from being met for the amounts which will be incurred regardless of future changes. Thus, PRPs should consider the potential of reopeners to delay their tax deductions and try to limit the amounts subject to those arrangements to levels where they have a realistic chance of avoiding liability.

Classification of Cleanup Cost Liability Under the Economic Performance Rules

The economic performance rules also impact the timing of cleanup cost deductions. An accrual method PRP can take a deduction for cleanup costs only when economic performance has occurred with respect to such liabilities. That will depend on how those liabilities are classified under the economic performance rules.

Income tax regulations proposed by the IRS divide liabilities into several categories for purposes of determining when economic performance occurs. If a liability requires the taxpayer to provide services to another person (Service Liability), economic performance occurs as the services are performed, even if the taxpayer pays someone else to perform the services on its behalf. But if the liability requires a payment or series of payments to another person and arises out of a tort, breach of contract (to the extent of incidental, consequential and liquidated damages) or other violation of law (Payment Liability), economic performance occurs as payment is made to the person to whom the liability is owed. Liabilities arising out of settlements of lawsuits alleging Payment Liabilities are also treated as Payment Liabilities.

If a PRP satisfies its cleanup liability by arranging for the performance of remedial work, then its cleanup costs appear to be Service Liabilities, meaning that economic performance will occur only as the work is performed. On the other hand, if the consent decree or judgment requires the PRP to make one or more payments to satisfy its liability, then it should be treated as a Payment Liability, although that result is less than clear due to the difficulty of classifying cleanup costs under the proposed regulations.

The approach of the proposed regulations is to use traditional categories of legal liability to treat various types of liabilities imposed by law as Payment Liabilities. But liability imposed under CERCLA and similar state laws does not easily fit within any of those categories. It clearly is not based on contract law. It is doubtful that cleanup costs can be characterized as liabilities arising out of a tort because such costs may be imposed in the absence of a showing that the PRPs' actions were a proximate cause and a cause-in-fact of the injury, a necessary element of tort liability. The liability also does not appear to result from a violation of law because the acts on which it is predicated often were carried out in accordance with all applicable statutes and regulations. Nevertheless, the intent behind the proposed regulations apparently was to treat all types of involuntary liabilities imposed by law as Payment Liabilities. Accordingly, the IRS should clarify that cleanup costs can be Payment Liabilities.

If cleanup costs can be classified as Payment Liabilities, PRPs choosing cash-outs and other options requiring prefunding of work will be able to secure deductions at the time they make irrevocable payment of their liability, but only if it is made to the person to whom that liability is owed. Under the proposed regulations, that person would appear to be the plaintiff in the cost-recovery action giving rise to the liability, such as EPA. In general, payments to trusts, escrows or other settlement funds will not constitute payment to the person to whom the liability is owed. If a PRP's obligation is classified as a Payment Liability, and a cost-recovery plaintiff assigns its right to receive payment to another person (including a trust), however, payment to that person will constitute economic performance.

Qualified Settlement Funds

The restrictions on the receipt of deductions at the time of contributions to trusts or escrows create serious problems for PRPs, particularly those involved in cash-out settlements, who are required to make payments to such funds to prefund work to be performed in later years. The delay in receipt of deductions until amounts are paid out of the funds can significantly magnify the financial impact of the cleanup.

Under rules proposed by the IRS, PRPs in many cases will be able to secure current deductions through use of special settlement funds, referred to as qualified settlement funds. A qualified settlement fund includes any fund, account or trust:

1. That is established pursuant to an order of, or is approved by, a governmental authority (including a court or EPA);

2. That is established to resolve or satisfy certain specified claims under CERCLA, arising from an event, or series of events, that has occurred; and

3. That is a trust under state law, or the assets of which are segregated from other assets of the transferor (or related persons).

Accrual method PRPs will satisfy the economic performance test at the time they make contributions to such a fund, just as if they had made the transfer directly to the claimants. A PRP will not meet that test, however, to the extent that the PRP has an unrestricted right to return of money from the fund at the time of the contribution, or to the extent that a such a right is certain to arise in the future. If the PRP can only receive a return from the fund with the approval of a court or EPA, however, that should not prevent a current deduction. Should a right to a return arise in the future with respect to amounts previously deducted, however, the PRP would have to recognize the amount involved as income at that time.

PRPs participating in cash-out settlements with EPA (as in the case of de minimis settlements) can use a qualified settlement fund to accelerate their deductions. PRPs participating in an internal cash-out arrangement, in which other PRPs agree to assume work obligations, should also be allowed to use qualified settlement funds, to the extent that those cash-out participants satisfy their obligations to EPA or other claimants by making cash payments. In such cases, the settlement papers should contain an acknowledgement by the claimants that the liability under CERCLA of the cash-out participants is satisfied to the extent of their payments to the fund. If the IRS seeks to deny deductions until the amounts are disbursed from the fund on the ground that the ultimate liability under CERCLA is not satisfied until such disbursements are made, the acknowledgment will provide a strong basis on which to sustain the deductions.

It is not clear whether PRPs who will be involved in performing cleanup work can secure deductions from contributions to qualified funds if they will receive payments from the fund for performing work. The IRS may contend that the arrangement constitutes a right of reversion from the fund despite the fact that the PRP must perform work to receive the payments. If EPA must approve disbursements to the PRP as the work is performed, however, then the PRP may be able to receive deductions for its contributions to the fund.

A qualified settlement fund will be treated as a separate entity, taxable on its income at the highest rate applicable to trusts, currently 31%. It will not recognize income from the receipt of contributions from PRPs, and will not receive deductions from distributions to satisfy the cleanup liabilities involved.

If a fund would meet the requirements to be a qualified settlement fund as of a particular date, except that no governmental order was entered at that time, PRPs can elect to have qualified fund treatment relate back to the date the fund met the other requirements. If the order is entered in a year following that date, however, the relation back will only be effective as of January 1 of the year that it is entered. Thus, the relation back election cannot be used to accelerate deductions into an earlier year, but can be used to have the fund treated as a separate taxable entity from the date it first existed in the year the order is entered.

The new provisions are proposed to be generally effective commencing January 1, 1993. Transfers to funds after 1992 will be fully subject to the new rules. Existing funds which meet the requirements for being qualified settlement funds will be treated as such beginning January 1, 1993, unless allowed otherwise by the IRS. Taxpayers who make or who made pre-1993 contributions to a qualified settlement fund will be treated as having transferred the amounts still held by the fund on January 1, 1993, as of that date, assuming that deductions have not already been taken with respect to those transfers. Thus, deductions for past contributions to cleanup funds may become available at that time.

An election is available to have the new rules apply in years prior to 1993. Using that election, taxpayers may be able to accelerate deductions with respect to transfers to qualified settlement funds made before January 1, 1993.

Although the regulations for qualified settlement funds have been issued in proposed form, and are subject to change, it is unlikely that the determination to allow deductions for CERCLA liabilities through the funds will be altered.

Tax Consequences Of Choosing Arrangements And Entities To Fund Joint Cleanups

Avoiding Income Realization in Arrangements for Prefunding Cleanup Work

Cash-out options and some work options for cleanups require PRPs to satisfy all or a part of their liability by paying amounts into various types of funds that will be used later to finance cleanup work. These prefunding arrangements can have dramatically different tax consequences depending on the circumstances involved.

If PRPs can sustain Payment Liability treatment for their obligations and satisfy them through irrevocable payments to EPA, another cost-recovery plaintiff, or an assignee of the foregoing, economic performance will occur as such payments are made. If ownership of an annuity is transferred to such persons, that will also constitute economic performance to the extent of the annuity's cost.

If the transferee is EPA or another entity not subject to tax, it will not realize income from the receipt. Furthermore, any income produced from interim investment of the funds or the income build-up on a transferred annuity will not be subject to tax.

If transfers directly to a claimant are not possible or desired, the settlement should be accomplished by use of one or more qualified settlement funds. The fund must be approved by a court or EPA, and the claims being settled should be specified in the documents organizing the fund. If a relation back or effective date election would be beneficial, it should be provided for in connection with the settlement. If PRPs performing work will receive payments from the fund, provide in the settlement documents for EPA or the court to approve disbursements before they can be made.

If PRPs involved in cleanup work have no obligation to contribute sums except as the work is performed, they will not care that their deductions are available only as work is performed. But, they must still take care to avoid unnecessary income recognition in accomplishing the cleanup. The risk is that without proper planning, the PRPs managing the cleanup work, or an entity organized for that purpose, will have taxable income from receiving money from prefunding PRPs with no offsetting deductions until later years if the money will not be spent until then. If the recipients acquire capital assets from the expenditure of the funds, that could further delay their deductions.

Qualified settlement funds can be used to delay the recognition of income from receipt of control over amounts paid by cash-out PRPs until such amounts are distributed to pay for work when the work PRPs may have offsetting deductions. Alternatively, the work PRPs can avoid income recognition altogether if they can sustain that they are acting as agent for the cash-out PRPs or their fund in directing expenditure of the amounts. That approach can also be used in conjunction with corporations or partnerships formed by work PRPs to avoid or delay receipt of income by those organizations.

The risk, however, is that the IRS will assert that the agency arrangement should be disregarded if it concludes that the PRPs or organization controlling the expenditures have too much discretionary power over their expenditure and can apply them to their own benefit. That challenge, if successful, would result in the holders having income from receipt of the amounts. The courts, however, have upheld even informal agency relationships in the face of similar IRS attacks, but there is no direct authority dealing with environmental cleanups. If the recipients are considered to have received income upon distribution from a qualified fund, they may also have deductions to offset that income if the amounts were spent in the year of their distribution.

Another option is to engage a tax-exempt cleanup entity to perform the cleanup and have a qualified settlement fund make payments to that entity. Any cleanup entity formed by the PRPs solely to perform work at a particular site would not qualify for tax exemption, however, because its purpose would be simply to satisfy the legal obligations of that specific group of persons. In contrast, cleanup entities formed by industry groups and others to provide cleanup services on a broad basis have qualified for tax exemption. Since the tax-exempt entity would not be liable for tax on investment earnings from the payments, it might be able to perform the cleanup at less cost to the PRPs by applying the tax-free earnings to the site work. In order to use this approach, however, the PRPs must be willing to give up control over the conduct of the work, with the tax-exempt entity acting as the general contractor.

Taxation of Corporations and Partnerships Performing Cleanups

Often, the PRPs having responsibility for the performance of the cleanup decide to associate together in a corporation to accomplish the necessary work. Usually, that decision is made to obtain whatever limitations on liability arising from the future cleanup operations are available under state corporate law, even though the participants know that they really cannot escape such liability under the environmental laws.

In taking that step, the PRPs often do not focus on the tax ramifications of their decision. A corporation generally is a separate taxable entity, meaning that its receipt of funds from the shareholders will likely be treated, in part, as a contribution to capital, and otherwise as taxable income of the corporation for the performance of cleanup services. Payments from cash-out or other PRPs owning no stock will likely be treated entirely as corporate income for the performance of cleanup services. Since the corporation will be performing work for its controlling shareholders, the IRS also has the authority to re-characterize amounts so that the corporation produces a reasonable profit, after all deductions, which of course will be subject to corporate tax.

Payments treated as contributions to capital will generally not be deductible by the PRP shareholders until the corporation is liquidated at the conclusion of the cleanup, which can significantly delay the deductions otherwise available to them as the work is performed. This can be avoided by organizing the cleanup entity as a partnership instead of a corporation. As partners, the PRPs involved will have the partnership's deductions from cleanup expenditures passed through to them for current deduction on their own tax returns. But they will also be required to recognize any income realized by the partnership, including from payments made by PRPs to prefund the cleanup (to the extent such payments are not treated as capital contributions to the partnership).

The use of qualified settlement funds to delay receipt of income from prefunding amounts until such amounts are spent on deductible cleanup costs has already been discussed. That technique cannot counter the capitalization requirement, however, if those funds are spent on capital costs. The corporation or partnership will be required to recover the cost of capital assets through depreciation or amortization, even though the receipt of the funds used by the organization to acquire such assets results in taxable income.

To minimize the potential for creation of income, the corporation or partnership (as well as the PRPs) should avoid acquiring ownership of assets used in the cleanup effort. If the cleanup can be conducted by an outside general contractor, that may even eliminate the need to have any type of business organization among the PRPs. If some type of PRP organization is necessary, its role should be as limited as possible. For example, it may serve solely as agent for the PRPs in overseeing the work of an outside contractor and disbursing amounts as agent for them. Its staff and overhead should be small, thereby reducing the amounts contributed as capital and the necessary profit resulting from its operations.

Conclusion

Armed with insight into the tax issues involving cleanups, a PRP will be able to make intelligent choices among the various options available, as well as suggest better alternatives to accomplish a cleanup. In evaluating the cleanup situation, the following questions should be answered:

- To what extent do the options involve reopeners that could theoretically reduce the PRP's proportionate share of liability after the date payment is made or work is performed, thereby delaying deductions? Do such reopeners provide a realistic chance for reduction of liability so that they are worth the tax detriment?

- Will any of the options cause the PRP to acquire a capital asset, including an improvement or betterment to its own property, which will prevent current deductions? If the resulting asset is not really useful to the business, can its acquisition be avoided under another option?

• Will cash-out or other prefunding options provide a deduction at the time of payment or only later as work is performed? If later, how long after payment will the funds be expended to perform work?

• Can the cleanup be accomplished without PRP participation (including through formation of a corporation or partnership) by retention of an outside general contractor?

• If the PRP participates in arranging for the performance of the cleanup, will it realize income from the receipt of prefunding payments from other PRPs before it has offsetting cleanup deductions (through participation in a cleanup partnership or otherwise)? Is use of a qualified settlement fund planned to prevent this?

• If a cleanup corporation or partnership is formed, will the scope of its activities be as limited as possible under an agency agreement with the PRPs?

• Will the prefunding amounts be transferred to EPA or another tax-exempt entity so that investment income will not be subject to tax? If so, has the arrangement been negotiated so that the PRPs receive the benefits through lower charges for the performance of the cleanup work?

Once these questions are answered, the PRP can make an intelligent choice among the cleanup alternatives available to produce the lowest after-tax cost possible.

Chapter 12

SEC Disclosures of Environmental Matters

Mark A. White
University of Virginia

Introduction

General requirements for the disclosure of material obligations, which by implication include environmental obligations, are set forth in the Securities Act of 1933 (1933 Act) and the Securities Exchange Act of 1934 (1934 Act). Later rules and several interpretive releases have clarified the position of the Securities and Exchange Commission (SEC) regarding the disclosure of environmental matters. This chapter identifies and describes a number of factors leading to current SEC requirements for the disclosure of environmental matters.

The Materiality Standard and Disclosure Obligations

Federal securities law requires that all "material" facts affecting the value of a publicly traded company be disclosed to current and potential investors. Material facts are "...those matters to which there is a substantial likelihood that a reasonable investor would attach importance in determining whether to buy or sell the securities registered."[1] The Supreme Court, in *TSC Industries v. Northway, Inc.*, extended this definition to include shareholder voting decisions.[2] The Court further refined the materiality standard in *Basic Inc. v. Levinson*, via the "probability/magnitude" test, in which materiality "...will depend at any given time upon a balancing of both the indicated probability that the event will occur and the anticipated magnitude of the event in light of the totality of the company activity."[3]

Material information on environmental matters includes a firm's anticipated expenses for complying with environmental regulations (e.g. disposal costs, administrative and legal costs, and new plant and equipment costs), pending litigation of an environmental nature and information regarding a firm's practices and procedures giving rise to particular environmental risks or contingencies. Under SEC Regulation S-K, this information may be disclosed in one or more of the following places:

(a) Item 101 of Form 10-K, "Description of Business"

(b) Item 103 of Form 10-K, "Legal Proceedings"

(c) Item 303 of Form 10-K, "Management's Discussion and Analysis of Financial Condition and Results of Operations" (MD&A),

(d) The company's annual financial statements and accompanying footnotes.

The particulars of environmental disclosure in each of these locations will be discussed later in this chapter.

---

[1] 17 C.F.R. § 240.12b-2 (1991).

[2] *TSC Industries v. Northway, Inc.*, 426 U.S. 438, 449 (1976).

[3] *Basic Inc. v. Levinson*, 485 U.S. 224, 229 (1988).

Specific Disclosure of Environmental Matters

In addition to a firm's general obligation to disclose material information, the SEC has developed and adopted several regulations specific to the disclosure of environmental matters.

The National Environmental Policy Act (NEPA) of 1969 was perhaps the spark igniting SEC involvement in environmental matters. NEPA required all federal agencies to incorporate protection for the environment into their regulations, policies and procedures. In a 1971 interpretive release, the SEC explicitly identified disclosure requirements for material obligations relating to legal proceedings arising from federal, state and local environmental protection statutes. The 1971 release thus reiterated a registrant's general obligation to disclose material facts, but did so with specific reference to its potential liability for environmental damages.

A petition filed in 1971 by the National Resources Defense Council (NRDC) led to SEC regulations in 1973 requiring disclosure of *all* environmental administrative and judicial proceedings, regardless of materiality. However, companies were allowed to group similar proceedings together and to provide only general descriptions unless a proceeding was material or the damages sought were greater than 10 percent of a firm's consolidated current assets. The 1973 regulations also closed a loophole allowing companies to avoid disclosure of environmental matters arising from "ordinary routine litigation incidental to the business."[4] Under the new regulations, litigation for environmental matters could no longer be considered either ordinary or routine. Shortly before adoption of the 1973 regulations, the NRDC filed suit in federal district court claiming that the SEC had not gone far enough nor fulfilled all of the requirements of NEPA. The court held in favor of the NRDC and required the SEC

---

[4] See 17 C.F.R. § 229.103 (1991).

to revise its regulations. Despite lengthy hearings and testimony, the SEC refused to change its position and eventually won its case in the U.S. Court of Appeals in 1979. In arguing its position, the SEC noted that its primary objective was to promote informed investment decisions, not regulate corporate behavior. Also in 1979, following administrative proceedings against the United States Steel Corporation, the SEC issued a strongly worded interpretative release requiring extensive disclosure and estimates of future capital expenditures necessary to comply with environmental regulations.

In 1981, the SEC proposed eliminating disclosure requirements for proceedings involving a governmental authority in which a fine of less than $100,000 was reasonably expected to prevail. The SEC adopted this proposal in 1982, justifying that the deletion of numerous, often lengthy disclosures of governmental proceedings would improve the presentation of more important environmental matters.

In May 1989, the SEC issued an interpretive release concerning disclosure in the MD&A section of a company's 10-K filing which included as an example a firm named as a "potentially responsible party" (PRP) by the Environmental Protection Agency (EPA) under the 1980 Comprehensive Environmental Response, Compensation, and Liability Act (CERCLA), or "Superfund." This release simultaneously clarified MD&A reporting responsibilities and communicated the SEC's position on the disclosure of actions pending under Superfund legislation.

Environmental Legislation and SEC Disclosure

The majority of a firm's environmental disclosure obligations arise from compliance with various federal, state and local environmental statutes and regulations. Although the impact of Superfund appears to be of greatest concern, other environmental laws may trigger SEC reporting requirements as well. Other major pieces of federal environmental legislation are the:

Clean Air Act The Clean Air Act (1970; amended in 1977 and 1990) established quality standards of two types—ambient air quality and emissions standards—and provided for the creation of the EPA to oversee their implementation and regulation. Under the 1990 Amendments, the EPA gained additional authority to issue administrative penalties of up to $200,000. Civil and criminal penalties for knowingly or negligently violating the air quality standards have been similarly enhanced.

Clean Water Act The original goals of the Clean Water Act (1972; amended in 1977, 1981 and 1987) were to eliminate the discharge of pollutants into navigable waters by 1985 and to achieve water quality of fishable, swimmable and recreational levels where possible. Limitations on effluent discharge and receiving water quality standards are the major policy tools used to effect these goals.

Resource Conservation and Recovery Act (RCRA) This Act, enacted in 1976, regulates the generation, transport, storage, treatment and disposal of current hazardous wastes. In 1984, the Hazardous and Solid Waste Amendments (HSWA) were added covering waste minimization, underground storage tanks, land disposal restrictions and the cleanup of hazardous wastes from hazardous waste facilities. Under the provisions of these Acts, manufacturers must properly package and label all controlled substances and provide detailed manifests to aid the EPA in its tracking and recordkeeping of hazardous wastes. Failure to comply with these provisions subjects both firms and individuals to substantial civil and criminal penalties.

Superfund Legislation The 1980 Superfund Act has been called the most expensive regulatory measure ever enacted in the United States, and the SEC has paid particular attention to obligations arising from its provisions. This legislation imposes liability for cleanup costs on any owner, transporter or generator of [hazardous] waste materials at a waste site. Sites are identified by severity for cleanup by the EPA on a National Priority List. The EPA has broad authority to manage hazardous waste sites—it can require responsible parties to clean them up or EPA may clean the site itself with funds from lawsuits or Superfund monies. Three aspects of the Act and its interpretation by EPA and the courts are especially pertinent: 1) strict liability, 2) retroactivity, and 3) joint and several liability. Under strict liability, businesses may be held liable even though they complied with existing legislation and are not found negligent. Further, the Act is retroactive, such that if the EPA can prove that a firm owned the land at the time during which the waste was disposed of, it may be held liable. The principle of joint and several liability allows the EPA to collect the full amount of cleanup costs from any one of the parties to the suit, irrespective of the amount of waste actually contributed by a particular party.

Potentially Responsible Parties (PRPs) in a Superfund suit may include the site's current owner or operator, past owners or operators, waste treatment or disposal contractors, and transporters of hazardous waste. In practice, the EPA generally relies upon the first three groups. The wide net cast by the EPA sometimes catches innocent parties unintentionally. For instance, under current law, banks and other lending institutions which become owners of hazardous waste sites through foreclosure may be liable for their cleanup. In 1991 the EPA proposed a rule providing broader protection for banks and other private creditors not participating in the firm's management.

Congress passed the Superfund Amendments and Reauthorization Act (SARA) in 1986, which broadened the number of sites subject to Superfund jurisdiction and increased the list of PRPs. Title III of SARA, also known as the Emergency Planning and Community Right-to-Know Act, requires firms to identify the names of chemicals used and the toxic hazards they present within their operations. This information is then made available for public inspection.

Form 10-K Disclosure Obligations

Disclosure requirements applicable to the nonfinancial portions of registration statements under the 1933 and 1934 Securities Acts are found in Regulation S-K and subsequent interpretive releases. Specific reference to the disclosure of environmental matters is made in three items.

Item 101, "Description of Business" In this item a registrant must provide a general description of the firm's operations and its industry. Specific information must be provided regarding "...the material effects that compliance with federal, state and local provisions which have been enacted or adopted regulating the discharge of materials into the environment, or otherwise relating to the protection of the environment, may have upon the capital expenditures, earnings and competitive position of the registrant and its subsidiaries."[5] Estimated capital expenditures for environmental control facilities must be reported, "...for the remainder of its current fiscal year and its succeeding fiscal years and for such further periods as the registrant may deem material."[6] Expenditures must thus be estimated for a minimum of two years.

Item 103, "Legal Proceedings" Pending legal proceedings against the firm or its subsidiaries must be disclosed in this section, with the exception of "ordinary routine litigation incidental to the business" noted earlier. Environmental administrative or judicial proceedings must be disclosed, provided they meet any of the three tests contained in Instruction~5.

---

[5] 17 C.F.R. § 229.101(c)(xii) (1991).
[6] Id.

(a) Such proceeding is material to the business or financial condition of the registrant;

(b) Such proceeding involves primarily a claim for damages or involves potential monetary sanctions, capital expenditures, deferred charges or charges to income and the amount involved, exclusive of interest and costs, exceeds 10 percent of the current assets of the registrant and its subsidiaries on a consolidated basis; or

(c) A governmental authority is a party to such proceedings and such proceeding involves potential monetary sanctions, unless the registrant reasonably believes that such proceeding will result in no monetary sanctions, or in monetary sanctions, exclusive of interest and costs, of less than $100,000; provided, however, that such proceedings which are similar in nature may be grouped and described generically.[7]

In an interpretative letter, the SEC ruled that designation as a PRP under the Superfund statutes does not, in and of itself, trigger disclosure requirements under Item 103, Instruction 5 although additional information regarding a firm's particular status may provide that knowledge.[8]

The availability of insurance and contributions from other PRPs must be weighed in determining materiality. Similarly, costs incurred for remedial action under Superfund legislation, though often substantial, are not considered "sanctions," within the context of Instruction 5(c).

---

[7] 17 C.F.R. § 229.103, Instruction 5 (1990).

[8] Letter to Thomas A. Cole, Esq., 17 January 1989, LEXIS 1989 SEC No-Act. 203; partially reprinted in 54 Fed. Reg. 22427, 22430 n. 30 (1989).

Item 303, "Management's Discussion and Analysis" (MD&A)
This item provides the opportunity for management to discuss
changes in liquidity, capital resources and results of the firm's
consolidated operations. As described in the May 1989 interpretive release, it is intended to provide "...material historical and
prospective textual disclosure enabling investors and other users
to assess the financial condition and results of operations of the
registrant, with particular emphasis on the registrant's prospects
for the future."[9] Accordingly, "...a disclosure duty exists where a
trend, demand, commitment, event or uncertainty is both
presently known to management and reasonably likely to have
material effects on the registrant's financial condition or results
of operation."[10] In a footnote, the SEC observes that the prob-
ability/magnitude of *Basic, Inc. v. Levinson* is not relevant to
Item 303 disclosure. The environmental example used by the SEC
to illustrate these principles was:

> *Facts:* A registrant has been correctly designated a PRP by
> the EPA with respect to cleanup of hazardous waste at
> three sites. No statutory defenses are available. The regis-
> trant is in the process of preliminary investigations of the
> sites to determine the nature of its potential liability and
> the amount of remedial costs necessary to clean up the
> sites. Other PRPs have also been designated, but the ability
> to obtain contribution is unclear, as is the extent of insur-
> ance coverage, if any. Management is unable to determine
> that a material effect on future financial condition or
> results of operations is not reasonably likely to occur.[11]

The SEC's ruling on this situation was:

> Based upon the facts of this hypothetical case, MD&A
> disclosure of the effects of PRP status, quantified to the
> extent reasonably practicable, would be required. For
> MD&A purposes, aggregate potential cleanup costs must be

---

[9] SEC Release Nos. 33-6835 and 34-26831 (May 18, 1989) [54 FR
22428].

[10] Id at 22429.

[11] Id at 22430.

considered in light of the joint and several liability to which a PRP is subject. Facts regarding whether insurance coverage may be contested and whether and to what extent potential sources of contribution and indemnification constitute reliable sources of recovery may be factored into the determination of whether a material future effect is likely to occur.[12]

Note that in this example, the company was "correctly" identified as a PRP, had "no statutory defense" to the action, was "uncertain" about its "ability to obtain contribution from other PRPs" or the "extent of potential insurance coverage" and was "unable to determine" that a "material effect" was not "reasonably" likely to occur. Mitigating circumstances may reduce the need for disclosure. If management is unable to determine that a known trend, demand, commitment or event is not reasonably likely to occur, then it must objectively evaluate the consequences of that event under the assumption that it *will* occur. Disclosure is required unless management determines that the trend, demand, etc. is not reasonably likely to have a material effect on the firm's financial condition or results of operations.

Disclosure in Financial Statements—FAS 5

A company's financial statements accompany its Form 10-K and may therefore be considered as part of its required SEC disclosure. For instance, Item 303, Management's Discussion and Analysis, is required under 10-K guidelines but is usually found in the firm's annual report. Guidelines for the disclosure of contingent liabilities, including those arising from environmental matters, are provided by the Financial Accounting Standards Board's Statement of Financial Accounting Standards No. 5, "Accounting for Contingencies," (FAS 5).

FAS 5 distinguishes between asserted and unasserted claims in determining disclosure responsibilities for contingent losses.

---

[12] Id.

For asserted claims, if a loss is "probable," i.e. has a greater than 50 percent probability of occurrence *and* can be reasonably estimated, then the firm must accrue the amount of the loss on its financial statements. For losses in which a firm can only estimate a range of probable amounts, it is required to accrue the minimum amount of the range and disclose the size of the range in a footnote. For probable losses in which no reasonable estimate of damage can be made, disclosure of this fact must be made in a footnote. If there is a "reasonable possibility," i.e. a probability in excess of 5 percent, of a contingent loss, then the firm must disclose the nature and, if known, the amount of the loss in a footnote to its financial statements. Management must disclose currently unasserted claims (in a footnote) only if it is probable that such claims will be asserted and there is a reasonable possibility of a loss occurring.

Lender Liability

Significant controversy surrounds the issue of lender liability under the Superfund statutes. Banks and other lending institutions are concerned about potential environmental liabilities arising from unplanned foreclosures on contaminated properties. Lenders in this position rely on essentially two defenses. The "innocent landowner defense" outlined in SARA provides an exemption for persons who were unaware of environmental contamination and who exercised "due diligence" before acquiring the property. An exemption also exists for persons who hold indicia of ownership (e.g. mortgages, deeds of trust, legal titles) primarily to protect a security interest and who do not participate in the management of the facility.

Recent court rulings have fueled uncertainties regarding lenders' potential environmental liabilities and responsibilities. Financial, administrative and general advice does not usually constitute "management participation," although in *U.S. v. Maryland Bank and Trust Company* the court found that the lengthy period of time between foreclosure and resale (four years) indicated that the bank acted to protect its investment rather than its security interest.[13] In *U.S. v. Fleet Factors Corp.*, a commercial factoring firm was found liable for cleanup costs if it possessed the capacity to influence treatment of a foreclosed firm's hazardous wastes.[14] In June 1991 the EPA issued a proposed rule clarifying the security interest exemption and allowing governmental lending entities or receivers such as the Resolution Trust Corporation access to the innocent landowner defense for properties acquired under involuntary transfers.[15]

Availability of Information

Financial statements and Form 10-Ks filed with the SEC are public information and can be obtained through a firm's corporate communications department or the libraries of many business schools. Private firms such as Disclosure, Inc. provide on-line access to this information and will send paper or fiche copies overnight if requested. Managers are required to report the amounts of over 300 toxic chemicals transported or released to the air, water or land on an annual basis by the Emergency Planning and Community Right-to-Know Act ("Right-to-Know") of 1986. The EPA compiles and publishes this data in the annual Toxics Release Inventory (TRI). On-line access to the TRI can be obtained through the National Library of Medicine in Bethesda, Maryland. The EPA also prepares quarterly reports for the SEC of enforcement actions it has taken against corporate polluters to aid in the latter organization's review of environmental disclosure obligations. This information is available to the public under the Freedom of Information Act.

---

[13] *U.S. v. Maryland Bank and Trust Company*, 632 F. Supp. 573 (D.Md. 1986).

[14] *U.S. v. Fleet Factors Corp.*, 901 F.2d. (11th Cir. 1990), *cert. denied*, 111 S.Ct. 752 (1991).

[15] EPA Release No. FRL-3966-3 (June 24, 1991) [56 FR 28798].

Numerous private organizations collect information on corporate environmental performance. The Council on Economic Priorities, the Investor Responsibility Research Center and Franklin Research and Development Corporation are three more well-known sources. Moody's Investors Service has required companies to provide financial data concerning possible environmental liabilities since 1990. Finally, a number of independent national and regional firms have recently been established which provide on-line access to a firm's environmental record, generally cross-matching data from several sources.[16]

Environmental Auditing and SEC Disclosure

Environmental auditing is a growing field as environmental legislation increases both in volume and complexity and firms find it more difficult to ensure they are in compliance with relevant statutes. Specialized teams examine sites, check prior records and evaluate a company's performance against varying standards of environmental conduct. Banks and financial institutions frequently utilize this service, for as noted earlier, they are very keen on protecting the value of their collateral. However, in the absence of standardized procedures and a legal framework, problems of interpretation have arisen, casting doubt upon the value of these endeavors. The EPA does not seem eager to make such audits compulsory, believing them to be more useful when conducted for internal use.

Summary

The SEC requires registrants and their subsidiaries to disclose contingent liabilities arising from compliance with federal, state and local environmental statutes and regulations in several places on Form 10-K and in a firm's financial statements. Emphasis on the disclosure of environmental matters is likely to

---

[16] Henriques, Diana B. "Tracking Environmental Risk," *New York Times*, 28 April 1991, p. 13.

increase as concern mounts over the proper disposition and long-term effects of hazardous wastes. Reluctant to risk the consequences of inaccurate disclosure, firms are more likely to err on the side of conservatism in estimating the probability and magnitude of potential environmental liabilities. Investors and the interested public would be wise to supplement readings of SEC-required disclosures with material obtained from outside agencies and organizations.

Bibliography

Archer, James G., MacMahon, Thomas M. and Maureen M. Crough. "SEC Reporting of Environmental Liabilities." *Environmental Law Reporter* (March 1990) pp. 10105-10111.

Afterman, Allan B. and Bruce N. Willis. *Handbook of SEC Accounting and Disclosure*, Boston: Warren, Gorham & Lamont, 1990.

Bloom, Gordon F. and Michael S. Scott Morton. "Hazardous Waste Is Every Manager's Problem," *Sloan Management Review* (Summer 1991) pp. 75-84.

Caron, Gerard A. "SEC Disclosure Requirements for Contingent Environmental Liability," *Boston College Environmental Affairs Law Review* (Summer 1987) pp. 729-763.

Dirks, H. John. "Accounting for the Costs of Environmental Cleanup—Where Things Stand Today," *Environmental Finance,* (Spring 1991) pp. 89-92.

Dominy, Garrett L. "Accounting for Environmental Contingencies and Losses," *Environmental Finance,* (Spring 1991) pp. 45-51.

"EPA and SEC are Allies on Chemical Disclosure," *Chemical Marketing Reporter* (4 June 1990) pp. 1, 26.

Erdevig, Eleanor H. "Lender Liability Under Environmental Law," *Chicago Fed Letter* (September 1991).

FASB Accounting Standards: Original Pronouncements (July 1973—June 1, 1988). Homewood, IL: Irwin, 1988.

"How Green Is My Company?" *The Economist*, 10 March 1990, p. 88.

Marcus, Amy Dockser, "Firms Ordered to Come Clean About Pollution," *The Wall Street Journal* (16 November 1989,)col 6, p. B1(E).

Newell, Gale E., Kreuze, Jerry G. and Stephen J. Newell. "Accounting for Hazardous Waste," *Management Accounting* (May 1990) pp. 58-61.

Rabinowitz, Daniel L. and Margaret Murphy. "Environmental Disclosure: What the SEC Requires," *Environmental Finance* (Spring 1991) pp. 31-43.

Rubenstein, Daniel B. "Accounting and the Environment: Lessons of Love," *CA Magazine* (March 1991) pp. 35-41.

Chapter 13

Environmental Ethics

Stuart A. Nicholson, Ph.D.
New Mexico Highlands University

What is Environmental Ethics?

Environmental ethics might be characterized as morally based rules of conduct for our (human) dealings with Nature. Environmental ethics, like other areas of applied ethics, are concerned with the moral "rightness" or "wrongness" of our conduct in a given domain. And, like other branches of applied ethics, environmental ethics can be applied at an individual or group level, and in the case of business, at the overall firm level. Thus, we may consider the environmental ethics of an individual's conduct on the job, or off for that matter, along with that of his employing firm as a collective whole or "unit." This chapter focuses on environmental ethics at the firm level. This partially overlaps with broader considerations of overall corporate social responsibility. Before delving into the business aspects of environmental ethics, an overview of the differing approaches is provided to help set the stage for a more practical discussion on how ethics can be integrated into daily business operations.

Understanding the Varying Approaches to Environmental Ethics

What, however, does environmental ethics, more specifically "nature," include? To most perhaps "nature" means wild animals, plants, and the environments they live in. But, is that all? Does nature just include wild things and wild places? What about human beings and everything they do? For the most part environmental ethics over the past several centuries, at least in the U.S. and England, has focused on animals, and primarily those useful to man.

Man, viewed as apart from and superior to nature, was simply not included. Although these traditional views have spanned a wide spectrum of variations—ranging from extreme reductionist views that animals were merely mechanical animations incapable of pain and suffering to "kinder and gentler" versions which emphasized Biblical imperatives of caring for God's creatures—the result was the same: Man sitting above and apart from nature could do whatever he saw fit.[1]

Several historical thinkers have suggested that this separation of man from nature, evident in Judeo-Christian doctrine, has contributed to negative environmental attitudes and behaviors toward nature.[2] In contrast, many more recent approaches to environmental ethics, and many of the belief systems of so-called primitive tribal societies, do view man as a part of nature. Specifically, the writings of Aldo Leopold, a key influence on the development of more recent environmental ethics in the U.S., have contributed to a wider adoption of the "man is part of nature" view in recent years. In describing his "land ethic," Leopold explained that the role of *Homo sapiens* has been

---

1 Nash, R., *The Rights of Nature*, University of Wisconsin Press, Madison, 1989.

2 White, L., "The Historical Roots of the Ecological Crisis," *Science*, Vol.155, 1203-1207, 1967.

changing from conqueror of the land community to plain member and citizen of it. "It implies respect for his fellow members, and also respect for the community as such....that man is, in fact, only a member of a biotic team is shown by ecological interpretation of history. Many historical events, hitherto explained solely in terms of human enterprise, were actually biotic interactions between people and land."[3]

Therefore, this chapter includes perspectives that present man as part of the environment. However, it does not encompass all existing approaches, which include about 30 books published on the topic since 1980. Furthermore, literature on primarily political movements such as the Greens, eco-warriors, and social ecology, all of which draw inspiration from various environmental ethics approaches have been excluded. Finally, eco-feminism has also been excluded because it incorporates complexities that are not easily understood. In fact, the eco-feminist approach has been expanded far beyond the "women and ecology" approaches which were often cited in the early 1970s.[4]

But where to start? There are three categories or pigeonholes that are often recognized and used in both applied ethics and business ethics. These are Rights, Justice, and Utilitarianism. Briefly, rights refer to entitlements to do or receive something. Justice encompasses questions as to fairness, equality, and equity, while utilitarianism entails maximizing benefits across a society.[5] The idea that natural entities such as animals, plants and landscapes should have rights, or at least recognition war-

---

3 Leopold, A., *A Sand County Almanac with other Essays from Round River*, Oxford University Press, New York, 1966.

4 Nicholson, S.A., and M. Fries, "Women, Society, and the Environment," *American Biology Teacher*, Vol.36, No. 5, 275-278, 311, 1974.

5 Velasquez, M.G., *Business Ethics Concepts and Cases*, Prentice-Hall, Englewood Cliffs, NJ, 1982.

ranting minimum deference, has existed for many centuries[6]. Many contemporary scholars object to *moral* rights for non-humans on the grounds that they have not been sufficiently or rigorously established. Dan Tarlock is a scholar who has identified four such objections, including impracticalities in enforcement. He does not, however, reject the idea that "interests" may be afforded to non-humans, as Christopher Stone has proposed in his book, *Earth and Other Ethics.* Whatever the "true" status of nonlegal "interests" (including moral rights of nonhuman entities), rights-seeking approaches are generally included under the "rights" category.

Another way of looking at approaches is to determine whether they are anthropocentric, biocentric, or ecocentric. Anthropocentric means human-centered, or judged exclusively from the human point of view. Alternatively, biocentric means life-centered (or from the biological viewpoint). Ecocentric is the term used to describe ecologically centered perspectives (or from the ecosystem's view). Finally, some approaches do not fit neatly into any single category, some may not seem to fit well anywhere, and of course, people may differ on how certain approaches should be classified.

Anthropocentric (or Human-Centered) Views

For several centuries many approaches to ethics have proposed the idea that humans and non-humans have natural rights.[7] In the 1960s & 1970s, the idea of asserting human rights, including "environmental" rights, was in vogue. Enthusiasts fashioned an "Environmental Bill of Rights" and dreamed of amending the U.S. Constitution.[8] Though unsuccessful at the fed-

---

6 See Note 1.

7 Ibid.

8 Landau, N.J., and P.D. Rheingold, *The Environmental Law Handbook*, Friends of the Earth/Ballantine, New York, 1971.

eral constitutional level, environmental rights type provisions have been adopted in some state constitutions.

Further, rights proponents have been influential in the United Nations, which has proclaimed man's right to "adequate conditions of life in an environment of a quality that permits a life of dignity and well-being." This has lead to the passage of more nature rights oriented provisions such as the "World Conservation Strategy" and the "World Charter for Nature."[9]

Biocentric (or Life-Centered) Views

In contrast to the anthropocentric rights approaches, there are several other approaches that attempt to establish the rights or human duties toward animals.[10] Going back further, awareness regarding animal rights in the West can be traced back to the fifteenth century.[11] Until quite recently, discussion of such rights emphasized domestic mammals. And, although contemporary biocentric approaches have expanded beyond domestic mammals, non-mammals have generally received secondary interest, and plants were routinely excluded by definition. Such discriminatory practices have been labelled "speciesism" and "animal chauvinism."

Ecocentric (or Ecologically Centered) Views

Beyond animals, some proponents have asserted natural rights or recognition for entities such as trees, wilderness, and even rocks. Regardless of whether such entities actually possess "natural" or moral rights, the debate continues, and legal rights or protections of such entities have expanded dramatically in

9 Dube, Y., "The Right to a Healthy Environment," *The Environmentalist*, Vol. 6, No. 3, 185-196, 1986.

10 Singer, P., "Animal Liberation: A New Ethics for our Treatment of Animals," New York Review Books, New York, 1975 and Regan, T. "The Case for Animal Rights," University of California Press, Berkeley, 1983.

11 See Note 1.

recent decades. Examples of such beneficiaries include marine mammals, endangered species, and wetlands.

Although legal protections for such entities were motivated by utilitarian and anthropocentric motivations, the fact that entities lacking economic utility have been included suggest the influence of other viewpoints. During the 1970s-80s several "eco-philosophers" put forward a range of ecocentric approaches[12]. More recently, another viewpoint has emerged, arguing for an approach that sees nature as a setting for collective moral and aesthetic judgments rather than as mere resources in need of management. Additionally, proponents of this would remind us that two ways we can value nature, namely for beauty and for love, are not concerned with market-type exploitation.[13]

Since the early 1970s, one of the strongest pleas for recognizing nonhuman rights beyond the organismic level has come from the "Deep Ecology" approach.[14] Of the several principles which constitute deep ecology, one key principle deals with the assertion that nonhuman life has value independent of human purposes, and the belief that humans "have no right to reduce this richness and diversity except to satisfy vital needs." Other followers of the deep ecology approach support the concept of "biospherical egalitarianism" which they define as "the equal intrinsic worth of all members of the biosphere."[15]

---

12 Scherer, D. *Ethics and the Environment*, Prentice-Hall, Englewood Cliffs, NJ, 1983.

13 Sagoff, M., *Has Nature a Good of its Own?* Paper delivered at Department of Ecology and Behavioral Biology, University of Minnesota, Minneapolis, 1991.

14 Naess, A., "Deep Ecology and Ultimate Premises," *The Ecologist*, Vol. 18, No. 4/5, 128-132, 1988.

15 Fox, W., "Deep Ecology: A New Philosophy of Our Time," *The Ecologist*, Vol. 14, No. 5-6, 194-200, 1984.

Finally, in the past few years a view has emerged that may go beyond Deep Ecology, at least philosophically if not influentially. The "biospheric ethic" was derived from Lovelock's Gaia hypothesis, in which it is asserted that the biosphere is a single, living organism that is, and has been, responsible for regulating the state of the atmosphere. This view maintains that it is in everyone's self-interest to survive and further implores humankind "to assist in maintaining the biosphere's stability or homeostasis in the face of change."[16]

Environmental & Social Justice

Since environmental causes are often seen as overlooking human welfare, critics have called for an environmental perspective that incorporates social justice. In particular, they have called attention to the exploitation of minorities through the practice of using their communities as sites for toxic waste treatment facilities and dumps. In the book *Dumping in Dixie*[17], the author discusses a social justice-oriented environmental movement with much broader human concerns than the mainstream groups. Those issues include equity, work place conditions, and basic community needs. Recent editorials have examined this on several levels, looking beyond the question of whether a given development will threaten or promote environmental restoration. The next logical question to ask is, "Will it impede or encourage communities in empowering themselves or will it further marginalize them?"[18] Finally, writers have commented on the integral linkage between man's and the earth's well-being along with man's obligation to exercise great care. They conclude that a thriving earth is not only necessary for

16 Goldsmith, E., "Towards a Biospheric Ethic," *The Ecologist*, Vol. 19, No. 2, 68-75, 1989.

17 Bullard, R.D., *Dumping in Dixie*, Westview Press, Boulder, CO, 1990.

18 Hildyard, N., "Liberation Ecology," *The Ecologist*, Vol. 21, Nos. 1/2, 1, 1991.

people's well-being, but that "its integrity must be respected...because every part of the earth counts for something in its own right."[19]

Looking Beyond Nonhuman Rights

In recent years there have been some elaborate philosophical arguments offering strong justifications for protecting nature, while not claiming to establish rights for nonhuman entities. One such justification has been called a "qualified version of ecocentric holism."[20] The contention is that while evolutionary processes and biotic diversity are not quite independent ends, wilderness and "preservation of species" may, in fact, be viewed as ends. Ecocentric holism results from the coupling of those views with an inegalitarian brand of biocentric individualism and special recognition for human rights. Another example of the holistic argument for preserving nature is:

> (1) Human beings have a duty to promote and preserve the existence of good in the world; (2) beauty, both artistic and natural, is part of that good; (3) natural beauty (in a broad sense that includes scientifically interesting properties of natural objects) is, in most cases, as valuable as artistic beauty and therefore as worthy of being promoted and preserved on non-existential grounds; and (4) because the creation of natural beauty is fundamentally contingent upon physical existence, in a way that art is not—(a) the need to preserve natural objects and systems is greater than the need to preserve works of art...[21]

From Resource Conservation to New Social Alternatives

The roots of utilitarian beliefs can be traced back to English philosophers such as Jeremy Bentham and to the U.S. govern-

---

19 Gibson, W.A., "Ecology and Justice," *Wilderness*, Summer 1986, 52-56.

20 Wenz, P. *Environmental Justice*, State University of New York at Albany Press, 1988.

21 Hargrove, E., *Fundamentals of Environmental Ethics*, Prentice-Hall, Englewood Cliffs, NJ, 1988.

ment through its federal resource management beginning in the early 1900s.[22] These policies include familiar concepts such as multiple use and the greatest good for the greatest number.

Particularly in the past decade, utilitarian approaches have been applied to development efforts in Third World countries under the title of "sustainable development." In the context of development projects funded by multinational banks, this concept has often turned out as natural *and* human resource exploitation, with some awareness and mitigation of adverse environmental impacts. There are several additional views of what sustainable development should mean, however. For example, in the more progressive approaches to natural resource management, "sustainability" entails far more. Namely, it calls for "an agriculture that is ecologically sound, resource conserving, and not *economically* degrading."[23] This is in stark contrast to "modern" mechanized agriculture.

Next, the well-publicized Brundtland Report provides additional ideas on what sustainable development should be. Although it includes environmental protection, the report also emphasizes the uplifting of the broad citizenry through indefinitely increasing economic growth.[24] This view—and others that emphasize economic growth without acknowledging or trying to accommodate inevitable negative environmental effects—have been roundly criticized by *ecological* economists[25], but rarely by

---

22 See Note 1.

23 Gliessman, S.R., "Quantifying the Agroecological Component of Sustainable Agriculture: A Goal," in Gliessman, S.R., ed., *Agroecology: Researching the Ecological Basis for Sustainable Agriculture*, Springer-Verlag, New York, 1990. Emphasis added.

24 World Commission on Environment and Development, *Our Common Future*, Oxford University Press, New York, 1987.

25 Soderholm, P., "Sustainable Development: A Challenge to Our World Views and Ideas of Economics," *Perspectives of Sustainable Development, Stockholm Studies in Natural Resources Management*, No.

"real" economists. Ecological economics, a rapidly emerging discipline, has much to say about environmental ethics because, in addition to dealing with the nature of environmental limits, it addresses issues of equity and distribution among subgroups and generations of Man, as well as between Man and other species.[26]

Making Sense of a Bewildering Array of Choices

Although abbreviated, the material covered thus far should have conveyed the great range of ideas that exist from valuing certain animals over others to including the entire biosphere. Some recent trends have also been discussed. These include: (1) divergence from strictly anthropocentric views, (2) the shift from viewing man apart from nature to that of including him within, (3) inclusion of social justice concerns, and (4) development of approaches not fitting traditional ethics categories, such as ecological economics, which includes both utilitarian and justice points of view. Finally, with some approaches it is difficult to tell which category, if any, they most logically fall in, and labels are not always helpful; for example, the approach of "environmental justice" could arguably also be categorized under environmental rights.

What's in it for Business?

Is an environmental ethics code good for business and is it as good for the environment as it could be? In contrast to the bewildering array of environmental approaches present in contemporary literature, the "Valdez Principles" offer a convenient "shopping list" of principles to deal with environmental is-

---

1, 1988 and Goodland, R., and H. Daly, "The Missing Tools," in Mungall, C., and McLaren, D.J., eds., *Planet under Stress: The Challenge of Global Change*, Oxford University Press, New York, 1990.

26 Constanza, R., "What is Ecological Economics?," *Ecological Economics,,* Vol. 1, 1-7, 1989.

sues.[27] These principles were discussed briefly in chapter 2 from the perspective of the investor. Now let's look at them again from the business management point of view.

The Valdez Principles

1. Protection of the Biosphere

We will minimize and strive to eliminate the release of any pollutant that may cause environmental damage to the air, water, or earth or its inhabitants. We will safeguard habitats in rivers, lakes, wetlands, coastal zones and oceans and will minimize contributing to the greenhouse effect, depletion of the ozone layer, acid rain, or smog.

2. Sustainable Use of Natural Resources

We will make sustainable use of renewable natural resources, such as water, soil and forests. We will conserve non-renewable natural resources through efficient use and careful planning. We will protect wildlife habitat, open spaces and wilderness, while preserving biodiversity.

3. Reduction and Disposal of Waste

We will minimize the creation of waste, especially hazardous waste, and wherever possible recycle materials. We will dispose of all wastes through safe and responsible methods.

4. Wise Use of Energy

We will make every effort to use environmentally safe and sustainable energy sources to meet our needs. We will invest in improved energy efficiency and conservation in our operations. We will maximize the energy efficiency of products we produce and sell.

---

27 Coalition for Environmentally Responsible Economies, *The 1990 Guide to the Valdez Principles*, The CERES Coalition, Boston.

5. Risk Reduction

We will minimize the environmental, health and safety risks to our employees and the communities in which we operate by employing safe technologies and operating procedures and by being constantly prepared for emergencies.

6. Marketing of Safe Products and Services

We will sell products or services that minimize adverse environmental impacts and that are safe as consumers commonly use them. We will inform consumers of the environmental impacts of our products and services.

7. Damage Compensation

We will take responsibility for any harm we cause to the environment by making every effort to fully restore the environment and to compensate those persons who are adversely affected.

8. Disclosure

We will disclose to our employees and to the public incidents relating to our operations that cause environmental harm or pose health or safety hazards. We will disclose potential environmental, health and safety hazards posed by our operations, and we will not take any action against employees who report any condition that creates a danger to the environment or poses health and safety hazards.

9. Environmental Directors and Managers

We commit management resources to implement the Valdez Principles, to monitor and report upon our implementation, and to sustain a process to ensure that the Board of Directors and Chief Executive Officer are kept informed of and are fully responsible for all environmental matters. We will establish a Committee of the Board of Directors with responsibility for environmental affairs. At least one member of the Board of

Directors will be a person qualified to represent environmental interests before the company.

10. Assessment and Annual Audit

We will conduct and make public an annual self-evaluation of our progress in implementing these Principles and in complying with applicable laws and regulations throughout our worldwide operations. We will work toward the timely creation of independent environmental audit procedures which we will complete annually and make available to the public.

* * *

Generally, large companies, including members of the Fortune 500 have balked at signing, because of "legal issues," particularly in regard to principles 8 and 10. In response to this problem and additional feedback, CERES is contemplating rewording the principles, after which it would again solicit acceptance by major U.S. corporations.

Turning to the principles themselves, what sort of ethics do they represent? A cursory analysis suggests they primarily fall into justice and utilitarian types. First, numbers 5-10 emphasize justice concerns, providing for safety, compensation, disclosure, and in-company representation. Those from numbers 2-4 stress utilitarian goals: sustainable use and prudent waste and energy management. Number 1, Biosphere Protection, could be interpreted as emphasizing rights (as may the protection provision in number 2); but it could also fit utilitarian or justice categories.

Let's look at the principles individually. Overall, number 1 is quite broad, and contains three separate statements: a general anti-pollution provision; a third directive to minimize contributing to four (only) presumably high-priority atmospheric effects; and another asserting a positive obligation to "safeguard" five (again, presumably) high-priority biospheric components which are essentially generic aquatic environmental domains.

One criticism of the first provision is its explicit omission of ecological properties, such as species interrelationships, and population and community characteristics. Is it therefore okay to damage these? Even if things ecological may be read into this provision by implication, there seems to be an overemphasis on the "magic media" of air, water, and land (earth). After all, these are primarily physical locations of specific *ecosystems*, which term includes the *inhabitants* of those locations. Neither the ecosystems nor their inhabitants are mentioned in this provision. The second provision, on safeguarding, also raises some questions, namely, what is meant by that term and how far does it extend? That is, are we talking only about real estate owned or managed by the company, or more? Another obvious limitation is that we only include "wet" type habitats (arguably the third provision in principle number 2 does cover land, but the wording is different). Furthermore, all we say is "habitats." How about the "inhabitants," and beyond that, the ecological structure and function? Finally, we can inquire into what the term "safeguarding" is intended to mean: Do we mean absolute protection in all cases, strict stewardship, or resource exploitation to the hilt?

Principle number 2, like number 1, is very broad and also contains three distinct statements regarding "sustainable use," conservation of non-renewables, and a *duty* to "protect." All of these appear to be land-based categories. Does "protect" in number 2 means the same as "safeguard" in number 1, or, more precisely, what *did* the authors mean and what was the intended geographic scope of the obligation? One obvious way number 2 differs from number 1 in its first provision, however, is in its use of "such as"; this implies coverage of natural resources beyond the three enumerated. But we can still question what is meant by "natural resources." A few definitions, as routinely used in statutes and the sciences, would have helped clarify some of the provisions. Turning again to the third statement in number 2 on protecting, we see that it contains an appendage phrase, "while preserving biodiversity," which looks as if it were an afterthought. Significantly, there is no equivalent phraseology as to aquatic habitats in number 1. Does this mean it is okay to impact biodiversity there, but not okay in terrestrial situations? Another problem with this provision is that it may be read to omit vast valuable areas of the biosphere, such as our numerous parcels that contain little or no wildlife but may include interesting plant communities. And, again, there is no explicit statement on "protecting" ecological attributes.

In contrast to principles 1 and 2, number 3 is relatively narrow. It simply calls for environmentally sound waste management. In a similar vein, number 4 focuses on energy; however, it raises some questions. It says to use "environmentally safe" sources. To many environmentalists this would mean limiting the options to those renewables which can only be used in a truly safe fashion, i.e., with minimal environmental side effects. How many companies (or other organizations) today in the U.S. are, or realistically could be, powered exclusively by solar, geothermal, and/or biomass? This principle, though laudable from many perspectives, may simply be too unrealistic at present. Since fossil fuels are not "environmentally safe" or sustainable, they would probably be considered unacceptable. Further, there is a potential ethical objection with this provision, namely, its First World bias; if corporate entities in less developed countries have no economically attractive alternatives to fossil fuels, must they close down?

The third provision in number 4 may also be unrealistic. Seemingly, if followed to the letter it would discontinue autos and other internal combustion modes of transport as we know them. Again, while that may be desirable, it is unrealistic. Would production of environmentally incorrect units cease on the day of signing? Or would not some sort of "phase-in" provision make sense, as has been used in many environmental laws? Though phase-ins have been severely criticized for not working on original schedule, many desired improvements have transpired, albeit gradually. Looking ahead, the product efficiency provision of number 4 would seem to conflict with the safe product provision of number 6. While a 1,000 lb solar car might be entirely energy efficient and harmonious, would it (at present) be truly safe and not just *environmentally* safe?

Principle number 5 focuses narrowly on risk minimization and it is curiously limited to employees and "communities in which we operate." It does not address concern for others who might be exposed. Or, again, how about environmental impacts to the nonhuman environment? For example, if we had some sort of high energy technology, or biotechnology, would this allow for damaging the ecology so long as we protect the limited people/classes mentioned?

Returning to number 6, the goals, while absolutely laudable, would seem unattainable at the present time. For example, let's look at adverse environmental impact. Wouldn't the first provision eliminate contemporary combustion engine industries, technical agriculture, nearly all forestry, mining, and fossil fuel plants, just to mention a few products and services that may adversely impact the environment. Another problem with this provision, as well as with others that use the term "minimize," is trying to understand the precise meaning of the term. Borrowing some environmental law concepts, do we mean best efforts technically possible or those which are economically viable? And within those concepts, what do we mean? For example, economic feasibility may mean no increase in costs, or perhaps not precluding a planned-for 10 percent increase in profits per year, or something else.

Also, number 6 introduces a *duty* to disclose environmental impacts. Do any (and could any) companies fairly do this, and, if so, how? Would this require companies to put, alongside product use warnings, more information on environmental impacts? Interestingly also, disclosure provisions (also required by numbers 8 and 10) do not seem to be explicitly called for in the environmental ethics approaches reviewed. However, it could be argued that without disclosures, many provisions could frequently be ignored; further, disclosure obligations are impliedly desirable if not necessary in social justice-type approaches.

Though principle number 7's admonition to *fully restore* the environment is entirely consistent with and central to many approaches reviewed, its "take responsibility" mandate would seem to require the company to "shoot itself in the foot" or surrender its rights in all environmental damages cases. It should be noted that most companies routinely deny and defend damages suits. Admitting liability, at least until a company is satisfied it did in fact "cause" the alleged harm, would run counter to "prudent" business practices. Would or should, for example, Valdez' obligations supersede obligations to shareholders?

Finally, there is a question as to what is meant by *"fully restore,"* taking into account current practices. From the ecological point of view, restoration means reestablishing ecosystems similar to that which naturally occupied the site.[28] Is this what is meant? It should be noted that current massive, multi-billion dollar Superfund and allied toxic waste cleanup efforts, termed "environmental restoration," fall far short of true (ecological) restoration.[29] This is also true of mine "reclamation."[30]

---

28 Jordan, W.R. et al., "Ecological Restoration as a Strategy for Conserving Biological Diversity," *Environmental Management*, Vol. 12, No. 1, 55-72, 1988.

29 Nicholson, S.A. and N.M. Safaya. 1992. "The Significance of Ecological Factors in the Restoration of Radiological Waste Sites," Paper presented at 1992 Waste Management and Environmental Sciences Conference, April 9-11, San Juan, Puerto Rico.

(Footnotes continue on p. 285.)

Number 8 is concerned mainly with disclosure of environmental harms and also environmental, "health, and safety hazards." However, apparently, companies do not need to disclose health and safety injuries or incidents. On the other hand, a company must disclose *all* environmental, health, and safety *hazards* posed by *all* operations. This could amount to multiple volumes for a major chemical company. The second provision in this principle provides blanket "whistleblower" protection, irrespective of the employee's motivations and conduct. Is this too broad?

When originally presented, number 9 called for inclusion of a member of the board of directors who was "qualified to represent environmental interests to come before the company." According to CERES (as of March 1992), this requirement is rescinded. Another requirement retained in number 9, however, calls for a "commitment of resources" to implement the principles generally (how much support?) plus monitoring and reporting on progress as well as informing the board and the CEO, who are to be "fully responsible" for *all* environmental affairs. This is a big responsibility!

Finally, number 10 calls for an annual self-audit of Valdez principles progress *as well as* legal and regulatory compliance progress, worldwide. As with number 9, the requirements in 10 do not directly track environmental ethics; rather, they are included to demonstrate that ethical principles are actually followed.

An Overview of the Valdez Principles

As might be expected from a procedure involving input from varied environmentalist and consumer-oriented group profes-

---

30 Wali, M.K. and S.A. Nicholson, "Reclamation Research in North Dakota: Ten Years Ago and Now," 399-411, *in* Kube, W.R., E.A. Sondreal, and C.D. Rao, eds., *Technology and Utilization of Low-rank Coals Proceedings*, Twelfth Biennial Lignite Symposium, U.S. Department of Energy, Grand Forks, ND.

sionals, the principles developed are noticeably general and do not identify specific standards of conduct. Further, there appear to be many loopholes, for example, provisions which espouse a certain protection, often stated as a duty, that explicitly omit vital aspects of "the environment," specifically, ecological elements and properties. It is recognized that the principles were intended as broad provisions; however, they do appear to contain some major ambiguities and uncertainties that might have been avoided, with, for example, inclusion of definitions, greater consistency (i.e., land vs. water ecosystem protections), and "scenario testing."

Furthermore, numbers 5, 6, and 7, include, alongside environmental protection, provisions for protecting individual human beings from harm. Explicit human-oriented protections are rarely spelled out in environmental ethics approaches generally; however, as stated, such provisions would be implicit in social justice-type approaches, as would liberal disclosure provisions in numbers 8 and 10.

Additional Sources of Environmental Guidance

Over the past few years several environmental ethical guidelines, rules, or tips pertaining to business conduct and operations have emerged. One important code somewhat similar to the Valdez Principles but without the apparent legal flaws found in principles 8 and 10, is an industry-generated code which several hundred companies, including some Fortune 500 members, reportedly follow.

In addition, numerous companies have developed their own formal environmental policies. Presumably, they are tailored closely to individual company needs and concerns. But how do such policies compare with the foregoing environmental ethical provisions and to what extent should they? Each company will need to decide this, assuming it wishes to keep using existing policies. Of course, another possibility is revision—perhaps adding provisions not already included, that are in accord with the company's goals and views. Another related source of internal guidance may be broader company ethics rules. These often include at least some general environmental provisions, such as: "Company X will make every effort to recycle and minimize waste." Though positive, such statements typically exclude vast areas of environmental concern.

Next there are numerous environmental laws which also provide standards for environmental conduct. Ideally, an environmentally ethical company would not only be in compliance, it would go beyond what is required legally. For example, it would release less pollution than what is permitted by law.

Beyond this there has been a mini-explosion of green consumer guidebooks containing evaluations purporting to reflect the environmental safeness of various name brand products. These books carry titles such as *The Green Consumer*, *The Green Consumer Supermarket Guide*, and *1992 Earth Journal*. Some will conclude—fairly or unfairly but, arguably, with good reason— that "green" ratings for certain company products reflect company environmental ethics and the existence of a separate, high-quality environmental code or policy within that company.

In addition to looking at the alleged "environmental correctness" of the various products that companies produce, *The Green Consumer Supermarket Guide* offers brief pointers on what companies can (and should) do to become greener. However, the tie-in between the "tips" and environmental ethical concepts, and even with major environmental impacts, is not always clear. To add to the confusion, this reference gives five pointers on how to be a greener company, five on "green guidelines," plus five (green related) relationship-type questions to ask. In any event, the bulk of the points deal with waste and energy management only. Although useful, the various provisions fall far short of being comprehensive. A longer list is contained in a recent work that offers consumers a means to "make a difference."[31] Again, the focus is more on practical "how to's" rather than attempting to provide across-the-board environmental guidance.

Where Do You Fit In?

Under the broad umbrella of being or becoming environmentally ethical, environmentally correct, green, or just environmental, there is clearly a tremendous range of choices and counter-choices in the written dogma. And what we have quickly surveyed is just the "soft" documentation, excluding the recognized social science disciplines, for example, law, policy, economics. And what about the hard sciences, particularly the *relevant* ones? If science attempts to define current and future environmental reality, can we or should we have an environmental ethical profile divorced from, and at times inconsistent with, our estimations of reality?

Probably not. Instead, perhaps we need a marriage, or at least a relationship between the "soft" and the "hard," to produce the best ethic. Additionally, the relationship should probably involve much blending of traditionally independent disciplines. This would mean a truly *interdisciplinary* approach to how we deal with the environment, which is the ultimate interdisciplinary problem.

What examples, if any, can we point to? Ethics that attempt to reflect environmental reality are good examples. Indications of this can be seen in the new "biosphere ethic," in some ecocentric strands, and in ecological economics. These emerging modes of inquiry are attempting to learn better about reality and how we ought to deal with it—without the limitations of traditional disciplines.

---

31 Earthworks Group Staff, *Fifty Simple Things Your Business Can Do to Save the Earth,* Earthworks, Berkeley, CA, 1991.

But as new explorers in ecological economics remind us, reality is a two-way street. Just as the more objective phases of inquiry must feed the "soft" or more values-oriented side, so too the converse. This means those of us in the quantitative disciplines must be open to information from the other side, and most importantly open to acknowledging the extent that our own biases, agendas, and world views color and control the "realities" we paint.

In short, we need to draw upon *all* perspectives to develop our environmental ethics. To do otherwise would not be just discounting "the ecology," it would mean eventually destroying our ultimate market, supplier and producer—the biosphere. Clearly, in the 1990s the direction in environmental ethics for business is no longer merely a "nifty" or "trendy" option—it is a matter of the utmost concern and responsibility.

Chapter 14

Eco-Terrorism's Corporate and Environmental Costs

By Steven S. Young, REM. CEA.
Pollution Engineering Magazine

NIMBY—Not in my back yard. Too many people in the United States believe that terrorism could never happen in their town or where they work—but it can!

Environmental Terrorism Timeline

The following is a selected list of publicly known environmental terrorist incidents in America and abroad.[1]

1977　The British Chief of an American-owned chemical facility in Ireland is brutally assasinated.

---

[1] The list is limited to research of government public records, computerized research facilities at Northwestern University, files from the Chicago Crime Commission, and the *Encyclopedia of World Crime*. This research is made available without risking legal or national security positions.

1981   Members of the IRA destroy a British coal ship off the coast of Donegal, spilling tons of coal into the water.

1981   Right wing members of the Falangists seize a petroleum camp near Santa Cruz, Bolivia.

1981   A bomb explodes on a Scottish oil terminal a quarter mile from where Queen Elizabeth is having lunch. The spill from the explosion is thought to have caused damage to the area's groundwater supply and soil.

1981   New York police discover a pipe bomb in a waste hauling truck as it travels to the United Nations building.

1981   American and African environmental interests in petroleum depot at Lesotho are damaged by South African mortar fire.

1982   Rockets strike an American oil tanker in Lebanon causing massive amounts of damage to an already damaged ecological system.

1982   The Kirkuk-Banias oil pipeline in Lebanon is bombed twice causing massive amounts of damage to environmental quality.

1982   Four rockets cause minimal damage to the Crey-Malville nuclear power plant. Unknown ecology activists claim responsibility.

1982   A fueling facility is bombed outside of Paulpietersberg, South Africa. Spills from the gasoline cause major contamination of soil and ground water supply.

1982   Oil pipelines are severed by terrorists near Dasht-i-Kelagai and Charikar, Afghanistan, causing major contamination of soil and groundwater supply.

1984 Bombing of points along NATO fuel pipelines in Belgium and West Germany cause a shutdown of pipelines and severe environmental damage.

1986 NATO fuel lines in West Germany near Vollersode are bombed. Fuels spills from bomb cause severe damage to German groundwater quality.

1986 A U.S. Military fuel pumping station is bombed. Two fuel trucks are also destroyed in the attack. A spill of over 1000 gallons of fuel is ignited.

1986 A Spanish construction site is bombed to protest the building of an American-funded waste treatment plant, killing a worker. The bomb, set to detonate at night, explodes during the day.

1987 A group calling itself the Animal Liberation Front creates a fire at a veterinary science facility in California. Damage is claimed in the hundreds of thousands.

1987 Two amonal bombs are exploded at a Spanish government petrochemical plant. Estimated cleanup and recovery costs range from $8 to $16 million dollars.

1988 Three Palestinian terrorists seize a bus near a nuclear power plant, with plans to destroy the plant.

1990 An arson-type fire is discovered in the home of the chief investigator for the Nuclear Regulatory Commission. Eco-terrorists and disgruntled employees are suspected.

1990 A meat packer in Iowa is indicted for selling tainted food. Members of his company plead guilty to government conspiracy charges.

1990 A research scientist in Wiltshire, England escapes a car bomb explosion. Environmental terrorists claim responsibility, saying they attempted to prevent the scientist from researching deadly effects of chemical weapons on animals.

1990 A West German industrialist in Mannheim, West Germany is arrested for aiding Libya to build a chemical weapons plant capable of destroying the environment in the Persian Gulf. It should be noted that indictments and arrests are being made for similar charges in West Germany for aiding Iraq.

1990 Japanese citizens are fined and deported from China for destruction of a rare insect species from the Yulong-xue Mountain Wildlife Preserve.

1990 A politically motivated sportsman pleads guilty to poaching charges in Bedford, Virginia. He cites that he broke fishing laws because they were unjust.

1991 Iraqi army releases thousands of gallons of oil into Persian Gulf and also ignites hundreds of oil-field fires.

Industrial Terrorism Scenarios

Those incidents graphically show the range and type of eco-terrorist attacks that can occur. Taking it one step further, lets now examine some hypothetical, yet realistic, events that could be in tomorrow's headlines.

The following is a list of possible environmental terrorist scenarios.[2]

---

[2] It is important to note that this list was developed from publicly acknowledged criminal records, files of the Chicago Crime Commission, computerized research files at Northwestern University, and the *Ency-*

- Psychologically disturbed scientist releases into the environment commercially developed, genetically modified bacteria prior to government approval.

- Hunters or vandals returning from trip shoot at what they assume are empty drums at side of road near plant. Barrels had been awaiting pickup by hazardous waste disposer. Contents of drum flow into nearby river via storm water sewer system.

- Religiously motivated terrorist pours rat poison into small public water supply.

- Politically motivated citizens group charges security gate of U.S. defense contractor, break windows of building, create sparks which ignite flammable materials stored inside.

- Disgruntled employee sabotages computer control system of waste treatment plant.

- Middle Eastern students sabotage vehicles in company parking lot, opening drain valves on several parked tank trucks containing liquid wastes or flammables.

- White supremacist group burns black-owned business permitting release of toxic air pollutants from processes.

- Politically active student assassinates government environmental official for current environmental policies which the student deems against his beliefs.

---

clopedia of World Crime. The writer and publisher of this article do not suggest in any way that these scenarios will or have taken place. Moreover, the writer and publisher do not suggest that the following acts are a way of solving political or religious disagreements with individuals, government, or private corporations. It should be further noted that this list was developed through a series of interviews with present and former government officials that asked to be unnamed.

- Ecological activists hold chemical company executive hostage until his/her company publicly changes their environmental policies.

- Environmental extremists break into a quarantined animal facility at an American port of entry to free them.

- Peace activists seize a tanker of flammable liquid to pour into an American city's sewer system in order to blow up a city block.

Applied Intelligence is Key

The industrial use of intelligence can help limit terrorism. "Intelligence" can be defined as information gained through conventional or unconventional means to prevent a terrorist action. Conventional means of gaining industrial intelligence include interviews with governmental personnel, the general population, media, and other public sources. Unconventional means of industrial intelligence gathering are governmental or private investigational services. Both types of intelligence gathering are usually through "secondary sources." Businesses should consult qualified security professionals for accurate primary source intelligence. Governments usually gain unconventional intelligence through satellite reconnaissance as well as human observation of terrorist activities.[3] Unconventional gathering of intelligence, by its very description, involves utilizing sources beyond normal legal means, in other words, "spying."

A profile of employees is useful for intelligence purposes in industry. It is important to know everything about your employees within the limits of the law—conventional intelligence. Unconventional information about employees could be gained by sources interviewing the employees about their work and their co-workers. This is one of the techniques, for example, a terrorist

---

[3] *Deep Black*, Journalist William E. Burrows.

organization would use to gain information about your facility. However, it is important for employers to keep in mind that the integrity of secondary source intelligence must always be questioned. It is also important to note that corporations in the United States are, by law, restricted to using conventional means to gather intelligence. Although questionable in its legality, unconventional intelligence gathering has been used abroad by some multi-national corporations.

Management should incorporate security intelligence into the early design development of a facility to prevent terrorism. The need for additional protection can also be assessed in an existing facility through an environmental audit. Both security and environmental consultants should be retained to work together to counter terrorism on sensitive processes or facilities.

By nature, the law enforcement community is a closed branch of the government. Therefore, any information obtained from them on environmental terrorism will be extremely limited. The government maintains strict confidentiality about their sources. For that reason, most security professionals would agree that companies should develop their own intelligence sources. In fact, companies often have more time, money, and personnel to devote to establishing intelligence sources.

Plant Location and Geography

The geography of a potential target is important to a terrorist. How easy is it to get in and out? Once you're in, how difficult is it to reach and take over the target? To some terrorists, the problem of (even) getting out after they have caused their destruction may only be of secondary concern.

The military establishes fortifications in an area that can easily be defended and difficult to attack. Ideally, it would be advantageous if industrial sites could be established in an identical manner. Realistically though, this is rarely the case. Plants locate near each other to share utilities, transportation and other resources. Plants also locate near large population centers. Therefore, water and gas supplies, storage areas, electrical transmission lines and computer operations become key targets for an attack. And while processes and facilities are targets, it must be remembered that there have also been many instances of terrorists acting against individuals.

An active measure that can be taken is to plan the landscaping around your plant to offer a clear view of the area night or day and in all types of weather. Landscaping should be designed to be an obstacle to attackers, preventing them from getting in or out easily.

Management reaction to any type of terrorism against humans or facilities is an extremely important protection factor. Terrorists study corporate structures to determine where the greatest damage to the system can be inflicted. Corporate structures and their reactions often parallel those of a government, in that large bureaucratic and conventional systems are considered easy prey by terrorists because they fail to react quickly and decisively to violent. On the other hand, terrorists will avoid attacking totalitarian-like systems where unconventional means of defense may be used against them. This observation is confirmed when the number of terrorist activities against the U.S. is compared to those against the U.S.S.R.

Terrorism and Intelligence

The intelligence activities of terrorist organizations are a problem that industry must learn to recognize. Under Community Right-to-Know and other laws, industry may be required to provide basic security information on the handling, storage, and processing of materials within their facilities. It is possible for terrorists to utilize the public disclosure portion of these laws to gain intelligence on security systems, unless companies use their right of confidentiality to protect information about sensitive areas and procedures. Even college and high school students, not bent on terrorism, have been known to design atomic weapons, "hack" into computerized systems, and carry out other disruptive and potentially dangerous activities based on information found in local libraries and other public information sources. Industries should critically assess their vulnerabilities based on the possibility of misuse of information that is readily available to the public.

Another aid to industrial terrorist intelligence gathering is corporate garbage. Security agencies throughout the world study solid waste materials in criminal investigations. Given the sensitive documents that are routinely thrown away, it is reasonable to assume that terrorists may sort through garbage to gain intelligence on both corporation operations and personnel. To counter this source of information, many corporations have turned to shredders to destroy documents. However, the destructive capability of shredders must be carefully judged. In addition to other sources, the Vietnamese gained information on United States intelligence operations through inadequately destroyed documents at the end of the Vietnamese conflict.[4]

Plant Security Measures

Physically protecting a facility and its processes is extremely important. Formal security procedures should be established with persons designated and specially trained to be responsible for them. Buildings should be built with limited access to their interior. Moreover, buildings should also be equipped with state-of-the-art intrusion prevention, fire protection, spill prevention, and other countermeasure systems. Bomb and bullet protection of buildings would, of course, be ideal, but is usually impractical. In

---

[4] Former Central Intelligence Agency analyst Frank Snepp concludes this information in his book *Decent Interval.*

any case, a terrorist would be more likely to destroy a more vulnerable temporary storage structure like a tool shed or an aboveground storage tank.

Securing the perimeter around an industrial site with electrified barbed wire and crash barriers may be necessary for some particularly sensitive types of facilities. Some companies may find it necessary to consider military-type building construction to combat terrorism. According to economist Arthur J. Alexander, effective physical security also protects your neighbors, and deters future acts of terrorism.

Guards (armed or unarmed) are also important to the physical protection of an industrial site. Trained members of an industrial security force should be familiar with all functions of the plant and how to react to differing situations. On-scene visual knowledge of a situation is important to prevent terrorism. If a choice has to be made, humans make better decisions than sensors and cameras. Industrial security forces also can serve as teachers[5] by establishing seminars and simulations to share their knowledge with the employees, and thus, possibly saving lives and equipment.[6] It is important to note that a single chapter cannot provide a complete lesson on industrial security. These are merely general suggestions from an experienced industrial security professional.

Electronic protection of an industrial area is also important to counter terrorism. Modern surveillance technology can sense more than a human. The failure of human intelligence resulted in the bombing of the United States Marine barracks in Lebanon in 1983.[7] Conversely, it must be remembered that electronic pro-

---

[5] *Terrorism and Personal Protection*, Security Specialist Don E. Wurth.

[6] Maintained by Wurth and military strategist Richard Clutterbuck.

[7] *Secrecy and Democracy*, Former Director of the Central Intelligence Agency Stansfield Turner.

tection is vulnerable to terrorists and should not be relied upon exclusively.

Terrorist Ideology

It is important to think like a terrorist to prevent industrial terrorism. That, of course, is easier said than done. Most individuals have no idea how a terrorist thinks, which points out the need to retain security professionals to help in planning.

Most terrorists do not have great economic resources. Therefore, they want to cause the most amount of damage for the least amount of cost.

Terrorists are always interested in the legitimacy of their actions.[8] Therefore, gaining attention for their actions is important to them and makes them feel effective. For this reason, management may need to present a low profile to the population before and after a terrorist action. In order to destroy the force of terrorism, industry and governments must destroy the legitimacy of an action in any way they can.

Terrorists tend to have a military ideology which they follow much the same as normal citizens follow common law. Most terrorist groups are interested in promoting an ideology that can appeal to the masses. Many terrorists are interested in generating class antagonism in order to further confuse and delay decisive action against them. Communist Karl Marx saw and wrote that industry could be a vehicle of class manipulation. Thus, industry is a primary target for revolutionaries.

Conservative journalist David Brooks in the *National Review* breaks environmental activism into three parts. Revolutionary environmentalists, like the Greens or student radicals, make up the first tier of his analysis. These groups tend to romanticize

---

[8] *Contemporary Political Ideology*, political scientist Roy C. Macridis.

environmental politics in an effort to reshape society along outdated anti-capitalist formulas. Many scholars contend that these groups have limited ties to each other. Their activism extends as far as their spring break. These groups are dangerous because they are not easy to track.

Brooks defines his second tier as "designer" environmentalism. He says this group is made up of professionals and conservatives. Brooks claims that members of this type of activism actually work for the U.S. Environmental Protection Agency. Brooks does not believe that they are much of a threat to anyone. In fact, he concludes that their finances may aid efforts for environmental protection.

Brooks defines a third group called "establishment" environmentalists. This group he considers to be the most dangerous and politically perverse of all environmental activists. They solicit funds through romantic advertisements that children watch on television. They portray themselves as heroes, although they actually cause more damage than they portray to cure. Some individuals hire publicists to create health scares. They create cheap publicity stands which endanger lives and the environment. Foreign governments attack them without success. They declare their views as absolute through the media, and they dare anyone to repudiate them. Victims of their physical and publicity attacks seldom recover fully. They look for political answers to environmental problems instead of scientific ones. Brooks further contends that elements of their intelligence networks have infiltrated the government at various levels within the environmental protection system. Brooks argues that their special interests in the name of environmental protection clog up the economy, endanger lives, and divert resources to themselves. The lesson of the Brooks article is that while it is acceptable to romanticize activism, it is incorrect to lose sight of political and scientific realities.

Terrorism and Behavioralism

The study of terrorism can be looked at as a study of human political behavior, or "behavioralism."[9] Behavioralism is an integration of all other social sciences. Behavioralists study consistencies in terrorist behavior to formulate answers to counter terrorism. Scholars like Allan Larson would disagree with behavioralists' formulations on terrorists' political behavior. According to Larson, behavioralism is considered a pure science. His book concludes that *unpredictable* political behavior like terrorism cannot be encompassed by a pure science. Terrorists are individuals with independent behavior. Therefore, patterns in terrorist behavior are not totally predictive of future behavior.

Industrial Study of Terrorism

It is difficult to analyze a terrorist act once it has been since completed, since terrorists take steps to eradicate traces that could be discovered during an investigation.[10] Therefore, industry and governments must plan and prepare for a variety of terrorist scenarios. Such scenarios lay a foundation for analysis of terrorists' motives, security breach opportunities, and financial risks.

Industry management must study terrorism with several things in mind.[11] First, industry should avoid any complicity with a terrorist. Second, industry should avoid any action which would subsidize and support a terrorist act. Third, industry should cooperate to apprehend and punish all terrorists to the fullest extent of the law.

---

[9] *Comparative Political Analysis*, political scientist Allan Larson.
[10] *A World of Secrets*, Intelligence expert Walter Laqueur.
[11] According to the book *International Law*.

Terrorism and Cost

Terrorism costs industry lives and money. Industry spends over $100 million dollars yearly on direct damage from terrorist attacks.[12] Indirect financial costs of terrorism are practically immeasurable.[13] However, at present, no real empirical evidence has been provided for the correlation between industry security expenditures and terrorist attacks on industry.

Terrorism and Labor Policies

Employee morale and loyalty are serious issues during the threat of terrorism. Terrorists will attempt to gain the sympathy of workers and residents in surrounding communities.[14] Wainstein concluded that worker sympathy for terrorists destroys the economic viability of corporations and dissolves economic productivity. Terrorists try to gain labor support by politically attacking working conditions and wages at plants. Purnell points out, though, that labor support of terrorism is short term. After the terrorists have gained the support of labor, they will exploit workers with the conditions they sought to change. Brian Jenkins' work shows how important it is for industry to establish good, strong lines of communication with labor and an improvement in labor morale to combat terrorism.

Adjusting the Corporate Mindset to Deal with Eco-Terrorism

As companies begin recognizing the risks and costs associated with eco-terrorism, it becomes necessary for corporate officers to draft and adopt a professional code of ethics by which the com-

---

[12] *Terrorism and Personal Protection*, kidnapping studies specialist Susanna W. Purnell.

[13] *Terrorism and Personal Protection*, terrorism specialist Brian M. Jenkins.

[14] *Terrorism and Personal Protection*, economist Eleanor S. Wainstein.

pany will deal with terrorist considerations. Whether it is presented as a new "corporate policy" or simply incorporated into the existing framework, it is essential that the company's position on eco-terrorism be readily apparent to all who are concerned.

Industrial Philanthropy and Terrorism

The scholars Barkey and Eitzen, claim that corporate social expenditures and terrorism are not linked.[15] However, many sociologists and behaviorists would disagree with them on key points. Specifically, they point out that terrorists might try to portray corporate social expenditures as similar to the frivolous consumption of tax revenues by a corrupt dictator.

Barkey concluded that industry could attempt to ease social unrest through social expenditures—donating to parks, schools, certain community groups, etc. However, it is important to note that industrial social expenditures may further alienate labor and neighboring populations. Local populations may see only a temporary social good coming from industrial expenditures. They may also conclude that the company is a tool of political manipulation by the government.

From another perspective, industrial social expenditures may discourage government support of programs against terrorism. Government may consider such expenditures support vehicles for terrorist operations. As an example, claims have been made about certain social activities involving supporters of the Irish Republican Army (IRA).

The social responsibility of industry is to increase profits. Attempts at political manipulation by companies through social

---

[15] Scholars include theologist David W. Barkey and sociologist D. Stanley Eitzen in the book *Terrorism and Personal Protection.*

expenditure can cause social unrest, which the same companies are ultimately unable to cope with.

Terrorism and Industrial Liability

Industrial liability principles for terrorism have not been greatly developed through case law. Courts generally look towards common law remedies to settle the question of industrial liability for terrorism.[16] Under common law, industry has a duty to reasonably protect and warn employees about the dangers of terrorism. However, jurist Charles Ruff does not develop the relationship of industrial liability to responsibility for warning the general population about terrorist acts.

Does industry have a duty to reasonably warn populations of terrorist attacks? Industrial use of intelligence must be questioned on this matter. Does an industry create eminent danger for populations? Is that industry liable for that danger? International law is vague in its interpretations of terrorism and industrial liability. Jurists must ultimately decide the legal threshold of industrial protection against terrorism.

Maintaining a Balance

Extreme unconventional means of dealing with terrorists are encouraged by many scholars. However, industrial management must remain careful that it does not become a terrorist in the process. In *Mein Kampf*, Adolph Hitler claimed, "The one means that wins the easiest victory over reason: terror and force." By stooping to the level of punishment that terrorists comprehend, we lose sight of ourselves as a civilized society. Unfortunately, this type of violent backlash response to eco-terrorism and environmental activism has already been the case in Canada and Brazil as seen in recent articles in *Maclean's* and *Discovery*

---

[16] According to Jurist Charles Ruff and other scholars in the book *Terrorism and Personal Protection*.

magazines. According to these stories, some businesses have resorted to theft and even assassination against environmental groups in an effort to maintain corporate security.

Appendix A:
Partial List of Environmental Terrorist Organizations

The following is a list of foreign political factions that reportedly have ties to some type of environmental terrorism.[17] The main target of these terrorist organizations appear to be American, conservation, and environmental interests in Europe. However, it is possible that one of these groups may plan an attack within the United States, given the events in the Persian Gulf War. It should be noted the political groups divide and regroup. Therefore, this list can only be considered current within limits. It is suggested that companies consult with local law enforcement officials for specific anti-american or eco-terrorist acts in their geographic location.

- Bassque Fatherland and Liberty (ETA) Spain and France
- Combatant Communist Cells (CCC) Belgium
- Iraultza, Basque Provinces of Spain
- Provisional Irish Republican Army (PIRA) Ireland
- Red Army Faction (RAF) Germany
- Revolutionary Cells (RZ) Germany
- Guatemalan National Revolutionary Unity (URNG) Guatemala
- Animal Rights Militia (ALM) Britain
- Eritean People's Liberation Front (EPLF) Ethopia
- Animal Liberation Front (ALF) Britain and United States

---

[17] This list is based on published government records, files of the Chicago Crime Commission, and the *Encyclopedia of World Crime.*

Appendix B:

Corporate Code of Anti-Environmental Terrorist Conduct

- Our company will offer a concrete perspective to individuals and groups that will disassociate themselves from an armed or violent conflict with our corporate interests.

- We will confirm the principle that serious deeds which harm the environment, company, and personnel will not go unpunished. To that end, we will work alongside members of the criminal justice community to prevent eco-terrorism at all levels.

- We will refuse to invite media attention to eco-terrorist activities even if those activities are against our corporate interests.

- We will refrain from use of force as long as possible to end an eco-terrorist activity. We realize that violence would place our corporate response on the same level as a terrorist act.

The author would like to thank the reference and bibliographic research staff at Northwestern University Library for their time and assistance with his computerized research. He would also like to acknowledge the help of Mr. John Jemilo, Esq., formerly of the Chicago Police Department, and the investigators and support staff of the Chicago Crime Commission.

Chapter 15

The Green Labeling Phenomenon: Issues And Trends in the Regulation of "Environmentally Friendly" Product Claims

by Thomas Bick and Ciannat Howett
Kilpatrick & Cody

Introduction: The "Green Labeling" Phenomenon

Over the past 20 years, Americans have become increasingly aware of and concerned about the degradation of their natural environment. Until recently, environmental pollution was seen as a problem largely created by industry and, therefore, one that could best be addressed by government regulation of industry. In the past few years, however, Americans have begun to examine the environmental impacts of their own actions and lifestyles as never before, including the environmental costs of their individual purchasing decisions.

Many manufacturers, retailers and advertisers are responding to this new consumer awareness by producing and promoting more environmentally benign products. Others, however, are attempting to take advantage of this trend by promoting products with misleading, or, at best, ambiguous environmental claims. Claims that products are "environmentally friendly," "environmentally safe," "recyclable," "recycled," "biodegradable," "compostable," "ozone-friendly," "landfill safe," or "incinerator safe," now appear on a wide variety of product packages, labels, and advertisements. This proliferation of "green label" claims has led to consumer confusion and, in many cases, consumer mistrust of environmental claims in general.

The growing perception that many green label claims are fraudulent has resulted in a variety of proposals from industry, government, environmental, and consumer groups for a regulatory system that gives consumers confidence that they are being fully and accurately informed of the environmental impacts of the products they buy.

This article looks at the green labeling phenomenon in the United States. It briefly addresses the scientific uncertainty that surrounds this issue, concluding that such uncertainty may well be the major factor complicating the development of a workable and broadly accepted regulatory system. The article discusses how litigation has traditionally been the major constraint on misleading product claims and concludes that such litigation will continue to be an important, though limited, means of challenging fraudulent green label claims. The article then discusses recent proposals for a system of uniform national standards—either enforceable or voluntary standards—against which the legitimacy of green label claims can be evaluated.

The article concludes that until broadly accepted standards emerge by which the true environmental effects of products and packaging can be judged, retailers and advertisers who use green label claims to promote their products will do so at considerable risk. Recent lawsuits by state attorneys general have underscored the potential for accurate green label claims, which are accurate in their literal sense, to be found misleading—resulting in lost profits, as well as tarnished public images for those involved.

The biggest challenge to government regulators and the regulated community will be to develop a system of public or private safeguards that convince consumers that green label claims are genuine. Many fear that recent proposals for such safeguards will create a regulatory process that is so cumbersome, costly, or complex that it will discourage industry from developing and advertising environmentally friendly products and packaging, at precisely the time that consumer demand for such products is at an all time high. Regardless of the type of regulatory system that evolves, one thing is clear: for the next several years there will be much uncertainty and confusion in this area, warranting considerable caution on the part of those who wish to profit from the green labeling phenomenon.

The Proliferation of Green Label Claims

A recent survey found that 26 percent of the 12,000 new household items placed on the market in 1990 boasted that they were environmentally beneficial in some way.[1] Manufacturers and marketers are responding to surveys which show that 29 percent of U.S. consumers say that they have chosen one product over another because of an advertisement or label touting the product's environmental benefits.[2] Significantly, national surveys have shown that over 90 percent of Americans would be willing to pay more for products if they were certain that those products were more environmentally sound than comparable existing products.[3]

---

[1] Fireman, *The Big Muddle in Green Marketing*, Fortune 91 (June 3, 1991).

[2] Holusha, *Coming Clean on Goods: Ecology Claims Faulted*, The New York Times (March 12, 1991).

[3] Environmental Marketing Claims Act of 1991, S.615, 102d Cong., 1st Sess., March 12, 1991.

Except in a few states, the terms "recyclable," "biodegradable," and other commonly used environmental labels have not been defined by statute or regulation. This absence of uniform definitions has allowed marketers and manufacturers to use these terms with little consistency and often with little attention to scientific accuracy. In response, the U.S. Environmental Protection Agency (EPA), the U.S. Federal Trade Commission (FTC), the U.S. Congress, and many state legislatures are exploring the need for uniform national standards and guidelines governing green label claims. In the meantime, pressure from consumer and environmental organizations has led the attorneys general of several states to bring lawsuits to crack down on allegedly fraudulent claims.

Many groups representing advertising and manufacturing interests favor uniform national standards as a means of reducing the confusion over the use and uneven regulation of environmental claims. These industry representatives are aware that public skepticism about green label claims is growing. In one survey, 47 percent of American consumers dismissed all environmental claims as "mere gimmickry."[4] Uniform standards for evaluating the environmental pros and cons of products— standards which consumers understand and trust—would go a long way towards reducing consumer skepticism—thereby promoting the development and sale of environmentally friendly consumer goods.

Industry also views uniform green labeling standards as a means of pre-empting inconsistent state and local standards. One of industry's biggest concerns is that state legislatures will create a patchwork of inconsistent state regulations. Industry representatives argue that uneven state and local standards will make it all but impossible for manufacturers who market nationally or who have multi-state distribution centers to place *any* sort of

---

[4] Supra note 1.

environmental claim on their products.[5] Even a minor change in a product label to comply with a new state law can cost a company millions of dollars. Many industries have already decided not to make any environmental claims for their products until national uniform standards have been established by the federal government.

So far, federal regulators have agreed with industry that a market-based solution to the problem of fraudulent green label claims is preferable to more intrusive methods of regulation. However, government representatives also emphasize that market forces can work to encourage environmentally sound purchasing decisions by consumers—and environmentally sound manufacturing decisions by industry—only if consumers become convinced that they have adequate and reliable information upon which to base purchasing decisions.

Studies have shown that consumers acquire most of their information about a product's characteristics from its label or package.[6] A 1990 study found that 52 percent of respondents who purchased a product with an environmental claim learned about the characteristics of the product from the material printed on the package. In short, the success of efforts to market environmentally beneficial products will likely depend on the ability of government and industry to convince consumers that green product labels are legitimate.

While many government policymakers believe there is a need for uniform, enforceable definitions governing green label claims, there is also a general belief that over-regulation can upset the balance of market forces by reducing industry

---

[5] *Federal Trade Commission Hearings on Environmental Marketing Guidelines* (July 18, 1991) (testimony of Dewitt F. Helm, Jr., President, The Association of National Advertisers, Inc.).

[6] Abt Associate, Inc., *Consumer Purchasing Behavior and the Environment; Results of an Event-Based Study* (November 1990).

incentives to educate consumers about the characteristics of their products. If manufacturers and marketers perceive themselves as constantly threatened with private litigation or government enforcement actions, they may simply elect not to make environmental claims of any kind. How to balance these competing concerns is, therefore, an important policy decision.

Scientific Uncertainty: The Problems of Evaluating the Legitimacy of Environmental Claims

The successful regulation of green labels requires a scientifically accurate means of evaluating the legitimacy of environmental claims. Unfortunately, policymakers and scientists attempting to define appropriate evaluation criteria have encountered several obstacles. A major problem is one frequently encountered by environmental regulators: the considerable degree of scientific uncertainty regarding the effects of many of man's products and activities on human health and environment. Compounding this problem is the complexity of comparing very different types of environmental impacts. The process of manufacturing product "A" may have a certain difficult-to-quantify effect on the earth's ozone layer. A substitute product "B" may have no effect on the ozone layer but, when improperly discarded in landfills, may leach contaminants into groundwater—contaminants whose toxic effects may not be precisely known. How does one compare these potential impacts, particularly when there may be a high degree of uncertainty regarding both? Those who attempt to make such comparisons—and then educate consumers on their findings—often find it difficult to communicate their conclusions in any meaningful way.

Invariably, product comparisons will require subjective value judgments. An example is the controversy over efforts to compare the environmental effects of cloth diapers and disposable diapers. A study by one research firm, Franklin Associates, found that, contrary to popular belief, reusable cloth diapers may not be the most environmentally sound option.[7] Washing diapers at home uses over 9,000 gallons of water per child per year, and the delivery trucks of diaper services consume fuel and pollute the air. On the other hand, disposable diapers take up space in landfills and, once discarded, are considered by some scientists to pose a health threat. How does one compare these very different environmental effects—and how are consumers to be informed of that comparison? Should product labels simply reflect the results of all pertinent environmental studies and let the consumer decide? If so, will this not force environmental claims to become so comprehensive and confusing that they will no longer be a useful method of communicating to consumers?

Adding to the confusion is the widespread disagreement over which method for disposing of a given product is the most environmentally sound. Recycling is generally considered to be the best solid waste disposal alternative, but recycling can increase energy use and create air and water pollution.[8] Similarly, claims that a product is degradable or compostable imply that these qualities are desirable or preferred. However, for products disposed of in a landfill, many solid waste managers consider degradability to be undesirable.[9] In fact, degradable products may frustrate efforts to increase recycling: the process of making a product degradable may also render it incapable of being recycled. Similarly, it is unclear whether mixed waste composting systems are environmentally desirable despite the many advocates of such systems. Some experimental mixed waste

---

[7] Supra note 1.

[8] Dennis Hayes, *Feeling Green about "green;" Sorting Out the Meaningful Environmental Claims Can Be Hard,* Advertising Age 46 (January 29, 1991). ("For example, some mills for recycled paper are chronic major violators of environmental laws.").

[9] *Federal Trade Commission Hearings on Environmental Marketing Guidelines* (July 17, 1991) (comments of J. Wirka, Environmental Action Foundation).

composting processes have resulted in traces of toxic contamination in the resulting compost.

In short, scientific uncertainty and the lack of a uniform measuring stick for comparing very different environmental impacts may prove to be the greatest obstacle to any attempt to regulate environmental claims. In light of these inevitable scientific limitations, some argue that green labels should simply summarize all the known environmental effects of a product. For example, the exact percentage of post-consumer recycled material in the product might be broken down and identified, the exact amounts of carbon dioxide emissions released in the manufacture of the product might be noted, and so forth. Critics of this position point out that such complicated labeling may not be effective in conveying information to consumers. Not surprisingly, a study commissioned by the EPA found that simple labels are much more effective in conveying information to consumers than more complex ones.[10] A second criticism of the "total disclosure" concept is that simply breaking down the various constituents and impacts of products will not aid consumers in making the most environmentally sound product choice. Few consumers, for example, will feel comfortable deciding whether a product that emits large quantities of carbon dioxide when manufactured, but is easily recyclable, is better or worse than a product that cannot be recycled and leaches a slightly toxic by-product when landfilled.

Because of these difficulties, there is an emerging consensus that some private or public body capable of estimating and comparing diverse environmental impacts will be a necessary component of any regulation or standardization of environmental claims—despite the scientific uncertainty that such a body

---

[10] Applied Decisions Analysis, Inc., "Environmental Labeling in the United States," Background Research Issues and Recommendations, *Draft Report 49* (February 2, 1990), as cited in Green Seal *Proposed Criteria and Standard for Toilet and Facial Tissue* 18 (June 17, 1991).

will have to deal with. In fact, the federal government and private organizations have already begun the difficult task of developing a defensible method of making such comparisons.

The method currently favored by the EPA is known as "life-cycle assessment" or "life-cycle analysis." This process was first used by industry in the mid-1970s, during the oil embargo to identify phases in the production process where energy use could be reduced. The idea was to assure that process changes to reduce energy use did not at the same time result in unacceptable environmental impacts. Life-cycle assessment develops quantitative measures for resource consumption and environmental impacts throughout a particular product or package's entire life cycle—from extraction of the raw materials used to make the product to disposal or recycling. Advocates of the method applaud its comprehensive, multi-dimensional approach as a welcome departure from past process- and impact-specific approaches.

Critics of life-cycle assessment argue that the method simply results in an inventory of impacts rather than a genuine risk assessment. Critics also believe the method tends to simplify reality by examining a select set of characteristics while ignoring others that are too difficult to quantify. Others argue that frequent changes in product characteristics and new insights into environmental impacts will quickly render the life cycle assessment of a given product obsolete. Perhaps most important, critics charge that this approach would be far too time-consuming and costly for all but a small percentage of the thousands of products in the marketplace.

Despite its drawbacks, life-cycle assessment—or some process similar to it—appears to be the trend of the future. The approach has been endorsed by EPA and is favored by many consumer and environmental groups. So far, life-cycle assessment appears to be the best means of assuring that the most important environmental effects of a given product or package are fully considered.

Private Litigation: The Traditional Approach to the Regulation of Environmental Claims

Until recently, the primary risk incurred by a company that promoted its product with a debatable environmental claim was a private lawsuit by a competitor under the Lanham Trademark act. Section 43(a) of the act confers a private right of action on "any person who believes that he or she is or is likely to be damaged" by any other person through the use of "any false designation of origin, false or misleading description of fact, or any false or misleading representation of fact" in connection with goods or services in commerce, including any container for goods.[11] Liability extends to the use in commerce of any word, term, name, symbol, or device which is likely to cause confusion, mistake, or misrepresentation as to the nature, characteristics, qualities or geographic origin of any goods, services, or commercial activities.[12] An injured party may bring action under the act where it has reason to believe that: (1) a statement, representation, or advertisement is false, or (2) a statement, representation, or advertisement, while literally true, is nonetheless likely to mislead or deceive its target audience.

A literally false claim may be judicially reviewed by a court without reference to the claim's impact on its target audience.[13] However, a court must examine the overall impact of such a claim in the context in which it was made. The sophistication of the receiving audience, the presence of disclaimers, and the marketplace context may all be important factors in determining whether a court will grant relief against a literally false claim.[14]

---

[11] 15 U.S.C. § 1125(a) (effective date November 16, 1989).

[12] Id.

[13] *Coca-Cola Co. v. Tropicana Prods. Inc.*, 690 F.2d 312, 317 (2d Cir. 1982).

[14] *Avis Rent A Car Sys., Inc. v. Hertz Corp.*, 782 F.2d 381, 385 (2d Cir. 1986); *Plough, Inc. v. Johnson & Johnson Baby Products Co.*, 532 F. Supp.

A plaintiff cannot satisfy the burden of proving that a claim is literally false under the Lanham Act merely by showing that the claim is not substantiated.[15] However, the defendant's reference to substantiation that is false or that does not support the claim, may lead to the entire claim being deemed a literally false representation.[16]

When a challenged claim is implicitly rather than explicitly false, the tendency of the claim to mislead or deceive the public is determined by reference to the perception of the claim's target audience. In such cases, plaintiffs must usually point to market research or consumer surveys to prove that the claim tends to confuse or mislead consumers.[17] Courts have held that surveys showing confusion levels as low as 15 to 20 percent of the consumer population were sufficient to sustain a "likelihood of deception" finding.[18] In this respect, it is interesting to note that a December 1990 survey by *Advertising Age* and the Gallup Organization found that out of 1,514 consumers polled, 47 percent were "not confident" that *any* environmental product claim pro-

---

714, 717 (D. Del. 1986); *Norton Tire Co. v. Tire Kingdom Co.*, 858 F.2d 1533 (11th Cir. 1988).

[15] *Proctor & Gamble Co. v. Cheeseborough-Pond's, Inc.*, 747 F.2d 114, 119 (2d Cir. 1984); *American Home Prods. Corp. v. Johnson & Johnson*, 654 F. Supp. at 590; *Toro v. Textron, Inc.*, 499 F. Supp. 241 (D. Del. 1980).

[16] *Proctor & Gamble v. Cheeseborough-Pond's, Inc.*, 747 F.2d at 119 (2d Cir. 1984).

[17] *Coca-Cola v. Tropicana Prods., Inc.*, 690 F.2d at 317 (2d Cir. 1982); *American Home Prods. Corp. v. Johnson & Johnson*, 577 F.2d at 165; *McNeilab., Inc. v. American Home Products Corp.*, 501 F. Supp. 517 (S.E.N.Y. 1980); *FTC v. Brown & Williamson Tobacco Corp.*, 778 F.2d 35 (D.C. Cir. 1985).

[18] *Coca-Cola v. Tropicana Prods., Inc.*, 690 F.2d 312, 317 2d Cir. 1982) (confusion level of 15% was "not insubstantial"); *R.J. Reynolds Tobacco Co. v. Loew's Theaters, Inc.*, 511 F. Supp. 867, 876 (s.D.N.Y. 1980) (between 20% and 33%); *McNeilab, Inc. v. American Home Prods. Corp.*, 501 F. Supp. at 525 (23%); *American Home Prods. Corp.v. Johnson & Johnson*, 436 F. Supp. 785, 793 (S.D.N.Y. 1977) (31%), *aff'd*, 577 F.2d 160 (2d Cir. 1978).

vided accurate information. Another 43 percent were only "somewhat confident" about the accuracy of such claims.[19]

Lanham Act plaintiffs need not show an intent to deceive or mislead to support a §43(a) false advertising claim. However, proof of bad faith in conducting product tests, or proof that an advertiser intended to communicate a false message, may be introduced to prove that an advertising claim is false.

The purpose of the Lanham Act is "to protect the interests of a purely commercial class against unscrupulous commercial conduct."[20] The rights of private parties to bring an action under the Lanham Act follows from this general purpose. Any business competitor, whether a direct or indirect competitor of the defendant, clearly has standing under the Lanham Act to sue for false advertising.[21] Consumers, on the other hand, have been held by a majority of courts to lack standing to sue under the act.[22] Standing has been granted in several cases to persons who, though not direct or indirect competitors of the advertiser, have suffered "competitive-type" harm from the false or misleading claim.[23]

---

[19] *Federal Trade Commission Hearings on Environmental Marketing Guidelines* (July 18, 1991) (testimony by Lynn Scarlett, vice-president, Research Reason Foundation).

[20] *Collivan v. Activities Club of New York Ltd.*, 442 F.2d 686 (2d Cir. 1971), *cert. denied*, 404 U.S. 1004 (1971); *Chromium Indus., Inc. v. Mirror Polishing & Plating Co.*, 448 F. Supp. 544, 554 (N.D. Ill. 1978).

[21] *Johnson & Johnson v. Carter Wallace, Inc.*, 631 F.2d 186, 190 (2d Cir. 1980); *PPX Enters., Inc. v. Audiofidelity Enters., Inc.*, 746 F.2d. 120, 125 (2d Cir. 1984); *Dallas Cowboys Cheerleaders v. Pussycat Cinema Ltd.*, 467 F.Supp. 366 (S.D.N.Y. 1979).

[22] A minority view holds that any person who believes that he or she has been damaged may sue under the § 43(a) of the Lanham Act. See, for example, *Arnesen v. Raymond Lee Organization, Inc.*, 333 F. Supp. 116 (C.D. Cal. 1971).

[23] For example, in *Thorn v. Reliance Van Co.*, 736 F.2d 929, 933 (3d Cir. 1984) (a major investor in a bankrupt company had standing to sue the company's competitor for false advertising that allegedly caused the bankrupt company's demise); see also *Camel Hair & Cashmere Inst. of*

A claim of false advertising may be brought under the Lanham Act against parties other than the manufacturer. Advertising agencies have frequently been enjoined under the act from continuing advertising campaigns found to be false or misleading.[24] Corporate officers have also been held liable as joint tortfeasors with the corporate manufacturer.[25]

Because a majority of courts have held that consumers do not have standing to bring false advertising claims under the act, consumers must now turn to state laws to contest product claims they believe to be false, deceptive, or misleading. Many states have "little FTC Acts" which include a provision granting consumers standing to challenge advertising and labeling claims.

In general, it is much easier under the Lanham Act to obtain injunctive relief than monetary damages. To obtain an injunction, a plaintiff need only show that the advertisement has a "tendency to deceive" consumers.[26] To recover damages, on the other hand, a plaintiff must establish that consumers were actually deceived by the false advertising and that the defendant

---

Am., Inc. v. Associated Dry Goods Corp., 799 F.2d 6 (1st Cir. 1986) (standing granted to a trade association to sue manufacturers and retailers who had misrepresented the content of cashmere in their coats); *Smith v. Montoro*, 648 F.2d 602 (9th Cir. 1981) (actor granted standing to sue a film distributor for allegedly removing the actor's name from the film's credits and substituting another actor's name).

[24] *Maybelline Co. v. Noxell Corp.*, 643 F.Supp. 294 (E.D. Ark. 1986), rev'd, 813 F.2d 901 (8th Cir. 1987); *U-Haul Int'l, Inc. v. Jartran, Inc.*, F.Supp. 1238 (D. Ariz. 1981), aff'd, 681 F.2d 1159 (9th Cir. 1982); *Tambrands, Inc. v. Warner-Lambert Co.*, 673 F.Supp. 1190 (S.D.N.Y. 1987); *Eastern Air Lines, Inc. v. New York Air Lines, Inc.*, 559 F.Supp. 1270 (S.D.N.Y. 1983).

[25] *National Survival Game, Inc. v. Skirmish, U.S.A., Inc.*, 603 F.Supp. 339, 341 (S.D.N.Y. 1985). In one case, liability under the act was extended to a booking agent of the rock group "Herman's Hermits" for misrepresentation because Herman was no longer a member of the group. *Noone v. Banner Talent Assocs., Inc.*, 398 F.Supp. 260 (S.D.N.Y. 1975).

[26] *Parkway Baking Co. v. Freihofer Baking Co.*, 255 F.2d 641, 648-49 (3d Cir. 1958).

lost sales as a direct result of the advertising.[27] Because of the difficulty of proving consumer reliance and actual damage, damages are rarely awarded in Lanham Act cases.[28]

The Regulatory Approach: State and Federal Efforts to Combat Fraudulent Claims

While the Lanham Act should continue to be an important source of restraint against misleading green label claims, the act is widely perceived to be too limited in scope and impact to instill consumer confidence in green label claims. Consequently, a variety of legislative and regulatory initiatives on the state and federal levels is also likely. This section reviews existing and anticipated regulatory approaches.

Federal Regulatory Scheme

Federal Trade Commission Initiatives

The federal agency charged with regulating product claims in labeling and advertising is the Federal Trade Commission (FTC). Established by the Federal Trade Commission Act, 15 U.S.C. §41, *et seq.*, to regulate unfair methods of competition, the FTC may exercise that authority in one of three ways: by bringing case-by-case enforcement actions, by establishing trade regulation rules, and by issuance of interpretive guides.[29] Over the years, the FTC has used all three tools to develop general rules and standards governing truth in advertising and labeling. On a few occasions,

---

[27] *Schutt Mfg. Co. v. Riddell, Inc.*, 673 F.2d 202, 206 (7th Cir. 1982).

[28] In one notable awarded, *U-Haul Int'l, Inc. v. Jartran, Inc.*, 601 F.Supp. 1140 (D.Ariz. 1984), *aff'd in part, modified in part, and rev'd in part on other grounds*, 793 F.2d 1034 (9th Cir. 1986), the Ninth Circuit affirmed an award of $20,000,000 in compensatory damages and $20,000,000 in punitive damages against Jartran after finding Jartran's advertising to be "malicious and in reckless disregard of plaintiff's rights."

[29] Federal Trade Commission Petitions for Environmental Marketing and Advertising Guides, 16 C.F.R. Cl. 1 (May 31, 1991).

the FTC has used this general authority to regulate environmental claims in product advertising and labeling.[30]

The FTC recently initiated regulatory action to establish uniform national guidelines for judging the validity of environmental claims. The commission has joined the EPA and the U.S. Office of Consumer Affairs in a joint task force known as the Federal Interagency Task Force on Environmental Labeling. Its objective is to establish clear and effective advertising and marketing guidelines for green label claims.

Support for national uniform federal regulation of environmental claims has come from many sectors. Individual manufacturers, trade associations, environmental groups and state attorneys general have petitioned the FTC and the EPA to promulgate national advertising rules governing environmental claims.[31] On July 17 and 18, 1991, the commission took the unusual step of holding public hearings to solicit comments to the proposed guidelines and to determine what form of action the

---

[30] *Ex-Cell-O Corp.*, 82 F.T.C. 36 (1973) (consent agreement with milk carton manufacturer concerning "biodegradable" and "environmentally-safe" claims on plastic-coated paper milk cartons); *Standard Oil of California*, 85 F.T.C. 1401 (1974), *aff'd as modified sub nom, Standard Oil Co. v. F.T.C.*, 577 F.2d 653 (9th Cir. 1979) (order against a gasoline manufacturer concerning misleading fuel emission reduction claims); and FTC Voluntary Industry Uniform Labeling Guideline Agreement as to phosphorus content and biodegradability of detergents (Aug. 6, 1973).

[31] The FTC has received formal petitions and several less formal requests that it issue guidelines on the advertising, labeling, and marketing of environmental claims. For Instance, the National Association of Attorneys General and the National Association of Consumer Agency Administrators independently adopted resolutions requesting FTC guidelines, the Mobile Chemical Company and First Brands Corporation independently submitted petitions for FTC to establish environmental claims guides; and the National Food Processors Association (NFPA) and ten other trade associations petitioned the FTC and submitted proposed environmental claims guides. The Cosmetic, Toiletry, and Fragrance Association and the Nonprescription Drug Manufacturers Association supported the NFPA proposals, but submitted revisions and amendments to NFPA's proposed guides.

FTC should take—whether a guideline, trade regulation rule, case-by-case enforcement, some combination of these approaches, or some other approach.[32]

Case-by-case enforcement is the traditional means by which the FTC has taken action against deceptive or unfair advertising and marketing claims.[33] One benefit of the case-by-case approach is that it allows the commission to examine the specific claim in its proper context. The FTC has stated that an integral part of a case-specific approach to environmental claims would be a major effort to publicize its decisions. Under this approach, the commission's position on environmental claims would evolve largely through individual case precedent, which would form the basis of enforcement actions against other companies engaged in the same or similar conduct.[34]

The drawback to this approach is that a company must be charged with deceptive and unfair trade practices before the FTC can judge the merit of a particular claim. Industry argues that in this era of scientific and regulatory uncertainty it is not fair to tarnish a company's reputation—and cause it to incur the expense of defense against an FTC action—when proper guidance as to how to comply with the law has not been provided.[35] Environmentalists argue that allowing standards to develop through case-by-case enforcement means relying on a process that is too time consuming and costly for consumers to participate in all but a few major cases.

---

[32] The FTC has held a general public hearing on an issue only once before in at least a quarter of a century. (testimony of Charles G. Brown, Coalition of National Retail Associations—July 18, 1991).

[33] Federal Trade Commission Petitions for Environmental Marketing and Advertising Guides, 16 C.F.R. Cl. 1 (May 31, 1991).

[34] Id.

[35] *Federal Trade Commission Hearings on Environmental Marketing Guidelines* (July 18, 1991) (testimony of the Council of Better Business Bureaus, delivered by Steven J. Cole, vice-president and senior counsel).

Despite these drawbacks, the FTC has rapidly expanded its case-by-case green label enforcement efforts. It is currently investigating the accuracy of over 30 environmental claims and plans to open many more such investigations soon. One of the most significant results of this initiative so far is the proposed consent order in *Zipatone, Inc. et al.*. Released for public comment in April, 1991,[36] the *Zipatone* settlement is the first FTC case involving ozone-safety claims for an aerosol product. The advertisement and labeling on the product contained the following statements:

> Ecologically-Safe Propellant and Zipatone's time-saving spray products use only ecologically-safe propellants. You get the job done quickly without damaging the environment.

Although the propellant in a Zipatone aerosol is not ozone-depleting, the primary ingredient in the spray is 1,1,1-trichloromethane, which has been classified as a Class I ozone-depleting substance under the 1990 Clean Air Act Amendments. The FTC's proposed consent order prohibits the company from making any further representations that a product containing a Class I ozone-depleting chemical is ecologically safe, ozone safe, or ozone friendly.

A second regulatory option available to the FTC is the promulgation of a trade regulation rule under Section 18 of the FTC Act.[37] Under this authority, the commission may conduct rulemaking to determine if a certain category of environmental claims are deceptive.[38] Significantly, such trade regulation rules are binding and can only be amended after full rulemaking

---

[36] FTC File No. 902 3368 (April 22, 1991).

[37] 15 U.S.C. 57(a).

[38] The Commission lacks authority to initiate rulemaking under a legal theory of unfairness. The FTC Improvements Act of 1980, Pub. L. No. 96-252, § 11(b), 94 Stat. 374, 379 (this proscription was extended through September 30, 1991 by provisions in the Commission's appropriation legislation).

proceedings. Equally important, trade regulation rules may preempt state and local requirements.

The major drawback of this regulatory approach is that the procedure for rulemaking is detailed and extensive, which means it is likely to be time-consuming and costly. It also tends to be inflexible: once a rule is promulgated it will tend to "freeze" the commission's position with respect to a given type of claim until the rule is formally amended.

The third option available to the FTC is the development of interpretive guidelines. Recent petitions to the FTC ask the commission to develop such guidelines for regulating environmental marketing and advertising. Section 6(f) of the FTC Act grants the commission the authority to provide interpretations of its substantive laws by issuing guidelines, advisory opinions, or policy statements. Guidelines are advantageous because they provide industry with clear and thorough direction on a number of prospective issues in a way not possible in individual case decisions. They also can be developed more quickly than case decisions or formal rulemaking. On the other hand, guidelines have the disadvantage of requiring the commission to determine policy on a wide range of issues without the benefit of the specific facts and context provided by case-by-case adjudications. In its request for comments, the FTC recognized that this prescriptive quality might "inadvertently either discourage beneficial claims or encourage deceptive claims."[39] Moreover, guidelines neither bind nor preempt state or local laws or regulations and, therefore, may not solve the problem of the patchwork of state regulation.[40]

---

[39] Federal Trade Commission Petitions for Environmental Marketing and Advertising Guides, 16 C.F.R. Cl. 1 (May 31, 1991).

[40] Some states do have "little FTC Acts" which require that FTC interpretive guides be given great weight and deference. See *eg*, Ala. Code § 8-9-16 (1975 & Supp. 1990); Alaska Stat. § 45.50.545 (1962 & Supp. 1990); Ariz. Rev. Stat. Ann. § 44-1522(B) (1986 & Supp. 1990); Conn. Gen.

Current FTC Guidelines Applicable to Environmental Claims

One argument against the FTC's issuance of guidelines for environmental claims is that such guidance is unnecessary in light of existing guidelines on what constitutes deceptive, unfair, or unsubstantiated advertising or labeling. Under FTC's Policy Statement on Deception, advertising must not be deceptive or have the capacity to deceive. An advertisement will be found deceptive if it involves a representation, omission or practice likely to mislead a consumer who acts reasonably under the circumstances to his or her detriment.[41] Thus, a claim which is literally true may nevertheless be misleading if it causes a consumer to draw incorrect inferences. For example, a consumer might assume that a product labeled "made from recycled materials" was produced from post-consumer waste, when in fact the product was made from pre-consumer waste using recycled factory scraps. Though literally accurate, the label still has the ability to "mislead" the purchaser of the product.

Under the FTC's Policy Statement on Advertising Substantiation, advertisers must have a reasonable basis for making an express or implied claim prior to an advertisement's dissemination.[42] When the substantiation is express, the advertisers must be able to support the claim by citing a specific study, set of studies, or consensus of opinion. If the substantiation is implied, the advertiser must possess the amount and type of substantiation that the advertisement actually communicates to consumers. If the claim lacks prior substantiation, the

---

Stat. Ann. § 42-110b(c) (1958 & Supp. 1990); Fla. Stat. Ann. § 501.205 (1991).

41   Federal Trade Commission Policy Statement on Deception, *appended to Cliffdale Assocs., Inc.*, 103 F.T.C. 110 (1984); *Southwest Sunsites, Inc. v. F.T.C.*, 785 F.2d 1431, 1435 (9th Cir.), *cert. denied*, 479 U.S. 828 (1986).

42   FTC Policy Statement Regarding Advertising Substantiation, *appended to Thompson Medical Co.*, 104 F.T.C. 648 (1984), Fed. Reg. Vol 49, No. 150 (Aug. 2, 1984).

reasonable basis for an advertising claim is determined by several factors: the type of claim, the product, the consequences of a false claim, the cost of developing substantiation for the claim, and the amount of substantiation experts in the field consider reasonable.

Under the FTC's Policy Statement on Unfairness, an advertisement may be deemed as "unfair," even if it is not deceptive or unsubstantiated.[43] The criterion for determining if an advertisement is unfair is whether there has been consumer injury. To justify a finding of unfairness, the injury must be substantial, not outweighed by countervailing benefits to consumers or competition, and not reasonably avoidable by consumers.

The Commission may enforce the above guidelines in a variety of ways, including issuance of "cease-and-desist" orders or, in more serious cases, seeking monetary redress for consumers. It may also require corrective advertising to clarify the misleading claims.

Proposed FTC Guidelines for Environmental Advertising and Marketing

Three sets of proposed guidelines were published for comment by the FTC in the *Federal Register* on May 31, 1991: (1) guidelines proposed by the National Food Processors Association (NFPA) and ten other trade associations; (2) a revision and supplement to the NFPA guides submitted by the Cosmetic, Toiletry, and Fragrance Association (CTFA) and the Nonprescription Drug Manufacturers Association (NDMA); and (3) *The Green Report II* issued

---

[43] Companion Statement to Letter from Commission to Honorable Wendell H. Ford and John C. Danforth (December 17, 1980) (Unfairness Policy Statement), *appended to International Harvester Co,* 104 F.T.C. 949, 1072 (1984), *appeal dismissed,* No. 85-1111 (D.C. Cir. 1985).

by a task force of attorneys general from eleven states.[44] The
NFPA-proposed guidelines include general statements on the
proper use and scope of six types of environmental claims:
recyclable, recycled, compostable, source reduction, refillable or
reusable, and general claims of environmental benefits. The
proposed guidelines list examples of when the claims would and
would not be considered deceptive. The CTFA and the NDMA
amendments specifically address claims relating to the ozone
layer and supplement the NFPA guides regarding recyclability
and recycled content.

The Green Report II offers the following proposals: (1) recycled
content claims should be specific, with separate percentages
distinguishing the factory waste from recycled post-consumer
materials; (2) assessments of the lifecycle of the product should
not be used until uniform methods for conducting such
assessments are developed; (3) environmental certifications and
seals of approval should be designed with care so that the public is
not misled; (4) claims should reflect actual existing disposal
options, clearly disclosing the general availability of the
advertised disposability or recovery potential of the product
where it is sold; (5) the terms "degradable," "biodegradable," and
"photodegradable" should not be used to promote products that
are currently disposed of primarily in landfills or through
incineration; (6) unqualified compostability claims should not be
made for products sold nationally unless a significant amount of
the product is being composted everywhere the product is sold, or
clear disclosure is made about the limited availability of this
disposal option; and (7) products sold nationally should use
unqualified recyclability claims only if a significant amount of
the product is being recycled everywhere the product is sold (if the

---

[44] *The Green Report II* was compiled by the Environmental
Marketing Task Force which is composed of attorney generals from
California, Florida, Massachusetts, Minnesota, Missouri, New York,
Tennessee, Texas, Utah, Washington, and Wisconsin.

product is recycled in many areas, a qualified claim can be made). One benefit of the *Green Report II* is that it puts manufacturers and advertisers on notice of the type of criteria the respective state attorneys general may use in evaluating the legitimacy of environmental claims.

The FTC is soliciting public comment on which concepts in the above proposals, if any, should be incorporated into the Commission's green label guidelines.

Environmental Protection Agency Initiatives

The EPA has announced that it plans to complete a draft of national guidelines for the use of environmental claims formulated by late fall of 1992.[45] Both industry and environmental groups have been pressuring the EPA to enact technically based standards and definitions that will advance a policy of environmental protection while preventing consumer deception. So far, the EPA has rejected the notion of creating standard environmental labels or a federal "seal of approval" for products. Instead, the agency has announced its intent to develop a guidance document to aid government officials and manufacturers in applying the life-cycle assessment method for determining the environmental soundness of various products, as well as establish standards for the legitimate use of environmental claims.

The EPA has put together a project team from the agency's Offices of Air and Radiation, Pollution Prevention and Evaluation, Research and Development, and Solid Waste to produce a comprehensive guidance document on the application of the life-cycle assessment method.[46] This intra-agency team is charged with developing a comprehensive methodology that can be used by industry, government officials, and consumers alike to evalu-

---

[45] U.S. Environmental Protection Agency, *Life-Cycle Assessment Methodology Development, Project Update* No. 2 (Summer 1991).

[46] U.S. Environmental Protection Agency, *Life-Cycle Assessment Methodology Development, Project Update* No. 1 (Winter 1991).

ate a product's effect on the environment throughout the product's life cycle—from the extraction of raw materials to make the product to its final disposal or re-use. The EPA has also created a technical advisory panel composed of representatives from state and federal agencies, consumer groups, environmental organizations, manufacturing and supply industries, professional organizations, and academia to provide input on scientific, technical, and communication issues raised by the green labeling phenomenon.

In August 1990, the EPA co-sponsored a workshop organized by the Society of Environmental Toxicology and Chemistry (SETAC) in order to identify the state-of-the-art in life-cycle assessments. The workshop resulted in a consensus that proper life-cycle assessments must possess at least three components: an inventory of inputs (such as raw materials or energy used in manufacture) and outputs (such as waste produced in manufacture); the translation of these inputs and outputs into environmental impacts; and the identification of improvements in a product's life-cycle which can reduce that product's total adverse impact on the environment. While the specifics of the EPA's final life-cycle assessment guidance are not yet known, it is clear that the agency stands committed to the life-cycle approach of evaluating the environmental impacts of consumer products. Whether this approach will become the standard in this country for judging the legitimacy of environmental claims remains to be seen.

Pending Federal Legislation

In addition to the federal and state initiatives discussed above, federal legislation has been introduced to clarify and standardize the use of environmental claims in product advertising, marketing, and labeling. Two bills were introduced in the last Congress that specifically address environmental claims regulation: S.615, the Environmental Marketing Claims Act of 1991, introduced by Senator Frank Lautenberg (D-NJ) on March 12, 1991; and its companion bill in the House of Representatives,

H.R. 1408, introduced by Congressman Gerry Sikorski (D-MN) on the same day.[47] In addition, the reauthorization bill for the Resource Conservation and Recovery Act (RCRA), sponsored by Senator Max Baucus (D-MT), contains a provision that would amend the Solid Waste Disposal Act to create a Products and Packaging Advisory Board.[48] This Board would develop recommendations for the EPA on national packaging and labeling standards that would maximize the recycling and reuse of packaging and minimize the quantity of packaging material in the waste stream.[49] Subcommittee hearings on all three bills were held in the first session of the 102d Congress and consideration of the bills is expected to continue in the second session.

Senator Lautenberg's bill and Congressman Sikorski's companion bill would require the EPA administrator to establish an Independent Advisory Board composed of members of consumer advocacy groups, industry groups, environmental organizations, and state and local governments to make recommendations regarding the regulation of environmentally friendly product claims. The bill would also require the EPA to develop a consumer education campaign to provide information to the public on the environmental effects of products and packages.

Under the Lautenberg/Sikorski bills, any person who intends to make an environmental claim for which a regulation has been promulgated would have to file a certification that the claim meets the requirements of the regulation. All such environmental claims would be required to address a specific environmental impact or attribute. In other words, general claims of

---

[47] See earlier bills, National Recyclable Commodities Act of 1989, S. 1884 (introduced by Senator Albert Gore), and National Recyclable Commodities Act of 1990, H.R. 4942 (introduced by Congressman Gerry Sikorski).

[48] The Resource Conservation and Recovery Act Amendments of 1991, S.976, 102d Congress, 1st Sess. (April 25, 1991).

[49] Id.

"environmentally friendly" or "environmentally safe" would not be allowed. All environmental claims would have to be substantiated by the best available scientific information and clearly indicate whether the claim applies to the product, the packaging, or both. The Lautenberg/Sikorski bills also would establish criteria to apply to claims of recycled content, recyclability, reusability, compostability, or degradability. The EPA administrator would be required to promulgate regulations that reflect the best available technology for encouraging higher performance levels in products and packaging and improvements in manufacturing techniques and waste management. The bills further provide that after two years of enactment, no environmental claim would be permitted unless the claim had been specifically defined by EPA regulation. Claims regarding the absence of a characteristic would also be regulated and would be allowed only if the characteristic is usually present in that type of product or package or if the statement would assist consumers in making product comparisons. Interested parties could petition the administrator to develop additional regulations. EPA could seek civil or criminal sanctions against violators through administrative or judicial enforcement actions. A citizen suit provision would authorize private enforcement actions if the EPA failed to take action.

State Initiatives

State Enforcement Actions

Unwilling to wait for the development of a uniform federal advertising standard, in November 1989 the attorneys general of eleven states (California, Florida, Massachusetts, Minnesota, Missouri, New York, Tennessee, Texas, Utah, Washington, and Wisconsin) formed the Environmental Marketing Task Force to establish guidelines governing environmental product claims. Led by Minnesota's Attorney General Hubert Humphrey III, the Task Force recently released *Green Report II*, which Humphrey describes as a "warning shot for companies so eager to cash in on consumer sentiment they commit green-collar fraud."[50] *Green Report II* lacks the force of law, but contains recommendations on how to comply with state false advertising laws.

Several states have taken legal action against manufacturers for alleged deceptive trade practices and consumer fraud arising from questionable environmental claims. Dozens of other state investigations are underway. The most highly publicized of these are the misleading advertising complaints brought by seven states, including New York and California, against Mobil Chemical Company, manufacturer of "Hefty" garbage bags. Mobil decorated its Hefty box with a pine tree, sunbeam and eagle, and proclaimed the plastic bags to be "biodegradable". While the bags are biodegradable if exposed to adequate amounts of air, moisture and sunlight, studies have shown the over 90 percent of the bags are buried in landfills, where there is not enough exposure to the oxygen, water, and light needed to trigger the degradation process. Thus far, Mobile has entered into settlement agreements with six of the seven states. These settlements require the company to discontinue its claims of degradability until appropriate federal guidelines are developed. Some of the settlements also require payment of monetary compensation.

In another well-publicized case, the New York Department of Consumer Affairs sued Procter & Gamble (P&G) for its advertisements claiming that "Pampers" and "Luvs" disposable diapers are compostable in municipal landfills.[51] P&G admits that very few composting facilities which accept disposable diapers exist in the entire country. Its packages of disposable diapers also display a three-arrow recycling symbol, without any indication of what the symbol means. The state charges that use of the symbol is

---

[50] Kiley, *"Green Report" Out To Clean Up Misleading Environmental Ads*, Chicago Tribune, June 9, 1991.

[51] Green, *Recyclable . . . or Just Fraudulent?*, N.Y. Times, April 21, 1991, at 11, col. 2.

misleading, because it is not clear whether it refers to the package, the product, or both, or whether it is simply an endorsement of recycling in general.

State Legislative Initiatives

While federal agencies continue to debate various approaches to establishing uniform national standards governing environmental claims, several states have already developed their own standards. These and similar state initiatives now in the works could result in a patchwork of differing state standards, much to the dismay of companies that manufacture or market products nationwide. These industries argue that the proliferation of so many different state standards will require manufacturers who market nationally to either eliminate environmental product claims altogether or vary their packaging to comply to each state's law—an expensive and often impractical proposition.

At least eleven states, including California and New York, have enacted laws or regulations specifically governing environmental claims by advertisers. California's law, which took effect January 1, 1991, regulates the use of the claims "ozone friendly," "biodegradable," "photodegradable," "recyclable," and "recycled."[52] Proposed legislation in California would ban the use of the word "recyclable" on all labels unless it can be shown that consumers have ready access to a facility willing to recycle that particular product. Illinois and Indiana have proposed similar legislation. Some states, such as Connecticut, have established consumer education programs to encourage the purchase of reusable and recyclable products. Others, such as Iowa and Florida, have enacted legislation that defines the term "degradable," thereby establishing a standard governing the use of this term to promote the sale of plastic bags, packaging materials and other items sold in those states.

---

[52] A.B. 3994

New York's legislation requires that a product or package have a minimum percentage of post-consumer and secondary materials content to qualify for the "recycled" label. Rhode Island's law requires both post-consumer and pre-consumer recycling percentages to be disclosed, but establishes no minimum percentage of total secondary materials content before the package or product may lawfully be characterized as "recycled." These differences in the requirements for labeling under the New York and Rhode Island laws illustrate the problem that conflicting state regulations will present to those who market nationwide: a product properly labeled "recycled" in Rhode Island may be improperly—and illegally—labeled in New York.

Some states without laws specifically prohibiting deceptive environmental claims have challenged green marketing campaigns under their general laws against deceptive trade practices. For example, Texas' suit against Mobil Chemical Company for its degradability claims for Hefty garbage bags was brought under the state's deceptive trade practices statute.[53] Companies marketing products in the many states with deceptive trade practice statutes similar to the one in Texas should make every effort to determine if state enforcers have developed their own internal green label guidelines.

Industry Self-Regulation of Environmental Claims

A consumer or competitor seeking to challenge an environmental claim may elect to invoke a private dispute resolution procedure rather than bring a formal lawsuit in court. In many cases, green label claims may be challenged in an arbitration

---

[53] In addition to these state-specific initiatives, at least one regional initiative is also underway. The Northeast Recycling Council (NERC) has recently adopted model standards that may lead to a regional labeling program. The NERC is composed of state officials from Connecticut, Maine, New Hampshire, New Jersey, New York, Rhode Island, Vermont, Pennsylvania, and Massachusetts.

conducted through the National Advertising Division of the Council of Better Business Bureaus (NAD).

The NAD was created in 1971 to act as a self-regulatory dispute resolution mechanism for the advertising industry. The NAD reviews complaints of false advertising received from any party, including industry competitors, consumer groups, or state and federal agencies. Although compliance with a NAD decision is voluntary, the rate of compliance is high. The NAD reviews advertising challenges on the basis of a "truth and accuracy" standard. Unlike a court in a Lanham Trademark Act case, the NAD will also consider challenges to the adequacy of an advertiser's substantiation. A decision of the NAD may be appealed to the National Advertising Review Board (NARB). The NARB is composed of members from the advertising community and the public.

As of the time of this writing, the NAD had mediated disputes involving three competitor challenges to green label claims. One of the cases involves a claim of biodegradability on a paint stripper and a claim of recyclability for its packaging. A second case involves a recyclability claim on a plastic soft drink container. The NAD found this recyclability claim misleading because it was not apparent that the recycled bottles were suitable for anything other than non-food use. Because the third case is still pending, its details have not yet been released. The NAD expects the number of cases brought to arbitration on environmental claims to grow significantly in the future.[54] It has also recently brought a number of cases to arbitration on its own initiative. The NAD plans to have a green advertising self-regulation system funded and operational by late fall or early winter of 1991.

---

[54] *Federal Trade Commission Hearings on Environmental Marketing Guidelines* (July 18, 1991) (testimony of the Council of Better Business Bureaus delivered by Steven J. Cole, vice-president and senior counsel for the Council of Better Business Bureaus, Inc.).

Third Party "Regulation" of Green Label Claims

Two major non-profit organizations, Green Seal and Green Cross, plan to issue their own environmental "seals of approval" for products that meet their standards for being environmentally beneficial. In the same manner as state and federal governments, these private organizations face the difficulty and uncertainty inherent in balancing trade-offs between the environmental advantages and disadvantages of a given product, and the lack of scientific certitude in quantifying those trade-offs. Both programs are voluntary and are funded by the payment of fees by manufacturers who wish to qualify for the seals.

The Green Cross program, which was initiated by four Western retailers, focuses primarily on verifying manufacturers' claims about the environmental characteristics of their products. So far, the program has limited its research to verifying recycled content claims on products and packaging. In a recent case, for example, Green Cross certified that Webster Industries' trash bags contain 80 percent recycled plastic.[55]

Green Seal is a non-profit environmental labeling and consumer information organization that issues environmental seals of approval as a means of directing consumers to environmentally preferable products. Green Seal sets standards for products on a category-by-category basis. The standards are established by evaluating the life cycle of a product from its manufacture to its final disposal.

After formulating a standard, Green Seal will release it in proposed form for public comment. The standard is then published and distributed to affected parties. Any party disagreeing with Green Seal's technical assumptions or conclusions may appeal to the Environmental Standards Council, a board com-

---

[55] Halverson, *"Green" Products Dominate Hardware Show; Vendors Discover Price Resistance to Some Products* 29, 5 (September 3, 1990).

posed of scientists, academicians, and experts. Standards will be reviewed and updated every three years to reflect new technology and information. In addition, Green Seal plans to provide a brochure at the point of purchase which describes the standards and their significance. Green Seal will also monitor the use of its seal by manufacturers, advertisers, and retailers.

Green Seal has recently released for comment its proposed criteria for awarding its seal of approval to manufacturers of toilet and facial tissue. Approved products would bear the green seal mark and the phrase "Reduced Environmental Impact Tissue." Only facial and tissue paper products made from 100 percent waste paper, at least 10 percent of which must be derived from post-consumer waste, would qualify. The products must be manufactured without using chlorinated or other toxic wastepaper de-inking solvents, and may be rebleached with chlorine compounds only if the rebleaching does not generate additional quantities of certain toxic chemicals. In addition, the products must be designed so as to minimize the generation of solid waste. The product must not contain dyes, inks, or fragrances, and must be packaged either in bulk or in 100 percent waste material that is free of added toxic metals.

Third-party seals of approval, such as Green Cross and Green Seal, can exert a powerful influence on consumers' purchasing decisions. A 1990 survey by *Advertising Age* and the Gallup Organization found that out of 1,514 consumers, 34 percent indicated that a certification program like Green Seal's would have a great impact on their purchasing decisions. Another 40 percent said it would have some impact.[56] In addition, qualifying a product for the Green Seal could prove to be a powerful defense

---

56 *Federal Trade Commission Hearings on Environmental Marketing Guidelines* (July 18, 1991) (testimony by Lynn Scarlett, vice-president, Research Reason Foundation).

against government or private-party challenges to the legitimacy of the products' environmental claims.

In *Green Report II*, the attorneys general task force cautioned that third-party seals of approval must be designed and marketed with a great deal of care to avoid misleading the public. A seal may give consumers the impression that one product is environmentally superior to another when, in fact, the other lacks the seal simply because its manufacturer chose not to participate—or could not afford to participate—in the certification process.

Another concern is that seal-of-approval organizations might decide to evaluate a given product category based on financial considerations. Green Seal has responded to such concerns by emphasizing that its standard-setting process is open to the public to safeguard against such abuses. Another criticism is that the use of a third-party seal, alone, is much like a generalized environmental claim—and suffers from the same disadvantages. The symbol alone does not communicate to the consumer what it is about the product that makes it environmentally advantageous.

Because of these concerns, many interested parties have recommended that the FTC regulate the use of private seals of approval. Green Seal counters that specific government standards are unnecessary. It supports case-by-case regulation of seal-of-approval claims using the FTC's Guides Concerning Endorsements and Testimonials in Advertising.[57] These existing FTC guides require that endorsements be given only by qualified experts and always reflect the honest opinions, findings, beliefs, or experience of the endorser. Endorsements must not be taken out of context and should not contain any representations that

---

[57] 16 C.F.R. § 255.0, 255.1.

would be deceptive or could not be substantiated if made directly by an advertiser.

Regulation by Retailers

Retailers serve as the link between the manufacturer and the consumer and are therefore in a position to greatly influence consumer buying. The function of a retailer includes stocking and arranging products on the shelves, promoting products through in-store displays and posters, and promoting products in advertisements.

Many retailers have begun to establish their own standards for substantiating environmental claims. For example, four western supermarket chains have formed a coalition to establish standards for such claims.[58] Among other things, the coalition has agreed not to carry a product with a claim that it is recyclable if only 50 percent or less of its contents are actually recyclable.

Some retailers have made claims or endorsements of their own that products they sell are more environmentally beneficial than available substitutes. Wal-Mart, the nation's second largest retailer, for instance, began using special shelf markers to highlight new products and packaging that it considered environmentally preferable.[59] These "Wal-Mart Recommends" markers identify the product improvement, such as when the product comes in less packaging material.

Retailers argue that they should not be held liable if they promote products by repeating a manufacturer's environmental claims. At the FTC hearings on proposed guidelines for environmental advertising and marketing claims, a representative of the National Retail Federation (NRF) emphasized that retailers are

---

[58] Sanchez, *Group Will Target the Environmental Claims of Products*, April 13, 1990, at 1, col. 5.

[59] Supra note 1 at 91.

simply not in a position to verify a manufacturer's environmental claim. The average supermarket carries over 30,000 items.[60] Retailers believe they have neither the resources nor the facilities to test environmental claims for this many products. Retailers point out that if they are held liable for manufacturers' claims, the availability of environmentally friendly products may be greatly reduced because retailers would refuse to stock products that make environmental claims for fear of potential liability. None of the proposed guidelines submitted for comments by the FTC address the liability of retailers for claims initiated by manufacturers.

Several state laws regulating environmental claims, on the other hand, include liability exemptions for retailers. For example, California's statute exempts a retailer who does not initiate a representation by advertising or placing the claim on a package.

Outlook for the Future

According to a 1989 New York Times/CBS poll, 80 percent of Americans believe that progress in protecting the environment must continue regardless of cost.[61] Such surveys suggest that consumer interest in purchasing environmentally benign products, and the resulting marketing of those products, will continue to increase.

The goal of promoting accurate environmental claims involves a unique integration of science, environmental policy, societal values and marketplace dynamics. There appear to be four broad options for achieving this end: (1) an across-the-board ban on all environmental claims; (2) the deregulation of environmental claims and reliance on competition, private litigation

---

[60] *Federal Trade Commission Hearings on Environmental Marketing Guidelines* (July 17, 1991) (testimony of Food Marketing Institute).

[61] Supra note 8.

and private-party "green seal" programs to police the market-place, (3) active government regulation of environmental claims, or (4) some combination of limited government regulation and reliance on marketplace forces.

Banning all environmental claims would probably not achieve either policy goal of guarding consumer interests or promoting responsible environmental practices. Industry would doubtless argue that this option would infringe upon its right to promote environmentally beneficial products and packaging. Consumers would complain of being denied readily available information on the environmental impacts of their purchasing decisions. While banning environmental claims may eliminate the current confusion, this option would likely result in consumer ignorance and frustration. It is in the consumer's best interests to know the characteristics of a product, and product labels are a practical way to provide that information. More important, banning all such claims may ultimately prove detrimental to the environment because consumers would not be encouraged to purchase goods based on their environmental impacts. Environmental claims educate and remind consumers about the impacts of products on the environment—from manu-facture to packaging to distribution to disposal or reuse.

On the other hand, deregulating of all environmental claims, and thereby relying solely on competition and private litigation to police the marketplace, may be an ineffective and inefficient method of achieving either policy goal. While private litigation would be one way of preventing consumer deception, the best vehicle for bringing such litigation, the Lanham Act, is now largely unavailable to consumers. Moreover, all competitors in a given market may simply decide to make similar environmental claims rather than challenge those claims under the act.

An advantage of Lanham Act litigation in this area of scientific uncertainty is that it places the burden of substantiating a claim on the manufacturer. However, because private litigation is usually both slow and expensive, its use as a tool to promote green markets will no doubt be limited, even if consumers were to be given standing to sue under the act.

Development of nationally uniform green label standards is already being pursued by states and the federal government. In all likelihood, these standards will be made binding in some way through statute or regulation. Because many of the scientific questions have not been fully resolved—and may never be—claims regulation must necessarily be based on the best evidence available. If regulation is to move ahead—as many believe it must—then some method of substantiation, such as life-cycle assessment, is likely to be adopted despite its imperfections.

In short, the trend of the future appears to be some form of legally binding green label standards, probably developed using some variation of life-cycle analysis or a similar method of evaluating environmental effects. Although industry warns that it may be compelled to drop all environmental claims if such standards are too rigid, that appears unlikely to happen. If consumer demand for green products is as high as studies indicate, then manufacturers will no doubt respond to this demand by finding a way to meet the government standards. At any rate, to remain competitive internationally, American manufacturers will have to accommodate themselves to the green labeling standards of other nations regardless of whether they adopt similar standards in this country.

In summary, three major trends appear to be taking shape. The first is the formulation of federal guidelines or regulations establishing uniform national standards, either by Congress or through the collective efforts of the FTC, the EPA, and the U.S. Office of Consumer Affairs.

The second is the development of private seals of approval, upon which consumers may rely without the need to evaluate in detail the environmental strengths and weaknesses of a particular product. Whether such private seals will have a significant impact on market demand remains to be seen.

The third trend is likely to be an increase in both private and government litigation. As challenges are brought on the state and federal level against manufacturers, advertisers, and others who make false or deceptive environmental claims, the body of common law governing such claims will grow. This body of law will provide a valuable supplement to federal regulation and will act as a harbinger for changes and innovations in the expanding and dynamic green marketplace.

In the meantime, before uniform standards emerge through the courts, the Congress or the agencies, there will continue to be much confusion over what does and does not constitute a legitimate green label claim. Manufacturers, retailers and advertisers who promote products and packaging using such claims will be doing so in a climate of uncertainty, at least for the next several years. Nevertheless, because the market demand for environmentally friendly products is likely to grow, opportunities exist for those willing to take the risk and meet that demand.

Index

Also Available from Government Institutes

Clean Air Handbook
By F. William Brownell and Lee B. Zeugin
Softcover, 336 pp., 1991, $74 ISBN: 0-86587-239-2

Clean Water Handbook
By J. Gordon Arbuckle et al.
Softcover, 446 pp., 1990, $79 ISBN: 0-86587-210-4

Directory of Environmental Information Sources, 4th Edition
Edited by Government Institutes' Staff
Softcover, approx. 350 pp., 1992, $74 ISBN: 0-86587-326-7

Emergency Planning & Community Right-to-Know Handbook, 4th Edition
By J. Gordon Arbuckle et al.
Softcover, 192 pp., 1992, $67 ISBN: 0-86587-272-4

Environmental Audits, 6th Edition
By Lawrence B. Cahill
Softcover, 592 pp., 1989, $75 ISBN: 0-86587-776-9

Environmental Communication & Public Relations Handbook
By Bruce Harrison et al.
Softcover, 165 pp., 1988, $59 ISBN: 0-86587-748-3

Environmental Due Diligence Handbook, 2nd Edition
By William J. Denton et al.
Softcover, 300 pp., 1991, $74 ISBN: 0-86587-245-7

Environmental Evaluations for Real Estate Transactions: A Technical and Business Guide
Edited by Frank D. Goss
Softcover, 250 pp., 1989, $69 ISBN: 0-86587-765-3

Environmental, Health & Safety Manager's Handbook, 2nd Edition
Edited by Thomas F. P. Sullivan
Softcover, 242 pp., 1990, $59 ISBN: 0-86587-219-8

Environmental Law Handbook, 11th Edition
By J. Gordon Arbuckle et al.
Hardcover, 670 pp., 1991, $65 ISBN: 0-86587-250-3

Environmental Laws and Real Estate Handbook, 3rd Edition
By Steven A. Tasher et al.
Softcover, 290 pp., 1992, $74.50 ISBN: 0-86587-257-0

Environmental Management Review
Edited by Government Institutes' Staff
Quarterly, U.S. $188/Outside U.S. $220, ISSN: 1041-8172

Environmental Regulatory Glossary, 5th Edition
Edited by G. William Frick and Thomas F. P. Sullivan
Hardcover, 544 pp., 1990, $59 ISBN: 0-86587-798-X

Environmental Statutes, 1992 Edition
Hardcover, 1,165 pp., 1992, $57 ISBN: 0-86587-282-1

Environmental Telephone Directory, 1992-1993 Edition
Edited by Government Institutes' Staff
Softcover, 256 pp., 1991, $59 ISBN: 0-86587-278-3

Fundamentals of Environmental Science and Technology
Edited by Porter-C. Knowles
Softcover, 200 pp., 1992, $24.95 ISBN: 0-86587-302-X

How the Environmental Legal and Regulatory System Works
By Aaron Gershonowitz
Softcover, 128 pp., 1991, $24.95 ISBN: 0-86587-244-9

Industrial and Federal Environmental Markets Report
Edited by Government Institutes' Staff
Three-ring binder, 320 pp., 1991, $185 ISBN: 0-86587-253-8

International Environmental Law Special Report
Edited by Government Institutes' Staff
Softcover, 400 pp., 1992, $85 ISBN: 0-86587-305-4

RCRA/Hazardous Wastes Handbook, 9th Edition
By Ridgway M. Hall, Jr. et al.
Softcover, 552 pp., 1991, $98 ISBN: 0-86587-270-8

Superfund Manual: Legal and Management Strategies, 4th Edition
By Ridgway M. Hall, Jr. et al.
Softcover, 442 pp., 1990, $95 ISBN: 0-86587-229-5

TSCA Handbook, 2nd Edition
By John D. Conner, Jr.
Softcover, 490 pp., 1989, $89 ISBN: 0-86587-791-2

Wetlands and Real Estate Development Handbook, 2nd Edition
By Robert E. Steinberg
Softcover, 218 pp., 1991, $72 ISBN: 0-86587-269-4

To order any of these publications or receive a complete catalog, please call: (301) 921-2355

or write:
Government Institutes, Inc.
4 Research Place, Suite 200
Rockville, MD 20850